DIVORCE
SHOCK

DIVORCE SHOCK

Perspectives on Counseling and Therapy

Edited by

Adrian R. Tiemann, PhD, CSW, CCS
Bruce L. Danto, MD and
Stephen Viton Gullo, PhD

The Charles Press, Publishers
Philadelphia

The Charles Press, Publishers
Post Office Box 15715
Philadelphia, PA 19103

Acknowledgment

The editors wish to acknowledge the support and encouragement of the American Institute of Life-Threatening Illness and Loss, a division of the Foundation of Thanatology, in the preparation of this volume. All royalties from the sale of this book are assigned to the Foundation of Thanatology, a tax-exempt, not-for-profit, public scientific and educational foundation.

The publication of this book was supported in part by a grant from the Lucius N. Littauer Foundation.

Library of Congress Cataloging-in-Publication Data

Divorce shock: perspectives on counseling and therapy/edited by
  Adrian R. Tiemann [et al.].
     p.   cm.
  Includes bibliographical references.
  ISBN 0-914783-61-0
  1. Divorce—United States. 2. Divorced people—Counseling of
  —United States. 3. Divorce therapy—United States. I. Tiemann,
  Adrian R.
  HQ834.D587   1992
  306.89—dc20   92-5969
                                                               CIP

Printed in the United States of America

ISBN 0-914783-61-0 (pbk.)

Editors

Adrian R. Tiemann, PhD, CSW, CCS
Department of Psychiatry, Coney Island Hospital,
Brooklyn, New York; Director, Mid-Life Crisis
Support Group, New York, New York

Bruce L. Danto, MD
Psychiatrist in private practice,
Fullerton, California

Stephen Viton Gullo, PhD
President, Institute for Health and Weight Sciences,
Center for Healthful Living, Manhasset, New York;
Assistant Clinical Professor of Psychology,
School of Dental and Oral Surgery, Columbia University,
New York, New York·

Contributors

Margery M. Battin, BA
Brockton Mental Health Center,
Belmont, Massachusetts

Henry Berger, MD, PhD
New York Hospital-Cornell Medical Center,
New York, New York

B. Meredith Burke, PhD
Demographer and Economic Consultant to
The World Bank and USAID; writer on health
and social policy, Cupertino, California

Bruce L. Danto, MD
Psychiatrist in private practice,
Fullerton, California

Joan M. Danto, MSW
Therapist in private practice,
Fullerton, California

Stephen Viton Gullo, PhD
President, Institute for Health and Weight Sciences,
Center for Healthful Living, Manhasset, New York;
Assistant Clinical Professor of Psychology,
School of Dental and Oral Surgery, Columbia University,
New York, New York

Judith Haber, PhD
Associate Professor of Psychology,
College of New Rochelle, New Rochelle,
New York

David Lester, PhD
Professor of Psychology, Stockton State College,
Pomona, New Jersey

Frank Limone, MSW, CAS
Chemical Dependency Unit, St. Agnes Hospital;
Counselor in private practice, White Plains,
New York

Madeline A. Naegle, PhD
Associate Professor of Nursing,
Division of Nursing, New York University,
New York, New York

Phelps M. Robinson, MD
Psychiatrist in private practice,
Newton, Massachusetts; Consultant,
Brockton Mental Health Center and McLean Hospital,
Belmont, Massachusetts

Bernard E. Rollin, PhD
Professor of Philosophy, Professor of Physiology
and Biophysics; Director, Bioethical Planning,
Colorado State University, Fort Collins,
Colorado

Shirley Scott, RN
Adjunct Faculty, Valencia Community College;
Nurse Thanatologist in private practice,
Orlando, Florida

Necha Cornelia Sirota, CSW
Department of Psychiatry, Coney Island Hospital,
Brooklyn, New York

Adrian R. Tiemann, PhD, CSW, CCS
Department of Psychiatry, Coney Island Hospital,
Brooklyn, New York; Director, Mid-Life Crisis
Support Group, New York, New York

H. Elliot Wales, JD
Attorney at Law, New York, New York

Juerg Willi, MD
Psychiatrist, Universitätsspital Zürich
and Psychiatrische Poliklinik,
Zürich, Switzerland

Contents

Preface

Adrian R. Tiemann, PhD, CSW, CCS

The dust has hardly cleared regarding the question of whether the American family is, through divorce, going to hell in a handbasket or enabling some of its members to actualize themselves; whether people have come to their senses and are once again celebrating the virtues of marriage; whether the current down-turning economic conditions are fostering a false image of intimate life by offering few alternatives to togetherness; or whether the latest population trends toward fealty are but epiphenomena on the long waves of societal fashion that will move toward some new norm of separated stasis.

If we trace professional consideration of the social, emotional and economic consequences of divorce upon family members, we see a change in attitudes since the turn of the century. At first its treatment was, as Weiss (1975) records, both romantic and moralistic. There were scattered autobiographical accounts that appeared in the popular press of the 1920s and 1930s, as well as a couple of sociological studies. With the end of World War II and the surge in divorce rates, some additional survey studies were undertaken. But there were no sufficiently converged models of the separating and divorcing process within the disciplines of psychology, sociology and social work to enable researchers in these different fields to examine the topics in fruitful collaboration. Each discipline invoked its own variables—the sociologists called upon socioeconomic status, length of marriage, number of children, religious affiliation, type of residence, ethnic background and the like, while psychologists focused on mate selection, personality factors, types of relationships observed, and social workers examined effects of marital discord versus the effects of divorce upon children and the family system, as well as looking at pragmatic issues such as support payments.

Bowlby's studies (1969, 1973) on attachment and loss among young children were pivotal in fostering this necessary convergence. For the sociologically minded, his studies provided a distinct social framework for psychological theories. They gave hard clinical data regarding psychic development for psychologists. And for social workers and allied health professionals involved in giving concrete services to disorganized families, they reaffirmed the importance of parental responsibility and nurturing.

Coupled with this research and the studies it sparked, the United States openly began to experience something of a revolution in intimate relations. (I say "openly" because according to historical and anthropological records, "arrangements" have existed virtually everywhere since time began.) In the 1960s the "do your own thing" ethos galvanized people into feats of interactional originality not seen since the days of Charles II, the Merry Monarch of England; significantly, there was the slow but steady emergence of gays from their closets. Linked to this "narcissistic" ethos was the bursting of divorce onto a landscape of steady marital contracting. Except for a peak following World War I and the expectable decline during the 1930s economic depression, marriage rates remained steady from 1900 to 1945. Divorce rates, on the other hand, doubled from about 2 percent between 1920 and 1940 to 4.3 percent in 1946. They then retreated again to just over 2 percent for 20 years. But the decade of the 1970s saw divorces climb to over 5 percent and peak in 1981. The 1970s also saw cohabitation, with its easier and undocumentable access to separation, take hold. There were 523,000 such households recorded in 1970, rising to 2,764,000 in 1989, about 30 percent of which had children.*

Provincial as most nationals are, we tend to ascribe observations like divorce rates to internal psychological problems or to external sociocultural factors. However, United Nations data on 58 countries, those keeping accurate enough records for statistical comparisons to be made, show peaks in three categories: length of marriage, age of partners and number of children. (Fisher 1987). These data profile a pattern of disruption among couples married four years between the ages of 25 and 29 with one or no children. Although comparable information is lacking for primitive cultures, anthropologists report that cohabitation of parents declines sharply for children over five. Such

---

*For instance, Fordham University researchers (Miringoff et al. 1990) constructed an index of child health for New York City's 1.8 million children from data on infant mortality, number of children living in poverty and reports of child abuse. The index, which in 1974 stood at 67 out of 100, had fallen to 33 by 1988.

findings suggest a biophysical link between social patterns and genetic strategies.†

When Reagan and then Bush were elected, traditionalism in the family saw an uneasy resurgence in our society, reflected in book titles such as *Is Divorce the Answer?* and *The Shaking of the Foundations*. Except among certain subpopulations conveniently labeled for the benefit of agents of social control as "pathological," gone from the popular media are extolatory reports on phenomena such as serial heterogamy in dyads and triadic bisexual unions. Subsequently, the widely noted publication in 1989 of Wallerstein's research on divorce follow-ups, without control samples, and Weitzman's 1985 examination of the economic consequences of divorce upon women greatly attenuated enthusiasm for no-fault divorce. This was so even though Chess' 20-year longitudinal study (1984) employing control groups showed that marital discord had a greater effect than divorce did on children's adjustment as young adults and on their own readiness to divorce.

And then, like an unexpected cosmic ray hitting poised-for-meiosis protoplasm, AIDS appeared out of nowhere. The existence of an apparently deadly disease that is lopping off a sizeable fraction of the population suddenly has made unconnectedness from a "safe" intimate as dangerous to men pursuing gratification of their presumed biological urges as the position that unconnectedness from a mate has traditionally placed on women throughout history. It is sociologically interesting how rapidly mores of sexual promiscuity changed in the gay population when the facts about HIV transmission could no longer be denied. Perhaps nothing gives more credence to the significance of mating behavior for males than the swiftness of this shift.

It should be noted here that marriage—which until recent times women were supposed to want above all else—is conceived by some contemporary social theorists more in terms of the convenience of the man who, by marrying, guarantees propagation of his seed, stability of his *secondary* role as mate and nurturance of his self. Supposedly, man needs these assurances so that he can perform his *primary* life's work of stalking and seizing the "wild dollar." In fact, due to current

---

†I say "strategies" because observers of the genetic scene note significant divergence from elements of social causation. For instance, fox fur breeders in the Scandinavian countries, where silvering first appeared, sought to control the gene needed for silvering by selling no studs or vixen with the characteristic to other breeders. Yet within a few years the gene, pursuing its own strategy it would seem, had appeared on fox farms as far apart as New Zealand and mainland America.

social arrangements, marriage is not "good" for women. They lose what I call "administrative identity," that anonymous reference marker (like one's social security number) with which various governmental authorities log one's existence and entitlements. Married women, marginal to the accepted definitions of expertise though expert in ways transcending specific curricula, are officially discriminated against (that is, by the federal government of the United States) in employment, benefits, pensions, assistance plans and targeted programs. This discrimination is further compounded at the lower levels of state and community, and then magnificently embroidered at the level of organizations of whatever-size firm, for such is the nature of human beings who operate on the basis of dimly remembered and archaic values from childhood that they seek to preserve, values they may never have had but were told they should want.

With more than two million spouses divorcing annually and untold numbers of partners deserting each other with or without marriage, it is immaterial whether the motivation is genetic, social or psychological, for the economic consequences to society of this revolution are no less enormous than the psychological effects on the immediate and extended family members, conservatively estimated to number some eight million. For instance, in 1989, among children under 18 years of age, over half of 9.8 million blacks, nearly one-third of 7 million Hispanics and over 10 million whites lived with only one parent (Lewin 1990). The mechanisms that normally arise to handle problems caused by social change and dislocation always show a significant time lag. During this hiatus, people muddle through the various events with piecemeal solutions. But in the case of the family we are dealing with a basic societal institution. Divorce, in posing a fundamental threat to that institution, gets to everyone's guts and thereby creates battle lines between the reformers themselves and between reformers and their traditionalist opponents.

Even in garden-variety divorces, important legal issues arise. Whatever the husband's status, the wife as unskilled homemaker is usually too weak to negotiate. And various entanglements encumber the process even for parties who are essentially in agreement about the arrangements. For instance, evaluation of pensions depends upon whether they are vested or not. In New York the failure of both parties to sign a separation agreement may lose one of them various divorce entitlements. Interestingly enough, even though ex-partners may assent to waiving entitlements, their lawyers may choose to sue—and naturally, they charge their clients for such efforts.

Given these parameters, what can one say about divorce that is vaguely stimulating, provides new insights and gives information that busy clinicians and mental health practitioners need? The answer lies not in the classification of divorce causes. Most of the authors who have contributed a chapter to this book seem to share the predominant psychodynamic assumption that because like tends to marry like, most people who divorce share characteristics that lead to their breakups in the same way that healthy partners attract each other and contract a stable marriage. A variant suggests that partners may have trouble adjusting to the birth of a child, whether one withdraws and the other enmeshes with the infant or both simply act inadequately as parents, leading to divorce. There are also events that place undue stress on the marriage, such as birth of a defective child or sudden death in a family. Finally, some marriages are seen to be unduly influenced psychologically by the presence or actions of in-laws, prior to contracting the union as well as during and after it, for better or worse.

However, not even psychodynamically oriented clinicians see pathology everywhere. Many recognize that if partners "grow" at different rates, one member of the couple outdistancing the other socially and emotionally, they may elect to follow their different paths singly or with other mates. And none can deny that shifts in values have led some emotionally distant partners, who once would have remained together for the sake of appearances or for the children, to finally decide to seek separate lives.

Among sociologically oriented clinicians, various factors greatly enhance people's ability to withdraw from marriages that they feel are unfulfilling or intolerable. These include: the ethic of individualism; the improving parity between men and women in certain realms of action; attitudes of greater acceptance of alternative family arrangements, including divorce; and an interaction between the affluent part of the population and societal mechanisms designed to take up the slack (such as Aid to Dependent Children). Among the unanticipated consequences of these last-mentioned welfare reforms are that they make it easier for women contemplating divorce to go through with it and they also reduce the guilt that a departing husband might feel over leaving his family by providing a cushion for his irresponsibility or punitiveness. Recently, a much-admired homeless man, who lived in one of New York's small Lower East Side parks, died. Gentrified neighbors who saw him daily and for whom he wrote or spoke occasional poems, expressed deep sorrow at his passing. This was not the case with his immediate family members, including his wife, children and mother, all of whom he conned into supporting him and ultimately deserted without a word. A veteran whose college education was covered under the GI Bill, this man never completed his courses and never held any job for more than a week. By asking how his irresponsibility toward his family was fostered or what social mechanisms failed to keep it in check, we locate unanticipated sources of social disorganization.

The contributors to this volume provide a new way of looking at how to come to terms with partners considering or undergoing the divorce process. Returning to my opening statement about Bowlby's contribution to our knowledge of development, we now see a clear therapeutic mandate for intervention, based not on theory but on hard research. For now our best evidence is that development proceeds according to the same principles throughout the life cycle and that the ingrained biopsychosocial personality is distinguished from the learned character structure in being relatively constant (McCrae and Costa 1984).

This is good news because it gives those who intervene much greater power when dealing with the developmental deficits in spouses that might lead to divorce. This power provides two benefits—first, it honors the individuality of each client and second, it provides a method for intervening.

Respecting the individuality of the client is a concept that in all forms of social intervention—legal, therapeutic, administrative—has been honored more in the breach than in the practice. As a person with a hysterical body physiology, pragmatic mental structure and scientific/romantic ideological mapping, I am well aware how poorly administrative, clinical and bureaucratic categories fit my needs. And I hear it daily in my clinical practice from clients whose remarkable peculiarities have been treated roughshod by organizational functionaries—those denizens of the paper trays whose gum-chewing indifference belies their total inadequacy to their appointed and often well-paid tasks.

The newer models of biopsychosocial development allow for different pacings, styles and ranges of self-development. That personality seems to be constant offers hope that as clinicians we may be able to help people become more truly themselves, the selves that, before the traumas of life interceded, they were meant to be.

Some clinicians view the unwarping of the misdirected psyche as "fundamental" change or "restructuring." These practitioners are psychodynamically oriented and generally follow traditional Freudian, object relations or self-psychological approaches. They usually treat only one person at a time and use the transference to reveal the kinds of relationships that client typically engages in. The enthusiasm of their initiates hints at a despair that anything less than total transformation can help.

Others, critical of this stance, call that goal overweening, reminiscent of the ultra-solutions of which Watzlawick (1988) so eloquently speaks. Their followers, in contrast, offer to help clients make a fundamental change in the tools used by their psyche to express itself (Fisch, Weakland and Segal 1982). This view sees the psyche as constant, its mechanisms of adaptation as modifiable to achieve greater competence.

I raise this point because the contributors to this volume have different orientations, and yet they all succeed equally well. Whether this is because changing a person's coping strategies results in a change in that person's character or whether when character is changed, coping strategies will follow suit matters little. Whichever emphasis is preferred seems immaterial except for contributing to doctoral theses. What does matter is that a person is enabled to become more competent and lead a more fulfilling life.

REFERENCES

Bowlby, J. *Attachment and Loss. Vol. 1: Attachment.* New York: Basic Books, 1969.

_____. *Attachment and Loss. Vol. 2: Separation.* New York: Basic Books, 1973.

Chess, S. Early Parental Attitudes, Divorce and Separation, and Young Adult Outcome: Findings of a Longitudinal Study. In *Progress in Child Psychiatry and Child Development.* New York: New York University Medical Center, 1984.

Fisch, R., J. Weakland, and L. Segal. *Tactics of Change.* San Francisco: Jossey-Bass, 1982.

Fisher, H.E. The four-year itch: Do divorce patterns reflect our evolutionary heritage? *Natural History,* October 1987.

Gold, J.H. *Divorce as a Developmental Process.* Washington, DC: Psychiatric Press, 1988.

Kaslow, F.W. Divorce and Divorce Therapy. In A.S. Gurman and D.P. Kniskern, eds., *Handbook of Family Therapy.* New York: Brunner/ Mazel, 1981.

Klein, F. *The Bisexual Option: A Concept of One-Hundred-Percent Intimacy.* New York: Arbor House, 1978.

Kohn, B., and A. Matusow. *Barry and Alice: Portrait of a Bisexual Marriage.* Englewood Cliffs, NJ: Prentice-Hall, 1980.

Lewin, T. Rise in single families found continuing. *New York Times,* July 15, 1990, p. 17.

MacInnes, C. *Loving Them Both: A Study of Bisexuality and Bisexuals.* London: Martin Brian & O'Keeffe, 1973.

McCrae, R.R., and P. T. Costa, Jr. *Emerging Lives, Enduring Dispositions: Personality in Adulthood.* Boston: Little, Brown, 1984.

Miringoff, M.L., et al. *The Index of the Social Health of the Children of New York.* New York: Institute for Innovation in Social Policy, Fordham University, 1990.

Peterson, R.R. The Socioeconomic Consequences of Divorce for Women. Unpublished doctoral thesis, Columbia University, 1984.

Waller, W. *The Old Love and The New: Divorce and Readjustment.* New York: Horace Liveright, 1930.

Wallerstein, J.S., and S. Blakeslee. *Second Chances.* New York: Ticknor & Fields, 1989.

Watzlawick, P. *Ultra-Solutions: How to Fail Most Successfully.* New York: W.W. Norton, 1988.

Weiss, R. *Marital Separation.* New York: Basic Books, 1975.

Weitzman, L.J. *The Divorce Revolution: The Unexpected Social and Economic Consequences for Women and Children.* New York: Free Press, 1985.

Introduction

Adrian R. Tiemann, PhD, CSW, CCS

Society's remarkable inattention to the manifestations of grief and grieving arising from divorce is a puzzling fact of contemporary existence. When it dawns on us that divorce is the most frequent outcome of marriage today, it spurs philosophic scrutiny. The philosopher Bernard E. Rollin undertakes this task in Chapter 1, "Divorce and Grief: Some Philosophical Underpinnings." He asks whether, surprising as it may seem, our trying to fit everything into the forced dualism of *nomos* (nature) and *physis* (convention or artifice) may not account for the neglect of the emotional consequences of divorce as well as serving as its justification. Most of us are only too aware that the pernicious effects of dualistic thinking upon human affairs is not limited to some aspects of modern medicine—for example, where, by ignoring the value components of health and illness, people become branded with labels of degradation such as "bulimic" and "alcoholic" that often have little to do with helping in their recovery but are more a salve to our own helplessness as experts in managing their care.

We saw this dualism operating daily in the 1980s frenzy of mergers and acquisitions, leveraged buyouts and insider trading scandals carried out solely "by the numbers." These deals were the commercial counterparts of matings and divorces in which the identities of the partners (the businesses involved) were largely ignored, as were their psychosocial needs (the management skills required), and their physical needs for safety and security (the bases of their retail markets). In looking back, we see that these matters of high finance were conducted more like children trading baseball cards than like investment bankers tinkering with the foundations of our economy in deals that were blithely legal but morally wrong. Our attitude toward these practices has come to assign priority to the numerical bottom line without addressing the bottom lines of less tangible factors upon which the society and both its economy and emotional stability ultimately rest—with long-term consequences, such as the death of the enterprises themselves following the changes attendant upon the merger, acquisition or leveraged buyout.

Dualism extends to our thinking about other species as well. It enables us to see them as incapable of feelings, objectifying their existence in the service of our own ends. Ultimately, it muddles our logic by requiring either-or categorizations even as it attenuates our empathy for their suffering. In a similar fashion, it blunts our response to the grieving of the divorced—who, classified as having undergone a now conventional dissolution of a conventional union, are denied human solace.

For the hold of convention upon the relationship of marriage is often more powerful and mystical, if invisible, than the physical or material bonds of kinship itself. It is as if we are more tied to the family we choose than to that into which we were born. What is convention, after all, but the effect of accumulated feelings people have toward situations cognitively inscribed in rules of conduct? And so, while the day-to-day relationship may end—as through death of one spouse—the bond, the relationship it signified and the identity of the bereaved derived from that bond are not necessarily lost. The death of the other rarely casts doubt upon the shared identity of the remaining member of the couple.

Divorce, which is the death by execution of the relationship while the parties continue to live on as ex-partners, is a very different matter. In this case, the partner, who is neither willing nor psychologically able to relinquish the other who has left and remated, has the uncanny experience of perceiving a part of herself as having joined another while abandoning him.

What would happen were divorce harder to obtain? Would society invest convention with greater meaning—perhaps enough more to blur the false dichotomy between nature and convention altogether? Or would it adopt another quick fix? With so many fundamental areas of society reeling under the impact of unethical practice wherein legality swamps morality and we assign priority to the numerical bottom line, skipping the incommensurable factors having long-term consequences, it is hard to know. We do know that divorce provides respite in the short run for one (perhaps both) members of the couple while forcing others in the system—children, in-laws and friends—to adjust to an outcome not of their choosing. Rollin tackles these hard questions.

In Chapter 2, "Divorce Trends: Societal and Personal Experience," B. Meredith Burke accomplishes the difficult task of melding two very different sets of observations together in a way that gives deep meaning and poignance to the term "perspective." She first summarizes the history of twentieth-century marital behavior, detailing the shifting patterns of both marriage and divorce as the latter became more available and common in the 1960s, to double in the 1980s. She then shares a personal narrative regarding her own divorce and the shock and chagrin she felt when she found her individual life fitting a societal statistic. Emile Durkheim observed at the turn of the century that in our unwittingly self-centered outlook, we believe ourselves to be unique as well as individually driven by forces such as desire. It is a shock, then, when we find our desires and despairs mirrored in the public so that our distinctiveness seems to vanish like water droplets in a rushing stream at spring tide.

What is it that propels these individual droplets forward on a similar course so that their separate destinies become as intermingled as water cascading over rocks in the rapids? When experts seek to help us achieve insight into human affairs by unraveling their "underlying" complexity, each hews to his or her own disciplinary bias. In other words, they "see" things within the limits of the incapacities that have been trained into them. For example, consider how different experts describe the "ultimate cause" of the rise in phenomena as disparate as alcoholism, crime or divorce. Biomedical proponents point to physiological factors—inadequacies or hypertrophy of endocrine, neural or metabolic systems for dealing with the particular stressors to which these effects are responses. Psychologists invoke internal dynamics—those demons brought about by psychic scars occurring during developmental phases, particularly of childhood. Sociologists attribute causality to social forces—signal events or trends in society that affect everyone in an age cohort alike. And ethicists ascribe it to changes in core values brought on by different understandings of our universe gained through advances in or reinterpretations of existing knowledge. There are a lot of hidden assumptions in all of these models, but perhaps the most self-aggrandizing assumption of each is its claim to possessing the key to understanding ultimate reality when they are, in fact, merely aspects of that complex process called life.

This brings us to perhaps the greatest shift in our thinking in the twentieth century: the reorienting of our focus upon process—*how* things go—as distinguished from their substance, their content—or *what* is going on. This focus more immediately brings to our attention the fact that neither element is separable from the other, except heuristically. In the nineteenth century, when the cataloguing of content (and the building of museums to hold that content) was all the rage, we scrambled to put order into the tumbling mass of data arising from the burgeoning natural sciences. Display case after display case then mirrored the processes of life on earth as we saw impaled eggs meta-morphose first to tadpoles and then to frogs.

The content-oriented tradition of thinking, however, leads us to reify concepts such as divorce. Reification is especially convenient for the law that regulates divorce behavior and requires concrete, opposi-tional definitions of veracity (is, is not; yes, no) more suitable to Piaget's third stage of intellectual development than to a finely tuned tool of dispute resolution in a complex world. A focus on process reminds us that there can be no physical referent of that ineffable human bond denoted by people's desire to be together. Nor can its sundering in their desire to be apart be viewed physically, for in the realm of existence we cannot touch perceptions, we can only *feel* them through one of our senses.

Just as feeling is a process, all of these chapters focus on the *proc-esses* experienced by the authors and their cases or acquaintances as they recount the narratives of transformation from coupled to sepa-rate. From the first moments of recognition that something is terribly wrong, through the anxious decision to go it alone, or through the disbelief and stupefying shock of realizing one was being cast off, we move. Individual as is our hurt, we are congregate in our suffering as we go through the intermediate phases of grief, anger, pain, numb-ness, ambivalence and self-deception that mark our attempts to come to grips with realities we often must, for our sanity, ward off as the threats to our existence they are. If we are lucky, we will, at our own pace, parallel others' progression to the end stages of self-reorganization where these events can be placed in a perspective that will enable the pain to be transformed into a resource. In this process we hear the human voice of suffering, of fear, of gradual insight, and in some happy cases, of eventual joyous discovery of a new self ready to join and love again. Perhaps more subtly we hear the voices of judgment, for how can human institutions *not* be judged as the designer shoes beholden to momentary tastes on aching feet that they are?

If we can ask why some marriages founder while others flourish, we can also ask why some marital therapies help couples reunite while others help them sunder. Melding theory with praxis, Adrian R. Tiemann, in Chapter 3, "Divorce in Clinical Sociological Perspec-tive," analyzes divorce both as a social phenomenon of multiple levels and as an often thorny clinical problem. As a social event, divorce has repercussions at many levels: biological, personal, social and societal-ethical. Cognitively, it also spans a time frame encompassing the past and the present as well as the future. Because of the intensity of emotions it arouses, even seasoned clinicians sometimes mistake its genesis and misunderstand it simply as an individual solution to an interpersonal problem, or to a long-standing dilemma of the self. It may well be the latter, but when it is not, then therapy based upon an assumption of intrapsychic conflict is bound to suffer inexplicable difficulties. As a consequence, the clinician's efforts may be targeted at the wrong level of the marital system or fail to consider other, more relevant levels of the system in context. This accounts for the fact that divorce counseling, mediation or therapy can be a shoal for the unwary clinician fresh out of graduate school with his or her theories neatly packaged as "solutions."

By presenting a framework for assessing at what level of the system the "insult" occurs that leads partners to consider divorce, Tiemann argues that a more appropriate focus can be determined so that clinical interventions can be targeted for maximal effectiveness.

Two examples are then given of divorce situations displaying effects at differing system levels and requiring, therefore, differing types of therapeutic interventions. The first is a lower-class ethnic family recently arrived from another country, and the second is a never-married couple battling over custody arrangements as part of their continuing "divorce" from each other.

SOCIAL CONTEXTS OF DIVORCE.

The social setting of divorce has a great impact upon how people experience its effects. Unfortunately, few people are cognizant of that social setting since it is their customary background for experience. Being comfortable with their environment, people tend to perceive that "if it ain't broke, don't fix it." Only recently with the change in the law creating "no-fault" divorce and enlarging the scope of custody arrangements have certain inequities in the social setting become obvious. Weitzman (1985), for example, found that economic inequalities between men and women seriously affect post-divorce adjustment.

This lack of awareness often leads people to experience an additional shock when they decide to or are forced to divorce. In Chapter 4, "Betrayal: The World in Disarray," Phelps M. Robinson and Margery M. Battin examine how widely experienced and yet unrecognized as such is the element of betrayal in marital separation. The authors then ask what implications this fact has for basic psychic functioning. If we assume that a person's cognitive and affective inner world serves to make prediction possible and is structured in the person's psyche (e.g., a "self") in a flexing synthesis dependent upon a certain degree of external stability, then what happens to that self when that expectation is violated and someone is betrayed? How does a person cope with information that is at odds with this inner structuring or identity? And what happens to that identity as a result of the disconfirmation?

The authors also ask whether all varieties of betrayal are the same. Looking at these questions in various contexts of social disconfirmation, they ask how the experience of rape, being disowned, suicide and divorce differ. Bringing to bear a variety of psychoanalytic, Piagetian and other models of development, they illuminate the consequences of external events upon internal psychic structures.

If the feeling of betrayal is one response to impending divorce, what does the pragmatic process of legal negotiation reveal about clients and the resources they bring to bear upon it? H. Elliot Wales, an attorney specializing in divorce cases, examines these questions in Chapter 5, "Divorce and the Expectations Offered by the Legal Process." Implicit in his analysis is what divorce is supposed to do for ex-couples that the marriage could not. We might ask, how does each partner seek to use the severed bond and what does this tell us in retrospect about the hopes and fears of each upon going into marriage? Are there fantasy expectations of retribution, economic reward and self-justification? And if one or both of them avoid using the severed bond as a weapon against each other, what do we learn from that fact about family structure or relations between men and women in our society, or the status of our social institutions?

As we know, fantasies can rarely be satisfied in the courts because our legal institution is not a dream machine but a practical tool and imperfect vehicle for conflict resolution honed by centuries of sentiment and reigned by privilege. As such, the law is no more capable of providing instant gratification than may have been the marriage into which both parties—perhaps unrealistically—placed their hopes for personal fulfillment.

We follow the question of what divorce negotiations reveal about ex-spouses with the question of how they respond when their ex-spouse dies. How do we imagine the woman who was divorced by her husband will feel when she learns that he is dying or has just died? Conventional wisdom tells us to expect that she will experience a certain sense of justification—"He's gotten what he deserves for leaving me."

What about her feelings if she divorced him instead? Would they be different? In Chapter 6, "Death of a Divorced Spouse: The Survivor's Dilemma," Shirley Scott discusses the results obtained from a questionnaire that was answered by 85 percent of a sample of 82 survivors (mainly women) regarding their reactions to their former spouse's death. It is interesting to speculate how someone unfamiliar with this work might estimate the results. What percentage would be expected to report having experienced a grief reaction—20 percent? 40 percent? 60 percent? More? And what kind of grief reaction would we typically expect such ex-spouses to feel? Would it be mild, moderate or severe? Without giving away Scott's impressive results, would it surprise the seasoned clinicians among you to know that of those grieving, 67 percent felt reactions ranging from moderate to severe?

As you might have gathered by now, a surprisingly large number of her sample felt grief upon the death of their ex-spouse. By analyzing the unsolicited comments returned with the questionnaires, Scott was able to develop four categories of dilemmas facing the ex-spouse at the time of terminal illness and death of the former mate. That these dilemmas were so problematic, that all derived from the process of accommodating to the death of the ex-spouse, and that they were as much caused by the reactions of the others involved in the process as they were due to the ex-spouse's own internal dynamics, tell us from a sociological perspective that some of our social mechanisms need retuning.

If Scott and Wales have detailed some of the negative elements of divorce upon ex-spouses, Necha Sirota, in Chapter 7, "Divorcing Women: Psychological, Cultural and Clinical Considerations," has turned her attention to what positive aspects it might hold for women. Since much of the societal subtext on divorce concerns what can be particularly devastating to women, Sirota frames it in the context of their development. Regardless of their feelings toward the separation, in what way can it be used as a growth experience potentially capable of freeing them to pursue their own destinies as they are rarely able to do under the strictures of a male-dominated societal ethic? Not incidentally do we note that the rising rates of divorce coincide with women's greater economic and social freedom, loosening the bonds that tied women economically and socially to the institution of marriage for survival.

According to Sirota, women with children who are divorcing today undergo an experience so singular it deserves separate consideration from the topic of divorce in general. First of all, there are factors within the experience that present the woman with difficulties as well as opportunities. Secondly, helping professionals must examine their own attitudes as they affect transference and countertransference issues that might arise should a woman considering divorce seek assistance. Thirdly, there are specific approaches and modes of intervention that can facilitate the woman's ability to use divorce as an event for optimizing growth.

On a psychological level, most analysts assert that *relationship* characterizes the major thrusts of women's identity, while *separation* characterizes that of men. In other words, women are expected to fulfill their intellectual, emotional and actional potentials within the context of marriage and through their husbands while men are not similarly constrained. After all, they customarily take his name. Because of this, the issue of separation poses the threat of loss of self to the woman that it does not pose to the divorcing man who carries his identify with him regardless of his marital status.

The question, then, is how divorce can provide a growth experience for a woman in the current societal context. As do all crises, divorce provides both a danger and an opportunity to its recipients. For women, the positive aspect is the opportunity to confront and master issues of separation and individuation that have traditionally been clouded over in our society. With such individuation, of course, comes the chance to broaden one's role functions.

In seeking to leverage therapeutic effectiveness, the practitioner has an ally in the stress of crisis itself that calls upon reserves of capability not normally accessible to its sufferers. During crisis, the self-system opens (some say "explodes" as the parts fly apart). Existing mental constructs and emotional patterns are opened to reexamination and, through therapy, reorganization. The raising of unresolved issues to the foreground permits the therapist to enter the client's world more readily and to be more effective in intervening.

A therapist who takes a neutral stance, is knowledgeable about the emotional stages of the divorce process as well as being able to place them in the social context, and who knows something about the legal and social ramifications of divorce (such as single parenting and custody rights) is able to facilitate the client's growth during a difficult time. He or she is able to do this by letting the client experience her ambivalences and anxieties without being pushed into a hasty decision one way or the other. In her chapter, which bridges the sections on the social context and treatment, Sirota provides valuable examples of the application of these principles to several classes of divorcing women.

CLINICAL CASE STUDIES

Previous chapters have alluded to the importance of self, identity and interaction in addressing issues related to marriage and divorce. Madeline A. Naegle, in Chapter 8, "Grief as a Central Component in

Separation and Divorce," asserts that adjusting to divorce is a process lasting for as many as eight years and requiring all members in the family to try to come to terms with the grief that accompanies all losses. In contrast with Sirota, she finds that for most people in society, the damaging potential of divorce outweighs its growth-promoting opportunities. Among the many losses family members face are loss of income, household, life style and daily routine, loss or modification of relationship with extended family members, loss of family rituals and loss or change in roles formerly assumed.

Naegle believes that adjustment to divorce is more a function of family interaction in response to the changing circumstances than it is of members' individual traits. Nevertheless, most people pass through similar stages in mourning. This knowledge helps to prepare clinicians for the inevitable turmoil that follows upon the heels of such a break, and tempers their tendency to assume countertransference responsibility. It also suggests a proactive focus upon here-and-now issues rather than a reflective and interpretive emphasis upon existing pathology. Naegle details the symptoms of loss and mourning, and points out differences in response that tend to occur among family members of different ages.

More serious are delayed or postponed grief reactions in which mourning is blunted or blocked by various defensive maneuvers. Not surprisingly, dysfunctional interactional patterns that preceded the divorce may persist, impeding the working through of grief.

In all cases, Naegle sees the therapeutic goal as the prevention of psychopathology and the creation of changes in the family that permit emotional realignment with the altered or newly created family structure. The intensity of grief experienced and the strength of the need for its resolution are determined by the degree of attachment remaining between the former spouses.

Therapists from different perspectives agree that the interactional nature of the family system requires a relationship-centered evaluation of the separation process. In Naegle's view, successful realignment of family relationships includes continuing contact between the children and both parents.

It might be obvious how divorce counseling would differ when one couple presents the clinician with a fused, antagonistic relationship and another presents with relatively well-differentiated selves who have come to an amicable parting of the ways. But development is a tricky course for everyone to negotiate, and people are rarely so easily categorizable that their treatment can be left to a cookbook formulation or to an Eliza.*

Judith Haber in Chapter 9, "Divorce and the Loss of Self," bypasses symptomatology in favor of a family systems point of view to identify the major causes of personal stress in marital disruption. Specifying Naegle, she identifies these elements as the levels of differentiation of self from other that each spouse has been able to attain.

Her therapeutic interventions are thus aimed at identifying points of fusion within the family system that are potential sources of loss of self. If psychic "damage" results from loss of self just as physical damage may result from loss of blood, then clearly, treatment either should help to keep the "blood flow" intact or "tie off" the offending vessels.† Interventions aimed at initiating the client's grieving spur differentiation by reducing fusion and thereby increase clients' coping abilities.

Notable for praxis in Haber's model of four treatment stages is an action component. Instead of waiting for insight to promote change, Haber posits an end stage in which the client takes positive steps. Beginning with the engagement of the client in treatment, her stages progress through an increased focus on self rather than blaming of the spouse, and through finding the missing pieces of self to defining (operationalizing) this self in terms of action.

Chapter 10 tackles the tricky question that follows the fadeout at the film where they "lived happily ever after" and asks how soulmates can want to be sundered. What can be wrong when two hearts beat as one? Isn't such closeness not only an ideal but really attainable? From a self-psychology psychoanalytic point of view as presented by Frank Limone in "The Perfect Couple," the answer is No. In fact, such perfection often masks various but profound forms of codependency arising from the insufficient nurturing of each partner throughout their growth as described in Winnicott's theory of infant development.

---

*"Eliza" is the computer psychotherapy program developed by Joseph Weizenbaum of Stanford University to demonstrate the foolishness of such reductionistic endeavors when the 1950s enthusiasm for technology threatened to overrule our common sense.

†In many religions, ceremonial blood is shed or consumed, signifying oneness ("Selfhood") with the "Exalted Other." See R. Cardoza, The ordeal of Moharram: Shiites in India mourn their savior, *Natural History*, September 1990, pp. 50-56.

What happens then? Inevitably, such patterns of co-dependency lead to disillusion. Under the pressure of daily life it is difficult to retain the romance. Subsequently the secondary gains from the belief that each partner is the other's "dream mate" (what Juerg Willi calls the marital collusion) evaporate. Fantasies in duplicate that they are, they could not survive and each partner is left not only bereft in loss but diminished as well.

Following one of the basic tenets of psychoanalysis, Limone believes that only through each client's development of a regressive relationship in the transference with the therapist can early deficits in nurturing be identified and remedied. Such regression fosters examination of fears of rejection, of what others think of oneself, and of dreaded anger, helplessness and loneliness.

We often hear aphorisms attesting to the potentiating effects of summation. "Bad news travels in pairs" exemplifies this process. In Chapter 11, "Divorce-Death Synergism and Depression," Bruce and Joan Danto address this issue in its ramifications for the clinician dealing with cases of marital separation. They identify one of society's failings as occurring through our natural proclivity to be helpful: when enough people present clinicians with the same set or class of problems, it easily becomes reified as a specialty. (The similarity of this issue to social problems and the rise of the incompetent welfare state is both inescapable and disheartening.) While on the whole this is good for patients, it can also unwittingly promote a form of "monocular vision" that excludes key elements of the malaise lying outside the domain of the specialty. Therapists may then ignore these elements as lying beyond their field of expertise or as unworthy of notice. Such inattention may have lethal results, as the authors note for the benefit of malpractice-wary practitioners. These situations are easily documented in case studies drawn from the popular press.

How the practitioner recognizes such synergism and treats it is taken up in the concluding section. Drawing upon newspaper accounts as well as their own varied practice, the authors address the question of when the effects of divorce and death may synergistically act upon the depressed person to potentiate suicide.

Many writers have likened the loss of a love to the loss of life itself. And clinicians have noted the similarity to the bereaved of mourning a love lost through death with a love lost in life. Eschewing the usual rationalization of theory, the authors of Chapter 12 aim for the heart of praxis: how to restore vitality to that life. Stephen Viton Gullo, along with Henry Berger, in "Love Shock: Therapy and Management in Loss of a Love Relationship," defines several stages of "love shock." By understanding the relatively invariant stages of impending or newly experienced loss, the therapist can maximize effectiveness with the patient.

But there is more to it than that. Beyond understanding, therapeutic power can be heightened in a nontraditional and technologically creative way. Since each client is responding to unique subjective cues deriving from the lost relationship, Gullo has devised a way of using audio cassettes to tap these specifics in order to aid recovery. Herein lies his uniquely valuable contribution. As psychic pain is at one and the same time the cause of most clients' visits to therapists' offices as well as the factor most responsible for treatment stalemates, any technique that helps to desensitize the person to the loss and lessen the intensity of pain suffered will improve client cooperation with therapy and accelerate the process of recovery.

Clinicians know only too well what devastating effects loss in early life can have upon a person. Some modern theorists even suggest that failures in self-development represent losses incompletely mourned.* Early loss is especially predictive of suicide attempts in later life. Regardless of how well-situated and "popular" someone may appear to be, external conditions may not nourish an "unprepared" or fragile psychic organization. In Chapter 13, "Love, Loss and Divorce: The Risk of Suicide," David Lester uses Marilyn Monroe's story as a case example of someone whose waifish charm was the basis of her appeal as a star. We all could identify with her because deep down she radiated her internal belief that she only appeared to "have it all," while at heart she was but a bereft waif awaiting our ministering care.

How does someone's psyche become organized as a waif? Lester examines the precursors of the star's personality in her history and family constellation. He notes the thematic significance and repetitiveness of loss and desertion in these relationships and her failed attempts at restitution through her many marital choices and the subsequent divorces that added to the toll of early loss she suffered.

Might matters have taken a different turn had she not been living alone at the time of her suicide? And what if Hollywood had not had such unrealistic standards regarding youth and beauty or the film industry's ethos were not so determinedly narcissistic? Lester implic-

---

*Kernberg (1989, p. 143) says that every integration of love and hatred activates guilt over the lost opportunity of the past that cannot be undone. In essence, therefore, integration of the self signifies a mourning process as idealizations of others are relinquished and more realistic appraisals involving positive and negative elements of the other are incorporated into the self structure.

itly addresses these questions and creates a compelling case for the operation of three risk factors to which all clinicians working with depressed clients should be alerted.

Because of our Aristotelian bias of linear causality, the concept of betrayal engenders confusion because onlookers tend to neglect its interactional and consequently recursive nature. In Chapter 14, "Divorce as Betrayal: When 'To Love' is 'To Be,' " Adrian R. Tiemann argues that one cannot accurately define betrayal without reference to a "self" experiencing and defining that betrayal in some relational context. Consequently, in contrast to the position taken in Chapter 3 that social factors can be causal, when divorce is perceived as betrayal, it is more likely to be an individual, intrapsychic matter best handled by depth therapy.

The elements of this experience and the terms of that definition are unique and different for each client. They must be unraveled as the crucial elements they are in charting the course of treatment, for they identify how the betrayed partner is an unwitting co-conspirator in the process. Finding and exploring that hidden alliance holds both the key to "repairing the self" and to preventing betrayal in the future. Tiemann concludes with a summary of a treatment case illustrating these points.

We have heard a lot lately about "projective identification." This is a difficult concept as intoned by some representatives of the psychoanalytic profession, as for example, Klein (1948). In her formulation, projective identification extends the defense of splitting. Parts of the ego are chosen from the rest of self and projected onto objects that stand for these projected aspects of the self. She hypothesizes that the first objects of these drives are extensions of the drives themselves derived from the infant's own libido or aggression that are then experienced as being directed toward him by that self-invested external object. "By projection, by turning outward libido and aggression and by imbuing the object with them, the infant's first object-relation comes about." Thus Klein mystifyingly asserts that objects are "created" to contain the infant's drives on the basis that no other explanation exists of the harshness of the primitive superego with its fantasies of destroying, mutilating and consuming those who frustrate its desires.

In translation we might say that projective identification is a response derived from the immature individual's inability to hold contradictory notions simultaneously. The people who first arouse an infant's loving or hating feelings are seen by the infant as personifications of those very feelings of love or hate, a not uncommon reaction even among adults. Since others invariably respond in their own unique ways to the infant's emotions rather than to its expectations, such as they might be, this interaction sequence helps to build upon the self through building up memories encompassing experiences with others.

Fortunately, in Chapter 15, projective identification becomes amazingly simple when described interactively by Juerg Willi in "Divorce and the Dissolution of 'Love as Oneness'" as particular forms of collusion between partners with complementary personalities. Nothing so important as mate selection can occur by accident, much though popular literature and advertising might promote the role of chance to serve their own ends. For, as therapists, we know that when people find others kindling their interest, that spark receives its fire from the primordial cauldron of their psyche's desire.

Willi has identified many complementary patterns of partner relationship, reminiscent of Jackson and Lederer's earlier typology. In this selection, which is among the longer chapters in this book and well worth a careful reading for its breadth of perspective, insight and wisdom, the "love as oneness" pattern that develops between extreme narcissists and their complementary narcissist partners is explored in detail. In addition to discussing the theoretical basis for partner choice, Willi provides an annotated transcript of a course of therapy with a narcissistic couple seeking through marital counseling to "divorce" more in the personal than in the legal sense. Particularly valuable are the sprinklings throughout the text of Willi's reflections upon his personal reactions to the pair undergoing the process and the insights these provided him in conducting the treatment.

REFERENCES

Jackson, D., and W. Lederer. *The Mirages of Marriage.* New York: Basic Books, 1950.

Kernberg, O., M.A. Selzer, H.W. Koenigsberg, A.C. Carr and A.H. Applebaum. *Psychodynamic Psychotherapy of Borderline Patients.* New York: Basic Books, 1989.

Klein, M., ed. *Contributions to Psychoanalysis, 1921-1945.* London: Hogarth Press, 1948.

Lichtenberg, J. *Current Infant Research.* Hillsdale, NJ: Analytic Press, 1983.

New York State Department of Education: *Bibliography on Divorce and Separation.* Albany, 1989.

Stern, D. *The Psychological Birth of the Infant.* New York: Basic Books, 1985.

Wallerstein, J.S., and J.B. Kelly. *Second Chances.* New York: Basic Books, 1989.

Weitzman, L.J. *The Divorce Revolution: The Unexpected Social and Economic Consequences for Women and Children.* New York: Free Press, 1985.
Winnicott, D.W. *Collected Papers.* New York: Basic Books, 1954.

1

Divorce and Grief:
Some Philosophical Underpinnings

Bernard E. Rollin, PhD

The subject of grief in response to the death of a loved one has been a perennial theme in art and literature across all historical eras and cultures. Most recently, the analysis of such grief has been the focus of intensive cross-disciplinary examination by fields including—but not limited to—psychology, psychiatry, medicine, anthropology and sociology. Of late, it has become clear that the grief response is not restricted to human beings; grief for a companion animal has now been recognized as widespread and worthy of serious concern and attention.

Equally provocative is the notion that grief may manifest itself in a variety of other modalities, occasioned by various forms of loss and having a variety of objects. We may grieve at the passing of a career; the waning of a talent; the irrevocable loss of an opportunity; the passing of love or friendship; the loss of faith, trust or innocence; the irrevocable passing of religious commitment, a belief, or youth. The logic and psychology of all such grief is worthy of exploration and conceptual analysis; the deep structure of these emotions may well belie the surface similarities.

One can but marvel at the fact that one of these grief and loss phenomena—that occasioned by divorce and dissolution of marriage—should command so little attention and scrutiny. We live in a society in which none of us is untouched by the effects of divorce; some 60 percent of our marriages end in divorce. Yet the ubiquitousness of divorce far outstrips our understanding of our responses to it. It is far from clear whether our culture even acknowledges, through its institutions or practices, the manifest fact that divorce can occa-

sion grief that rivals and even surpasses grief at death loss. Not only
in degree, but also in virtue of certain logical features, such grief can
differ significantly enough in kind as to constitute a special set of
problems.

Why has relatively little social attention been devoted to examining and understanding the concept of divorce grief and loss? Though I
cannot prove my claim, I would venture to suggest that this failure
results at least in part from the powerful hold that a traditional
dichotomy exerts over our thinking—the dualism of *nomos* and *physis*, or nature and convention. As I have discussed at length elsewhere, this division of the world into what is true by nature versus
what is true by art, artifice, social or cultural decision is as old as
human thought itself. It can be found in the earliest pre-Socratics, the
most avant-garde structuralists, and virtually everyone in between
(Rollin 1976). And as I have also discussed in a variety of papers, our
implicit presumption that all phenomena fall clearly and fully into
one category or the other wreaks havoc with our ability to conceptual-
ize a variety of interesting cases that are, in fact, an admixture of
nature and convention. There are a number of clear examples where
this has dramatically occurred.

In a number of essays (Rollin 1979, 1983), I have attempted to
show that seeing the world through this dualism has pernicious
effects on modern medicine. Modern biomedicine schematizes itself
as a science, and as such, as laying bare the way things are by nature.
The human being is seen as a biochemical machine, and diseases and
illnesses are seen as empirically detectable breakdowns in that
machine. What this ignores, of course, is the valuational nature of
health and disease: the fact that one cannot have a concept of sickness
without a paired concept of health, and that the concept of health is a
valuational and culturally variable one. What we choose to call
healthy or ill is a matter of value as well as fact; no set of facts forces
us to call something sick or well. But as we believe that biomedicine is
strictly a matter of seeing what is there in nature, we allow physicians to make value judgments for all of us without anyone realizing
that this is what they are doing. To assert, as the U.S. medical community has done, that obesity is a disease rather than a cause of
disease; or that alcoholism or child abuse are diseases rather than
evils; or that hyperactivity in children or suicidal tendencies in an
adult are diseases rather than behaviors society should discourage
represents at least debatable value judgments masquerading as new
insight into nature.

In an earlier presentation (Rollin 1984), I argued that the dualism of nature and convention is responsible for the medical community's demonstrable inability to deal with the dying elderly in that it sees such people as products of a natural process in which intervention is futile and in which scientific effort is mocked. In old people, the machine *will* eventually break down regardless of what physicians do. Because physicians are trained to do and to cure, they shun this mockery of their mission and deploy their skills where they can make a difference, neglecting (as nurses tell me), that medicine must be care as well as cure.

Our scientific and philosophical inability to recognize thought and feeling in other species is also conditioned by the dualism of nature and convention. From Aristotle to Descartes to Kant and Wittgenstein, thought has been equated with language, and language with freedom. Animals do not freely manipulate conventional signs; they are allegedly locked into preprogrammed mechanical responses. The howl of the dog is as the cuckoo of the clock, bespeaking well-functioning machinery, not mind. If conscious at all, the animal is locked in the eternal now, for only conventional signs can soar beyond the moment. All of this in turn has hardened our moral response to animals and their suffering, and has helped us to build our culture on foundations of suffering without guilt (see Rollin 1986a, 1986b, 1987).

Our perennial attempts at understanding classification—both biological and artistic—have been based in seeing the world through this dualism. And so those who say that good classification reflects what is have eternally wrestled with those who say that good classification creates what is—realists against nominalists. As I have tried to show elsewhere, proper classification has elements of both. Given a theory such as evolutionary biology, empirical natural tests of classificatory hypotheses such as protein sequencing emerge. Thus our theory *(nomos)* directs us where to look in nature *(physis)*. By the same token, the conventional ground rules of science can lead us to highlight or to ignore certain natural phenomena, as Darwin's science saw facts of animal thought in the world and twentieth-century science denied them (Rollin 1981).

Our valiant biomedical attempts to discover in nature when death occurs (or life begins) again reflects the either/or of nature-convention. What is forgotten here is that we don't just discover the moment of death, we decide it. And the decision is not forced by the facts, but indicated by them, given ancillary values we hold. A flat EEG defines death in a culture not impressed with mere vegetative existence—eminently plausible but not logically necessary.

As these examples point out, the world does not present itself as divided neatly into what is natural and what is conventional. At most, we find a spectrum running, for example, from the natural signification of clouds meaning rain to the conventional signification of what the word "cloud" means in English. But for clouds to mean rain we must notice or care; this is at least partly a matter of culture. And for words to mean, we must naturally understand that they refer and connote. So we are forced to acknowledge that, at least in these cases, the phenomena in question evidence the mix of nature and convention, not the schism historically postulated.

Implicit presumption of this dualism seems to be at least part of what is involved in social attitudes towards divorce loss and its neglect as a legitimate object of study and concern. After all, since divorce (unlike death) is seen as a conventional, socially created termination of a conventional, socially created relationship, we are not disposed to see the grief it can elicit as natural. We rather are inclined to see it as somehow artificial and self-indulgent. Our tendency is to view such grieving with impatience, reacting not as we would to legitimate grief, occasioned for example by the death of a father, but rather as we would to a child's (to us) trivial grief over the loss of a replaceable artifact—for example, a toy. One can get another toy or another husband.

A key point that must be stressed in response to such a widespread attitude is that just because something is conventional (that is, in my nondualistic view, something on the conventional end of the spectrum) it is not necessarily unreal. Conventional connections can be as powerful as natural ones, and their hold on our minds and hearts can be as great or even greater than natural ones. If one doubts this, a simple thought experiment can make the point quite eloquently. We know that "by nature" people cannot walk in air and fall when they step off cliffs. By the same token, the words we use to designate things are paradigmatic of what we hold to be conventional and artificial. Yet a moment's reflection will make it clear that we can far more easily imagine a man walking off a cliff and not falling, in violation of "natural law," than we can imagine the English word "red" written in green ink and "green" written in red ink.

The hold of convention is powerful, yet invisible. On one occasion while in Rome, I was involved in an altercation with a man I felt had been rude. As I walked toward him, he moved away quickly, walking backward and beckoning to me. The more quickly I approached, the more quickly he backed away and the more frantically he beckoned. "Dammit," I yelled, "If you expect me to come to you, hold still." I was nonplussed when a passing American residing in Italy informed me that the gesture I took to mean "come here" meant "go away," since Italians gesture with the *backs* of their hands.

Most assuredly, marriage and divorce connections and dissolutions are more like beckoning than they are like physical laws of cause and effect. Like gestures and words, divorce and marriage vary considerably from culture to culture and from age to age. Many societies don't have institutions of marriage; still others don't have divorce. Among those that do have marriage and divorce, the variation in rules governing them is dazzling. All of these points notwithstanding, the crucial thing for our discussion is this: in a society like ours, where divorce and marriage are socially real, the grief engendered by the sundering of these "conventional" ties can be as profound and as great or even greater than that engendered by the "natural" process of death.

Though the social profundity of marriage and its dissolution has been weakened during the past few decades in our society, there is no question that the marriage bond still exerts a powerful tie. In fact, one could argue that entering into marriage represents a change in one's personhood, and one's self awareness of that personhood, at least as powerful and profound as that occasioned by entering into puberty. Perhaps more so—one is often not aware one has entered puberty, but one is quite aware of getting married or divorced. In women, of course, marriage is represented by the most powerful of conventional symbolic tokens, the change of name and thus of identity. By the same token virtually all Western religious rituals during the marriage ceremony stress the almost magical transformation of personhood occasioned by entering into marriage. The Catholic ceremony, for example, traditionally made use of the following text (which has recently fallen into disfavor for feminist political reasons):

Husbands, love your wives, even as Christ loved the church and gave Himself for her, in order that by cleansing her by means of the washing in water He may sanctify her through His word, so that He may present the church to Himself gloriously, having no spot or wrinkle or any of such thing, but holy and blameless.

In a similar way husbands ought to love their wives as their own bodies. One who loves his wife loves himself. For no one ever hated his own flesh, but he nourishes and carefully protects it, just as Christ treats the church, for we are members of His body. "On this account a man shall leave his father and his mother and shall be joined to his wife, and the two shall become one flesh."

There is a great, hidden meaning in this, but I am speaking about Christ and the church. Nevertheless, let each of you love his wife as much as himself, and let the wife revere her husband (Ephesians 5:21ff).

Note in particular the notion of two becoming one, a metaphysical union that brings to mind language usually only evoked in reference to the Trinity!

The Protestant ceremony shares a similar if less dramatically stated message. Phrases like "holy matrimony," "mystical union," "joined in holy estate," "perfection of a love that cannot end," "oneness of the life before you," "two bodies but only one life before you," abound in the examples I have examined, both traditional and contemporary. And the Mormon faith sees the union of marriage as one literally made in heaven.

One friend of mine, who is a prominent conservative Protestant theologian, spoke frankly to me of the fundamentally irreconcilable conflict between the Protestant view of marriage and the social prevalence of divorce. (In his daughter's school district only 15 percent of children live with both biological parents.) The Protestant view of marriage, he told me, entails a person being so bonded with another that their lives are now inseparable. Certainly the presumption of marriage is permanence. Yet social attitudes are quite cavalier toward marriage and divorce. The churches have been forced to accept this situation, although theologically the view remains the same.

Though one may cavil at the metaphysical notion of two becoming one, there is a literal truth here that depicts genuine psychological, conceptional and social reality. Thus, for example, many if not most people who are married for any length of time do become one. Trivially, they anticipate their partner's responses and reactions and see themselves through their partner's eyes; most profoundly, they even define their own selves in relation to the other. Speaking autobiographically, I know that I would not be the same person if my relationship with my wife were expunged from my history; so much of what is me is based in so much of what is her. Socially, many women have primarily been defined as "so and so's wife," thus irrevocably tying their social personhood to their marriages. And if Heidegger is correct in suggesting that the unity of one's life consists in balancing in the present past events and future projects, one's unity of self consists in large part in experiences provided by marriage.

Thus, for some people, and I suspect for most (with observant Catholics as a paradigmatic example), marriage can create a bond between individuals as strong as any natural bond of birth or family, although it is "conventionally" rather than "naturally" engendered. Indeed, in many cases the bond is far stronger than a natural one; there are circumstances where one would not substantially grieve the loss of another when one is tied by natural bonds, as in the death of a father one never knew.

Thus I am suggesting a rather strong thesis: despite its conventional origin, marriage may create a significant part of one's personal identity, self-awareness and sense of self. Who one is can be said to be linked irrevocably with one's relations with another. As one of my colleagues has put it, marriage involves logical and psychological relations sufficiently strong to license the claim that upon becoming married, one experiences an ontic transformation of one's self. Built into this transformation is, of course, the realization on some level that the relationship will inevitably terminate through the fact of biological death. Obviously, given two people, one must die before the other. Thus, we may distinguish between the inevitable death of one party to the relationship, and the death of the relationship, which is another matter altogether. It is the latter that occurs in divorce but not in death.

In divorce the relationship dies, the parties to the relationship do not. And the expectation of such dissolution is not conceptually built into the forging of the relationship—hence the standard phrase in marriage ceremonies telling us that what God has wrought, no man may rend asunder. Now it may of course occur that the relationship between the two parties has indeed died, with both parties to the marriage equally distanced from their initial bonding. Such a case is not likely to cause grief; relief is probably the natural consequence.

But what happens if one partner is not ready to relinquish the relationship? From the perspective of the person seeking the divorce, the other person is relationally dead—the organic tie or internal relation has become an artificial graft that didn't take. But from the perspective of the partner not willing to relinquish the relationship, and therefore not willing to relinquish the other partner, something fundamental is being torn away. Thus far, of course, the latter case parallels the situation of a spouse's dying; after all, most people are unwilling to relinquish the other or the relationship at the point when the spouse dies.

But there is one manifest disanalogy. In the case of death, we must, after all, expect it on some level. Thus the reality of the death of the other forces itself on a person relentlessly and inevitably, though we sometimes hold on to the other in dreams and hallucinations for some time. On some level, we know that it is *de facto* impossible to get the other person or the relationship back; Orpheus notwithstanding, there is no returning from death. But no such cleansing certainty forces itself on one in divorce. Thus one may see the other partner daily or weekly. One can reach out physically and touch the person as one did for 20 years of marriage, yet at the same time one can't. The other person—and thus the relationship—however much beloved, is physically present but ontically or metaphysically removed. This is perhaps analogous to those terrible nightmares in which one screams but cannot be heard. This situation in turn provides yet another potential source of grief not present in the case of death—a sense of helplessness, powerlessness, and failure. No one can stop death; but not everyone gets divorced and many achieve reconciliation or even remarriage to the original partner. "Why then can't I reappropriate the relationship," says the grieving divorced person? "What did I do wrong?" So the natural sense of loss may be compounded by a sense of failure and inadequacy, especially if the spouse is marrying someone else.

In a sense, loss through divorce may be more difficult to deal with than loss through death, for divorce holds out and tantalizes with the false promise of reuniting with the lost loved one. In the language suggested earlier, part of yourself is walking around, yet you can't get in touch with it, or get rid of it either. It is probably for this reason, in part, that some people cannot even bear to talk to each other after a divorce and do their best to act as if the other is dead or invisible. Dead is dead, but watching part of yourself become part of someone else while lost to you forever must be close to unbearable.

Even in the case of divorced couples where no such lingering love and attachment remains, and where the divorce is sincerely mutual, the effect may exist in children who are biologically as well as culturally tied to the absent parent, who had no voice in either the initial bonding of marriage or in its dissolution, who had no voice in the divorce but can always imagine Mommy and Daddy back together, and who often feel responsibility for the breakup. I am personally left cold by the rationalization mechanisms perpetuated in our society to shield divorced parents from seeing this pain and grief.

The child is told "you have two families now, you get Christmas and birthday and other special times twice." More likely, they don't really get it once. It is my sorrow for these forgotten and innocent victims of divorce that leads me to be cynical about and unaccepting of many of the reasons given for divorce: "I need to self-actualize"; "I have outgrown my spouse"; "I need my space." I do not think we have yet seen or appreciated the full extent of the damage that divorce does to children, to their concept of marriage, and ultimately to society.

Thus we can see that grief over loss of a spouse through divorce has the conceptual and psychological possibility of being more complex and difficult to work through than grief occasioned by death.

This in turn is compounded by society's failure to appreciate what occurs, especially since many divorced people are not so affected. Society, guided by the nature-convention dualism, does not admit to the profundity of the import that sundering conventional ties can have. Yet a moment's reflection reveals that dissolution of social bonds can be as acutely and chronically painful as death. The case of Orthodox Jews who act as if a child is dead if he or she converts makes this point dramatically: the social death engendered is at least as much a source of grief as biological death. In the case of divorce, the grief is walled off and trivialized by a social tendency toward cliches like "You can always marry again"; "Divorce is no big thing these days."

What then can be done socially to deal with the grief occasioned by divorce? One heretical solution which I favor, though I shan't argue for it here, is making divorce much harder to get, especially where children are involved. It is fairly evident that if people could not simply escape a problematic marriage as easily as they do, at least some people would be more likely to make it work. More immediately, people need to be educated to the idea that "conventional" does not mean trivial or unreal, and thus that grief at dissolution of a "conventional" bond like marriage is neither pathological, deviant, illegitimate, nor self-indulgent. At the very least, it must become common knowledge that such grief is nothing to be ashamed of or trivialized, but is an entirely intelligible reaction to a breaking of bonds that tears at the very core of one's self.

REFERENCES

Rollin, B.E. *Natural and Conventional Meaning: An Examination of the Distinction.* The Hague: Mouton, 1976.

_____. On the nature of illness. *Man and Medicine* 4(3):157-172, 1979.

_____. Nature, convention, and genre theory. *Poetics* 46, 1981.

_____. The concept of illness in veterinary medicine. *J. Am. Veterinary Med. Assoc.* 182:122-125, 1983.

_____. Nature, Convention, and the Medical Approach to the Dying Elderly. In M. Tallmer, et al., eds. *The Life-Threatened Elderly.* New York: Columbia University Press, 1984.

_____. Animal consciousness and scientific change. *New Ideas in Psychology* 4(2):141-152, 1986.

_____. Animal pain. In M.W. Fox and L. Mickley, eds. *Advances in Animal Welfare Science 1985-86.* The Hague: Martinus Nijhoff, 1986.

_____. *The Unheeded Cry: Animal Consciousness, Animal Pain, and Scientific Change.* Oxford, England: Oxford University Press, 1987.

2

Divorce Trends:
Societal and Personal Experience

B. Meredith Burke, PhD

The editor of this book unwittingly placed upon me two nearly irreconcilable charges: write a chapter drawing jointly upon my expertise as a professional demographer and upon my personal participation in the divorce experience of the 1970s. There are two reasons why I doubt my ability to complete this assignment gracefully. The first is stylistic: the disinterested tone by convention I assume as a social scientist cannot be reconciled with the conversational tone I assume as a first-person reporter. The second is point of view. The social scientist more accurately describes, the farther in the past a social change occurred and the greater the number of people affected by it. The individual must perforce live and experience her life in the present. She gains a sense of control by assuming she is the initiator in her own life rather than one of a multitude caught in a wave of social force.

I have decided to write a two-stage essay. Part one will be a brief history of this century's marital behavior. Part two will be a narrative weaving the bewilderment I felt when the world around me did not conform to expectations, with my later comprehension that my perceptions had been right, the old had changed.

There are two ways to describe demographic behavior such as marriage and divorce: for the population as a whole, or for the individual. In the former case we use measures such as the number of marriages or divorces per 1000 general population or per 100 marriages.

In the latter case we ask what is the likelihood of a person of stated age and sex (the main demographic discriminants, followed by race) or of a given birth or marriage cohort (persons born or married in the same year) experiencing a certain social transition, how long will he persist in the new social state, and how will he or she exit it?

To understand who got divorced in the 1960s, 1970s and early 1980s, we must first see who got married in the years preceding. Except for a hike at the end of World War I and a decline during the Depression, U.S. marriage rates were relatively stable from 1900 to the start of World War II. Thereafter, the proportion ever marrying (all figures pertain to those surviving to age 15) increased sharply for both sexes born between 1905 and 1915, then continued to rise more gradually for all those born up through the circa 1940 birth cohort. For men born circa 1900, 89 percent ultimately married. For the circa 1940 cohort the proportion was 96 percent. Comparable female figures were 92 and 97 percent, respectively.

Then even more swiftly than it had risen, the proportions marrying among age groups 15 to 29 declined. So sharp was this decline that U.S. Census experts (admittedly a conservative lot) estimate that for those born in the 1950s only 90 percent of both sexes may ultimately marry: proportions lower than for any preceding twentieth-century birth cohort.

If one looks to those in the next older age group for a model of expected or at least standard behavior, someone with a 1950s childhood would have seen a very different model from someone whose childhood was spent in the 1960s and 1970s. The median age at first marriage (the 50th percentile in the age distribution of those first marrying in a given year) dropped fairly steadily from 22.0 years for women and 26.1 for men in 1890 until it bottomed out at 20.3 for women and 22.8 for men during the 1950s (Table 1).

Table 1.
Median Age at First Marriage, by Sex: 1890-1988

Year	Men	Women
1988	25.9	23.6
1985	25.5	23.3
1980	24.7	22.0
1975	23.5	21.1
1970	23.2	20.8
1965	22.8	20.6
1960	22.8	20.3
1955	22.6	20.2
1950	22.8	20.3
1940	24.3	21.5
1930	24.3	21.3
1920	24.6	21.2
1910	25.1	21.6
1900	25.9	21.9
1890	26.1	22.0

Note: A standard error of 0.1 year is appropriate to measure sampling variability for any of the above median ages at first marriage, based on Current Population Survey data.

Source: U.S. Bureau of the Census, *Current Population Reports*, Series P-20, No. 433, *Marital Status and Living Arrangements: March 1988*, Table A-2.

    Then, in the mid-1960s, nuptiality behavior changed. Postponing a discussion of why this occurred, I will note it affected women first. (The marital behavior of the black population has increasingly diverged from that of the white. This not being a technical study of divorce, I am using data for the total U.S. population, 85 percent of whom are white.) Median age at marriage for women rose to 20.8 years in 1970, 22.0 in 1980, and 23.6 in 1988, the last being a historic high. For men, median age at marriage rose from 22.8 in 1960 to 23.2 in 1970, 24.7 in 1980, and 25.9 in 1988.

    This increase in marriage age is more strikingly demonstrated by the increases in the percent single never married in the post-1960 era. These proportions soared, especially for the post-1947 cohorts (Table 2). Just one year's difference in birth cohort made for a dramatic difference in marriage experience. In 1960 the proportion single among women at 22 was 25.6 percent; for those at age 23 it was 19.4 percent. By 1970 these proportions were 33.5 and 22.4 percent, corresponding to birth cohorts 1948 and 1947, respectively. By 1988 three-fifths of the women aged 20 to 24 and over three-quarters of the men aged 20 to 24 had never been married. For women aged 25 to 29 the proportion single had trebled since 1960 to 30 percent; for men it had more than doubled to 43 percent.

Americans born in the 1930s had a paucity of alternative role models. These cohorts behaved with astonishing uniformity: not only did nearly all of them marry and have children, but they did so in lockstep progression. The difference between the 25th percentile and the 75th, technically known as the interquartile range, was 3.8 years.

Table 2.
Percent Single (Never Married), by Age and Sex:
1988, 1980, 1970 and 1960

	Women			
Age	*1988*	*1980*	*1970*	*1960*
Total, 15 years and over	22.9	22.5	22.1	17.3
Under 40 years	40.4	38.8	38.5	28.1
40 years and over	5.1	5.1	6.2	7.5
15 to 17 years	97.7	97.0	97.3	93.2
18 years	92.4	88.0	82.0	75.6
19 years	86.0	77.6	68.8	59.7
20 to 24 years	61.1	50.2	35.8	28.4
20 years	78.7	66.5	56.9	46.0
21 years	71.6	59.7	43.9	34.6
22 years	58.9	48.3	33.5	25.6
23 years	56.0	41.7	22.4	19.4
24 years	43.7	33.5	17.9	15.7
25 to 29 years	29.5	20.9	10.5	10.5
25 years	39.0	28.6	14.0	13.1
26 years	32.6	22.7	12.2	11.4
27 years	27.4	22.2	9.1	10.2
28 years	26.3	16.0	8.9	9.2
29 years	22.2	14.6	8.0	8.7
30 to 34 years	16.1	9.5	6.2	6.9
35 to 39 years	9.0	6.2	5.4	6.1
40 to 44 years	6.2	4.8	4.9	6.1
45 to 54 years	5.1	4.7	4.9	7.0
55 to 64 years	4.0	4.5	6.8	8.0
65 years and over	5.3	5.9	7.7	8.5

Table 2.
Continued

Age	1988	1980	1970	1960
	Men			
Total, 15 years and over	29.9	29.6	28.1	23.2
Under 40 years	51.1	48.8	47.7	39.6
40 years and over	5.5	5.7	7.4	7.6
15 to 17 years	99.3	99.4	99.4	98.8
18 years	98.0	97.4	95.1	94.6
19 years	95.1	90.9	89.9	87.1
20 to 24 years	77.7	68.8	54.7	53.1
20 years	88.5	86.0	78.3	75.8
21 years	88.7	77.2	66.2	63.4
22 years	80.4	69.9	52.3	51.6
23 years	72.7	59.1	42.1	40.5
24 years	61.2	50.0	33.2	33.4
25 to 29 years	43.3	33.1	19.1	20.8
25 years	56.6	44.3	26.6	27.9
26 years	49.5	36.5	20.9	23.5
27 years	44.5	31.5	16.5	19.8
28 years	33.2	26.8	17.0	17.5
29 years	31.9	24.0	13.8	16.0
30 to 34 years	25.0	15.9	9.4	11.9
35 to 39 years	14.0	7.8	7.2	8.8
40 to 44 years	7.5	7.1	6.3	7.3
45 to 54 years	5.6	6.1	7.5	7.4
55 to 64 years	4.9	5.3	7.8	8.0
65 years and over	4.6	4.9	7.5	7.7

Figures for 1970 include persons 14 years of age.

Source: U.S. Bureau of the Census, *1960 Census of Population*, Vol. 1, *U.S. Summary*, Table 176.

From the late 1970s on, individual behavior became more diverse. Consequently, the interquartile range for women rose to 7.7 years in 1986. One-fourth of all first-time brides were over 27.7 years of age. For grooms this range lengthened from 6.5 years in 1962 to 9.0 years in 1986. One-fourth of all first-time grooms in 1986 were above age 31.1.

DIVORCE BEHAVIOR

Whether measured as the rate per 1000 total population or the rate per 1000 married women, the U.S. divorce rate increased very slowly but steadily for about 100 years, 1860 to the early 1960s. Only the immediate post–World War II years saw a sharp, temporary hike (Table 3). Between 1951 and 1964 no more than 1 percent of all married women were divorced annually. Then for 15 years the divorce rate rose, until it fluctuated around a plateau twice the earlier rates, or about 2 percent of married women or five divorces per 1000 total population. Another way of looking at the phenomenon is to note that in the mid-1960s about 500,000 divorces occurred annually, involving one million people. From 1975 onward, over one million divorces occurred annually, involving two million people.

Divorce has been more commonplace in American life than folklore would have it: about one-fifth of the marriages for men and women born in 1900 are estimated to have ended in divorce (Schoen et al. 1985, Table 4, p. 110). Although this proportion has risen for each birth cohort this century, fascinatingly enough the proportions of marriages ending in divorce by age 35 were almost identical for each of the 1920, 1930 and 1935 birth cohorts, both male and female. Then, at ages corresponding to the period 1970 onward, the gap between these widened, with each successively younger cohort more likely to divorce.

Table 3.
Estimated Number of Divorces and Annulments and Rates,
with Percent Changes from Preceding Year:
United States, 1920-1984

Year	Number	Percent Change	Rate per 1000 Total Population	Percent Change	Rate 1000 Married Women 15 Years of Age and Over	Percent Change
1984	1,169,000	+ 0.9	5.0	+ 2.0	21.5	+ 0.9
1983	1,158,000	– 1.0	4.9	– 2.0	21.3	– 1.8
1982	1,170,000	– 3.5	5.0	– 5.7	21.7	– 4.0
1981	1,213,000	+ 2.0	5.3	+ 1.9	22.6	–
1980	1,189,000	+ 0.7	5.2	– 1.9	22.6	– 0.9
1979	1,181,000	+ 4.5	5.3	+ 3.9	22.8	+ 4.1
1978	1,130,000	+ 3.6	5.1	+ 2.0	21.9	+ 3.8
1977	1,091,000	+ 0.7	5.0	–	21.1	–
1976	1,083,000	+ 4.5	5.0	+ 4.2	21.1	+ 3.9
1975	1,036,000	+ 6.0	4.8	+ 4.3	20.3	+ 5.2
1974	977,000	+ 6.8	4.6	+ 7.0	19.3	+ 6.0
1973	915,000	+ 8.3	4.3	+ 7.5	18.2	+ 7.1
1972	845,000	+ 9.3	4.0	+ 8.1	17.0	+ 7.6
1971	773,000	+ 9.2	3.7	+ 5.7	15.8	+ 6.0

Table 3.
Continued

Year	Number	Percent Change	Rate per 1000 Total Population	Percent Change	Rate 1000 Married Women 15 Years of Age and Over	Percent Change
1970	708,000	+ 10.8	3.5	+ 9.4	14.9	+ 11.2
1969	639,000	+ 9.4	3.2	+ 10.3	13.4	+ 7.2
1968	584,000	+ 11.7	2.9	+ 11.5	12.5	+ 11.6
1967	523,000	+ 4.8	2.6	+ 4.0	11.2	+ 2.8
1966	499,000	+ 4.2	2.5	–	10.9	+ 2.8
1965	479,000	+ 6.4	2.5	+ 4.2	10.6	+ 6.0
1964	450,000	+ 5.1	2.4	+ 4.3	10.0	+ 4.2
1963	428,000	+ 3.6	2.3	+ 4.5	9.6	+ 2.1
1962	413,000	– 0.2	2.2	– 4.3	9.4	– 2.1
1961	414,000	+ 5.3	2.3	+ 4.5	9.6	+ 4.3
1960	393,000	– 0.5	2.2	–	9.2	– 1.1
1959	395,000	+ 7.3	2.2	+ 4.8	9.3	+ 4.5
1958	368,000	– 3.4	2.1	– 4.5	8.9	– 3.3
1957	381,000	– 0.3	2.2	– 4.3	9.2	– 2.1
1956	382,000	+ 1.3	2.3	–	9.4	+ 1.1
1955	377,000	– 0.5	2.3	– 4.2	9.3	– 2.1
1954	379,000	– 2.8	2.4	– 4.0	9.5	– 4.0
1953	390,000	– 0.5	2.5	–	9.9	– 2.0
1952	392,000	+ 2.9	2.5	–	10.1	+ 2.0
1951	381,000	– 1.1	2.5	– 3.8	9.9	– 3.9
1950	385,144	– 3.0	2.6	– 3.7	10.3	– 2.8
1949	397,000	– 2.7	2.7	– 3.6	10.6	– 5.4
1948	408,000	+ 15.5	2.8	– 17.6	11.2	– 17.6
1947	483,000	– 20.8	3.4	– 20.9	13.6	– 24.0
1946	610,000	+ 25.8	4.3	+ 22.9	17.9	+ 24.3
1945	485,000	+ 21.3	3.5	+ 20.7	14.4	+ 20.0
1944	400,000	+ 11.4	2.9	+ 11.5	12.0	+ 9.1
1943	359,000	+ 11.8	2.6	+ 8.3	11.0	+ 8.9
1942	321,000	+ 9.6	+ 2.4	+ 9.1	10.1	+ 7.4
1941	293,000	+ 11.0	2.2	+ 10.0	9.4	+ 6.8
1940	264.000	+ 5.2	2.0	+ 5.3	8.8	+ 3.5
1939	251,000	+ 2.9	1.9	–	8.5	+ 1.2
1938	244,000	– 2.0	1.9	–	8.4	– 3.4
1937	249,000	+ 5.5	1.9	+ 5.6	8.7	+ 4.8
1936	236,000	+ 8.3	1.8	+ 5.9	8.3	+ 6.4
1935	218,000	+ 6.9	1.7	+ 6.3	7.8	+ 4.0
1934	204,000	+ 23.6	1.6	+ 23.1	7.5	+ 23.0
1933	165,000	+ 0.6	1.3	–	6.1	–
1932	164,241	– 12.6	1.3	– 13.3	6.1	– 14.1
1931	188,003	– 4.1	1.5	– 6.2	7.1	– 5.3
1930	195,961	– 4.8	1.6	– 5.9	7.5	– 6.2
1929	205,876	+ 2.8	1.7	–	8.0	+ 2.6

Table 3.
Continued

Year	Number	Percent Change	Rate per 1000 Total Population	Percent Change	Rate 1000 Married Women 15 Years of Age and Over	Percent Change
1928	200,176	+ 2.0	1.7	+ 6.3	7.8	–
1927	196,292	+ 6.3	1.6	–	7.8	+ 4.0
1926	184,678	+ 5.3	1.6	– 6.7	7.5	+ 4.2
1925	175,449	+ 2.6	1.5	–	7.2	–
1924	170,952	+ 3.5	1.5	–	7.2	+ 1.4
1923	165,096	+ 10.9	1.5	+ 7.1	7.1	+ 7.6
1922	148,815	– 6.7	1.4	– 6.7	6.6	– 8.3
1921	159,580	– 6.4	1.5	– 6.2	7.2	– 10.0
1920	170,505	–	1.6	–	8.0	–

Source: U.S. National Center for Health Statistics, *Vital Statistics of the United States, 1984*, Vol. III, *Marriage and Divorce, 1984*, Table 2-1

This increased likelihood showed itself in two different commonly measured ways. The first is as above, the increase in the cumulative proportion of marriages ultimately ending in divorce. Using data through 1980 Schoen and co-workers calculated that for the female birth cohorts circa 1920, 1930, 1940 and 1950, the percent of marriages ending in divorce would rise from 29 percent to 32, 37 and 42 percent, respectively. For men, the corresponding percentages would be 30, 34, 41 and 46 percent.

However, in a more recently published study using marriage rather than birth cohort data from the Census Bureau's June 1985 Current Population Survey, Teresa Martin and Larry Bumpass calculate still higher marital disruption (Martin and Bumpass 1989). Correcting for recently demonstrated sources of downward bias in two standard divorce data series, they project that after 40 years 64 percent of first marriages contracted between 1980 and 1985 will end in separation or divorce, separation accounting for 5 percentage points. For all marriages intact in June 1985 (some of them contracted 60 or more years ago), the authors estimate that 21 percent are likely to disrupt if current rates persist (Martin and Bumpass, p. 40). The 10 percent decline in the crude divorce rate between 1980 and 1987 they attribute to the changing age distribution of the adult population and the stabilization of certain rates.

Among the implications of such figures is the normalization of marriages terminating in divorce rather than in the death of one spouse. For the circa 1940 male birth cohort Schoen calculated that there was an equal likelihood of their first marriages ending in divorce or in their own deaths (only 18 percent ended in widower-hood). For those only five years younger, he estimated that 44 percent of their marriages would end in divorce versus 39 percent by their own deaths.

For women, a marriage is far more likely to end in widowhood than in the wife's death. Up through the 1920 birth cohort, about half or more marriages ended in widowhood (49 percent) compared with 22 percent in their own death and 29 percent in divorce. For the 1940 birth cohort the comparable proportions were 44, 19 and 37 percent: a marriage was now twice as likely to end in divorce as in a wife's own death. Widowhood, however, was still the most likely outcome. For those born circa 1950 (most of whose first marriages were contracted during the 1970s) these projections are 41, 17 and 42 percent. Martin and Bumpass's model, which assumes the rates of the 1980s continue unchanged, implies that for women born circa 1960 roughly 25 per-cent of first marriages will end in widowhood, 10 percent in wife's death, and 65 percent in divorce.

The other way of measuring change in divorce behavior is to look at the ages by which a stated proportion of marriages have ended in divorce. For American men born around 1890, not until age 55 did 15 percent of their marriages end in divorce. Men born in 1910 reached this proportion by age 40; men born between 1920 and 1935 reached it somewhere in their early 30s. Men born in 1945 were about 27 when 15 percent of their first marriages to date had ended in divorce. Wom-en's experience was near-identical, with the ages shifted downward by about two years (Schoen et al., Table 4). This accords with the usual two-year age difference between bride and groom in first mar-riages.

REMARRIAGE BEHAVIOR

For most Americans marriage is a preferred state. Although fewer than one in four widowers and one in ten widows born in the 1930s will ever remarry (reflecting an average age of widowhood of their mid-60s), Schoen calculated that more than four out of five divorced men and three out of four divorced women would remarry. These projections were based upon the 1980 census and vital statistics from the 1970s and pertain primarily to the white population.

However, there are good reasons for believing these estimates are too high. First, paralleling first marriage rates, remarriage rates (per 1000 divorced persons of state age and sex) declined sharply between

1970 and 1983 (NCHS, Wilson 1989). Secondly, as the age of first marriage has risen, the decline in the proportion of first marriages which involve a teenage bride has been particularly precipitous. Notably, women married for the first time in their teens have comprised a majority of all remarried women. In the June 1985 Current Population Survey, Martin and Bumpass found that whereas 35.4 percent of brides in first marriages between 1970 and 1985 were in their teens, 61.8 percent of all brides in second marriages had first married in their teens. As the authors point out, "this is a consequence of the higher rate of dissolution of teenage first marriages and the higher remarriage rate associated with returning to the marriage market at younger ages" (Martin and Bumpass, p. 46). Logically, the age at divorce must be rising along with the ages at first marriage, and the newly divorced are increasingly among age groups with lower remarriage rates.

Among divorced women, the remarriage rate declined 26 percent between 1970 and 1983, from 123 per 1000 to 92. For men, the decline was 31 percent, from 204 per 1000 to 142. These can be translated into percentages of the group remarrying: 9 percent of divorced women and 14 percent of divorced men remarried in 1983. In that year over 20 percent of divorced women in their 20s remarried versus under 7 percent of women aged 40 to 44. For those who do remarry, the mean interval to remarriage increased gradually from 2.5 years for divorced brides remarrying in 1970 to 3.3 years for their 1983 counterpart, and from 2.2 years to 3.0 for divorced grooms (NCHS, *Remarriages and Subsequent Divorces: United States*, 1989).

A declining rate of remarriage is perfectly consistent with an increase in the number of remarriages. Because of the huge increase in the population of divorced people, between 1970 and 1983 the number of divorced brides rose from 404,000 to 736,000; of divorced grooms, from 423,000 to 773,000. About one in three American brides and grooms in 1983 had been married before, up from one in four in 1970 (NCHS, 1989, p. 5). Indeed, the general marriage rate per 1000 population has not gone down with the sharp postponement of first marriages described above because of the countervailing gain in the number of remarriages.

A final note on remarriages comes from Martin and Bumpass. Adjusting for the effects on the survival of remarriages of the greater proportion of brides who first married as teenagers (a behavior which affects the survival of subsequent marriages as well) and the lower educational attainment of those in remarriages (presumably reflecting the truncated educational careers of those who first marry young), the authors find no higher risk of disruption of second marriages as compared to first (Martin and Bumpass, p. 47). The higher dissolution rates for remarriages so often offered as evidence that persons who remarry are less stable and more divorce-prone than first-time brides and grooms are entirely artifacts of the different demographic composition of the remarrying population.

THE DIVORCE REVOLUTION:
PERSONAL OBSERVATIONS

Shortly after I separated from my husband in late 1977 (at the age of 30), I commented to a recently divorced woman friend some five years my senior that I was having difficulty in adjusting to my new state. "You see," I confided, "over the years I've fantasized remaining a spinster or being a wife, or even a widow . . . but somehow I never thought I would be divorced." "Which of us did?" my friend responded.

In turn, the editor of this book remarked to me that many women born around 1930 did not even consider that divorce was an option, no matter how unsatisfying or soul-deadening the marriage. By the time of my marriage in the mid-1970s, no newlywed could be unaware that this was a possibility, some of them openly saying, "If it doesn't work out, then . . . ."

As a trained social scientist, I am familiar with the literature trying to explain in economic and sociological terms why and how the divorce rate soared in the post-1985 era, many of the reasons being the same as those cited for the decline in fertility. It has been stated that marriages were no worse than before, but women had less need to stay in a bad marriage. The greater availability of jobs made them less dependent. (But this ignores that female labor force participation rates had been increasing steadily throughout the postwar era for women over age 35, including during the low-divorce-rate 1950s. Furthermore, this completely ignores the problem so acute in the 1970s of the displaced homemaker.)

It is also alleged that expectations of the emotional and social rewards from marriage rose, so that definitions of a good and a bad marriage changed. The needs of the individual dominated that of the group in the "Me first" decade of the 1970s, so people were more selfish and had less tolerance of an unfulfilling marriage. Finally, those born in the postwar era took marriage less seriously than their elders and "wouldn't put in the hard (psychological) work" a lasting marriage requires to get through the rough spots.

As generalizations, I find all the above unsatisfying. I have never met anyone who set out to become divorced, although I have met many people both long-term married and divorced who admit to having had doubts about their marriages while in the engagement phase. Still, even those who by their wedding day rated the ultimate chance of divorce as non-negligible married in hopes that the shortcomings in the relationship could be worked out in the intimacy of marriage.

With one exception which I will describe below, I also have never encountered someone who accounts for a divorce by explaining "everyone is doing it, so we thought we'd jump on the social trend." Firstly, up until about 1980 most people did not think of themselves as members of a group whose divorce susceptibility was rising rapidly. Only with historical perspective can one realize that a given shift in behavior was no fluctuation but a signal of a new behavioral pattern. Secondly, even as Americans began to understand that high divorce probabilities were here for a long run, if not to stay, they still experienced their own lives individually. Asked to account for the circumstances leading to their divorce, most people will cite personal incompatibilities, events which resulted in a divergence of long-term goals, or a bad turn of fate which sundered their spousal relationship rather than strengthening it.

These are the (stated) reasons for twelve (first) divorces among members of the 1940 to 1949 birth cohort with whom I am familiar:

1. Husband took a gun to them (two cases).
2. Completed graduate school and one spouse did not wish to confront the demands of a "grown-up" non-student marriage.
3. Completed graduate school and both realized they had no more joint goals and no desire to forge new ones with that spouse.
4. Spouse had an emotionally abusive personality and spouse's therapist feared for the sanity of the partner.
5. The day after the first anniversary husband turned over and announced he wanted a divorce (unclear whether there was "another" woman).
6. Wife insisted upon adopting children with major medical problems and, after several years of a chaotic household environment, the husband issued an ultimatum "either the children go, or I do."
7. Married in early 20s and after husband enrolled in professional school, he ignored the emotional and companionship needs of his wife and child.

8. Got pregnant as a means of dropping out of college, refused the offer of a safe illegal abortion, married the father and divorced three years later.
9. Married so compatible a spouse when both were in their early 20s that when their first serious discord arose seven years later, neither knew how to work it out, and they were too naive to seek counseling.
10. Sibling disabled in freak accident and to assist with medical costs, wife took a job which ended in her becoming a national expert in a field far removed from her original career goals and evolving into a very different person from the one her husband married.
11. After ten years of irresolvable sexual incompatibility, one spouse opted out.

Although there may be some common factors (e.g., immaturity), show me a cohort pattern in the above! Certainly some of these cases fit the categories described above in that people were unwilling to tolerate indefinitely unmet sexual or emotional needs; they would not tolerate coexistence with someone in the absence of shared goals; and would not modify their behavior to please or satisfy their spouse. But it is understandable that to the participants these were all manifestations of individual behavior and not of membership in the birth cohort of the 1940s.

On the other hand, I would maintain that one group of men and women did see themselves as representative of a whole class of people, and these were those born in the 1930s or very early 1940s. At least three patterns of marital disruption became so common that even at the time the participants knew their experiences were not unique, although this knowledge did not necessarily alleviate the pain surrounding the breakup.

First were members of CR (consciousness raising) groups. Generally speaking, these were women who read Betty Friedan after they had contracted (an early) marriage under the old separate roles and spheres rules and who for a variety of reasons could not renegotiate new marital ground rules with their husbands. (One of the best novels describing this pattern is *Ella Price's Journal* by Dorothy Bryant.) These reasons included concealing their growing dissatisfaction with the old rules until one day they presented their unwary spouse with a list of demands which essentially asked the spouse to compress into one day the value changes which had taken many months to evolve in the wife; total refusal by a husband to consider a change in marital roles whether because he valued the comfort the old offered him or because he felt threatened by the new (or both); sufficient stored-up anger at the husband that there was no longer any desire to stay in and work at that particular marriage; and an urgent need to live on one's own in order belatedly to experience a stage between being a child of one's parents and a wife to one's husband which their early marriages had short-circuited.

These women were unique in that they not only knew they were not alone in initiating divorce when and why they did, but that in a curious way they were freed to initiate divorce precisely because of the solidarity they experienced from their "sisters" who were going through the same. Many of them had perhaps overly optimistic expectations of what life would be like on their own, not foreseeing how quickly most husbands would renege on child support payments or how poorly equipped they were to support themselves and their children in a still very sexist labor market. On the other hand, today many of them speak appreciatively of the opportunity to explore new ways of organizing their lives, new interests and new careers, new styles of parenting freed from the pressure to act in accordance with the status quo, and most importantly, of the opportunity to learn what their true tastes and values were once they no longer mirrored their parents or their husbands.

One non-participant in this experience remarked to me in some bewilderment, "Ten years later most of the women I knew who had taken the initiative in divorcing their first husbands were remarried to men very similar to those very husbands. Moreover, they admitted as much!"

"Yes, but those second marriages were not the same as the first because the women had changed during the process/interval of divorce." From the onset of the new relationship, these women could now negotiate a different package so to speak, one reflecting their sense of greater personal power and self-worth and their knowledge that they could survive on their own.

The second common pattern of divorce had its source in that most characteristically 1970s movement, "Open Marriage." Open marriage hit that same age group and the earlier marrying of the 1940s generation. One can view it variously, first as an outgrowth of the 1960s testing of all traditional rules—marital and nonmarital—which prompted a desire to "do one's own thing," or second as the need for experiences prevented by what were in retrospect the too-early marriages of the 1950s.

One can also see it as a counterploy by men who did not want to cede power and change roles in their traditional marriages but who could gain sexual variety guiltlessly while ceding freedom in at least one sphere to their wives, thereby sustaining an illusion that the underlying roles and power balance had shifted. Open marriage may also be viewed as an envious response by their near-elders to the delayed marriage and greater premarital sexual experimentation by the Baby Boom generation. The post-1960 diffusion of the contraceptive pill in a sense permitted both types of sexual freedom: it sharply reduced the likelihood of either a premarital or an extramarital pregnancy.

My personal observation is that open marriage was a sure route to divorce. It breached the sanctity and exclusivity which underpin Western marriage. It ultimately allowed one or both partners to charge exploitation. Finally, it certainly did not shift power to a wife who was negotiating for a greater say in the structure of the marriage.

The third common divorce pattern was related to the two above. This was for the increasing divorce rate among well-established marriages where the husband walked out on his loyal homemaker wife. We can speculate that early marriages before the adult personas of either husband or wife had fully formed may have resulted in more of a mismatch between husband and wife. Separate spheres were heightened by the postwar growth of age and sex-sequestered suburban housing tracts (Philip Slater perceptively recorded some consequences of this in *The Pursuit of Loneliness*). In a society which expects husband and wife to socialize together, differences in daily experience may attain a significance lacking in totally sex-segregated societies.

The high incomes of those born in the 1930s relative to their elders and their parents at comparable life stages have been cited by Richard Easterlin as one factor prompting their youthful marriages. This comparative affluence may also have made it easier for these men to believe they could support two households, even though the record demonstrates how few of them carried out obligations to their first families.

Finally, for those who were experiencing a nest emptying out while they and their partners were only in their early to mid 40s, the knowledge that they could expect to spend another 25 years as a couple may have led them to evaluate their spouses more critically than previous generations had at that point. Nineteenth-century women continued childbearing until nearly age 40 and could expect to die before their children were on their own. Women born in the 1930s typically compressed three births between ages 20 and 26 and then attained "demographic menopause" with very low birth rates in their 30s.

For whatever reasons, thousands of women who had faithfully kept their half of the traditional marriage vows, who had made a home for husband and children, and who had assumed they had an unassailable claim to continued support and their husbands' pensions found themselves displaced from their adult role. Many had never worked for pay outside the home; others not since their marriages 20 years or more before. The "Putting Hubby Through" degree of which many had boasted turned out to command nothing for them in their own job searches; and the legal position that one spouse's postmaritally acquired degree(s) constitute joint property gained initial acceptance only in the mid-1980s.

One value does underlie all the choices discussed above: that the individual is entitled to rectify choices which turn out to lead to significant degrees of unhappiness for the self. A second value has led to increasing frustration within the structure of traditional marriage, and that is the growing acceptance that women are entitled to develop and exercise talents which can be expressed only outside the domestic sphere. It is infrequently remarked that the middle-class generation coming of age after World War II was the first in world history to lack a servant class. Through the 1930s the relatively smaller white-collar class always had at least a "hired girl" to relieve the mistress of the house of the drudgery of repetitive or physically demanding chores. The supply of farm girls, immigrants, and blacks was self-renewing. The curtailment of immigration in the 1920s, the diminishment of rural migration as the society achieved urbanization, and the opening up of factory employment to women of all backgrounds during World War II dried up the supply of servants in the postwar period.

It is one thing to accept the duties of being mistress of one's household when that post has both managerial and self-development components. It is another when the mistress herself performs all the ceaseless work of physically maintaining a single-family house (no building superintendent to call on) and of tending to three children born in quick succession. The youngest generation participating in the Divorce Revolution to date are those born in the 1950s. The women of this cohort saw their mothers act as household servants and themselves perform household chores while their brothers went off more or less scot-free. Both the civil rights and the women's movements of the 1960s attacked the supposition that certain groups by virtue of race or sex membership were fated to be society's servants.

The women marrying in the 1980s include a far greater proportion committed to egalitarian marriage than any previous generation. To their sadness and anger (and I maintain to the detriment of societal well-being), those who entered the institution of marriage in this decade have too commonly discovered that neither their partners nor the structure of society at large are equipped to support this. Housework remains the political issue it was termed in the 1960s (and by the feminists of 1900 as well). Communal living has remained an interesting oddity, irrelevant to the vast majority of married Americans who live in their own nuclear family residence.

When women discover that husbands who can accept them on an equal basis as classmates and colleagues still regard them as household domestics once they accept the role of "wife," they frequently leave. Studies have supported what many of us have seen personally, namely that no matter how egalitarian a marriage has been in its early stages, the advent of a child usually resurrects traditional role separations and greatly increases the domestic work load of the wife with only a meager increase in that of the husband.

As I have written elsewhere, traditional marriages in traditional societies are stable in part because there is general agreement on the accepted courtship ritual and roles of husband and wife. Americans are confronting the fact that when a social institution is transformed, the process is neither smooth nor immediate. By the early 1970s, a commonly heard complaint by men was that when they behaved like gentlemen and opened a door for a woman, she was as apt to announce loudly "I can do it myself" as she was to say "Thank you." A still later criticism rooted in the new equality was: "She earns as much as I, yet she always expects me to pick up the bill!" (This was definitely a "yuppie" joke as the great majority of women remained poorly paid compared to men.)

Both sexes failed to recognize the fact that in a transition period people usually accept both some old and some new values, frequently in conflict. Mentioned above was the women's complaint that men who accepted equality in the workplace did not accept it at home. For their part, men would complain that their wives wanted dual career/ dual housework marriages yet would want to retain their entire paychecks for themselves ("What's yours is ours and what's mine is mine."). People's motivations arguably became more complicated, and the discovery after marriage that one's views on proper marital behavior were incompatible with those of one's spouse concomitantly became more frequent.

Against this backdrop young adults tried to find unstodgy, fashionable role models who were partners in solid, lasting marriages. These models held out reassurance that a new marital balance was possible which would permit both partners to develop their talents, nurture each other, and physically maintain a household nonexploitively. The same generation who, it is alleged, formed their image of ideal family life on the television shows of the 1950s, now looked to media-prominent couples for this model of new marital bliss.

Just as many couples in the same circle are traumatized and more than a little threatened when an "ideal" couple announces an impending divorce, so many Americans are angry and disillusioned when a seemingly stable media marriage dissolves. I am reminded of the much-discussed divorces of actress Jane Fonda and politician Tom Hayden, after 15 years of marriage and one child, and of actress Meredith Baxter Birney and actor David Birney, after 14 years and three children. The former was considered suitable for a serious column on this topic by Anne Taylor Fleming in *The New York Times*. As Americans of the late '80s and early '90s have learned all too well, there is no guaranteed "happily ever after."

LIVING THROUGH A REVOLUTION:
A PERSONAL ACCOUNT

It is not easy to live through a social revolution. Hardest of all is realizing that it is not just your life which is not working out according to plan, but that you have lots of company in this social upheaval. Entering college in 1962 at age 15 and graduating in 1967 at age 20, I traversed the great divide. In spring 1963, nearly every senior girl in my Berkeley dorm was engaged to be married immediately upon graduation. One close friend married two years later in what was then considered a late marriage. That summer I attended the wedding of a high school friend who had just completed her sophomore year of college and, just before her 20th birthday, married a man with a freshly conferred B.A.

Four years later I turned down a proposal from my senior-year boyfriend even as I served as sounding board to a classmate who feared if she turned down a current proposal from a man she did not love, she might never get married. At graduate school at Cornell, I discovered myself to be the sole woman in the course-taking stage of the demography major. One woman was completing her dissertation in the department, and two women were minoring in it. The former and one of the latter were six years older than I and married; the remaining woman was two years older than I and ultimately married and had children nearly two decades later.

I took the next year off from graduate school and headed to Boston. A good many of my friends there were married and paired off, including those in their late 20s and several who were only a year or two out of undergraduate school (of six couples closest to me, I know at least four are now divorced). Jobs that fall of 1968 were plentiful for college graduates, who were still scarce and commanded a premium wage. The expectation for those of us who were still single was that we could enjoy Boston's dating scene for a year or two while we found ourselves a mate.

Over the next six years the social scene turned completely around. The ending of the Great Society, the Vietnam War and the presidency of Richard Nixon coincided with the Energy Crisis, diminished employment prospects for the large number of Baby Boom college graduates, and lower productivity and wage growth for the typical American worker. I spent most of this time in and out of graduate school, buffered from much of this because I didn't see myself as ready to assume an adult life.

I remark upon the shifting social scene because I came to marriage as a product of ten or more years of social change. Only when I moved to Washington, D.C. and turned 27 did I discover that a whole universe of college-educated, socially normal people unmarried in their late 20s and even their 30s had come to pass outside of the university where deferred marriage had always been more common. In Washington entire neighborhoods, let alone apartment buildings, existed for the unencumbered single, where there was no expectation one should be married by a certain age. Only there did I bond with other women whose lives where evolving similarly to my own—and where I could begin to define myself as part of a well-defined group instead of as a too-fussy spinster.

The Divorce Revolution directly affected me in two ways. The man I married was available only because of his divorce from his first wife of 20 years' standing. Then I myself became a divorce statistic after 18 months of marriage. Although many years later I learned that some of what I consider the pathologies of my marriage were not unique, they were definitely not related to cohort influences.

Whether through divorce or through death, marriages can end in one of two ways: abruptly or drawn out. I still do not know which is the more painful. Divorces which emerge from a slow growing apart by husband and wife should be relatively painless because they mark the formal end of passion. For me the trust necessary to relax in the intimacy my husband and I had shared was broken in one episode. I was in mourning for the many months we remained together, part of me hoping for a miracle which could burn away the emotional scar tissue and renew what originated as a bond of total acceptance of each other. I know now that the necessary emotional changes might have taken decades, if indeed both of us could have agreed on what needed to change.

In retrospect, I weathered the initial year of separation rather solitarily. I could not identify with divorced people in general, and I soon learned how nearly impossible it was to find someone who could empathize with the depth of the misery I was suffering. I felt rather like someone recovering from a miscarriage or stillbirth. Many people made light of my marital experience, or at least I thought they did: "Married less than two years? No children? You'll get right over it, you were hardly married, lucky for you!"

I felt I didn't belong in a group like "Parents Without Partners." First of all, I only had the three stepchildren whom I never saw after I left their father. Secondly, I assumed from the accounts I heard that these groups were largely composed of people in their late 30s and over, who were recovering from long-term marriages. I myself had offered advice on occasion to such people, who felt totally unprepared to re-enter a dating scene they had left one decade and a revolution ago. I frankly could not see what such a group could offer me.

Also, I was very defensive with people. I had heard so many couples who had stayed together condemn people of my generation: "If only they would work harder on their marriages, they wouldn't be getting divorced so much." I took this as a personal attack, never considering they might be offering themselves reassurance. What was "enough"? I wondered. Inwardly I would frequently fantasize, crying out, "I tried! I really tried!" and carrying around a written certification from our therapist to that effect.

I attempted to tell myself that the people who mattered to me all knew the effort I had made to salvage my marriage and if they didn't, it was too bad. But for many, many months I felt like shrinking inside myself when I had to confess to being divorced.

I had a sense of unreality that year, anyhow, whenever I met new people in a group such as a church. I would look at them and think, "They think they are meeting me, but can't they see that they're meeting an amputee, that part of me is missing?" I had felt so coupled that I was incapable of feeling I was a complete person just by myself.

I was accompanied by personal mantras which persisted far longer than I am willing to confess on paper. They were not very novel. The first was, "Who would ever believe . . . ." The ending phrase of this would vary from "this could happen to us" to "a thing so perfect could end up in ruins," "a thing destined to last a lifetime could die so swiftly," "two people with such accord could end up not even friends."

The second one was "If only . . . ." If only he had not made a certain hurtful remark; if only I had had the knowledge or the maturity to have handled something differently; if only an apology had been made at a time when forgiveness might have been possible. The third mantra was a feeling rather than a phrase, a sense of deep wrongness with a world which allowed a relationship such as ours had originally promised to be to go awry. These mantras were like my car radio, turning on whenever I entered my car, and couldn't swaddle my inner ear with the distractions of my household routine.

These were an obsession which abated very slowly. Surprisingly in one used to library research, I never thought of searching the literature on divorce for help. I think the deluge of self-help books in this area began a few years too late for me, while I encountered Robert Weiss' excellent study, *Marital Separation*, three or four years later, after I had already passed through many of the milestones he described.

For many months I was very sad. I had hoped that the sadness which had afflicted me during the marriage would lift with the separation, but my sense of loss (even though in sane moments I knew this was of potentialities) was unbounded. I think now that I might have found the most help in a support group for young widows, assuming there were such a group in 1977. But that never occurred to me. Somewhat contradictorily, even in my anguish I felt such an easing of tension from removal from a home that had turned on me that I did not for one moment consider I was a candidate for counseling.

Dating was a no-problem area. I took a self-consciously congratulatory stance that I, at least, had no reason to go out and madly date a string of men to prove I was "still" attractive. After all, 18 months out of the dating scene could scarcely occasion "re-entry shock." The truth was, I was so emotionally drained that I lacked the energy to go through the standard getting acquainted process. Secondly, about every three months that year either an old flame would end up in Washington, or I would end up in some city or other where an old boyfriend lived. I found that these occasional meetings satisfied my "dating" needs.

The third reason I felt no urgency to resume my dating life was rooted in one of those deep inner feelings most of us have from time to time but conveniently remember only if they prove accurate. From the first moment of separation I held an inner conviction deeper than any other I have experienced to date—namely, that I had grown so much during my marriage that I had become more psychologically marriageable and would indeed meet a perfect mate within a year. Years later I would make a joke about this presentiment, reminding my listeners that this one in fact had not come to pass. Yet it acted as a spiritual balm, bringing me a peacefulness and a restful time out I sorely needed.

I had my first real post-divorce date approximately two weeks after my divorce became final following a year's separation. I could not and cannot discern any difference between a typical date before marriage and after divorce, with the sole exception being that I no longer needed to maintain the social pose of sexual inexperience. For nearly four years post-divorce I would have said the same of my relationships with men.

Then I met the first man I could seriously entertain as a prospective mate. I then learned that I had many scars left from my marriage, scars which never had surfaced while I was living by myself again. I was shocked at how much fear I carried, fear that I might not be able to protect myself any better than I had before, fear of being emotionally vulnerable again, fear I would not be strong enough to make my non-negotiable ground rules clear from the start.

Since I was also my partner's first serious romance following his divorce a couple of years before, he, too, displaced onto me emotions he had not resolved with his ex-wife. If he was repelled by the demands I was making so explicitly about what I would need in a life lived together, I was repelled by the residual bitterness toward women I discerned in his voice. Although our romance didn't work out for a number of reasons—several far removed from ones associated with our respective divorces—the unworked-through traumas had certainly contributed. Some time later, when I finally understood what had motivated my own behavior, I wrote a formal note of apology with an explanation of why I had acted as I did.

A year ago I encountered my ex-husband quite by chance and scarcely recognized him, so changed was he. To my reassurance, I found myself somewhat bored and with no need to prolong the meeting. So on those infrequent moments when one of the old mantras resurfaces, I counter them with the results of my "reality testing."

I had dated seriously for nearly 13 years before I got married. I have now been divorced for that long. For many of the post-divorce years—too many, I suppose any professional psychological counselor would say—I would take care to mention my ex-husband in any first conversation with a new friend. Many new acquaintances would therefore assume that I was freshly divorced. I think my behavior represented as much my flashing my credentials entitling me to acceptance in the world of the grown-ups as it did a need to feel I had at least once been attached to another person.

I perceive marriage as the great divide which one must cross to become a full-fledged adult able to meet others as equals. My experience has reinforced this sense. Several years after my divorce I performed a favor through a mutual friend for a sociologist I had never met. Afterward I pressed quite hard to meet her, and eventually we set up a lunch date. Perhaps I looked younger than my age, but I had the impression that this woman, maybe ten years older than I, was speaking as if to one very junior to her in the ways of the world. So I casually but deliberately let drop how long I had been divorced and some details about some consultancies I had performed abroad. Her manner toward me totally changed, and thereafter she addressed me as a "chum." Later I was proud when a woman I very much liked was surprised, after two months of knowing me, to hear I was divorced. I felt this showed I had come a long way.

Am I over my divorce? Have I gained closure, to use today's jargon? Truthfully, I don't know. I don't know how other people experience either the event or the process. I had forged new family ties, then I had to cast them off and could say, "I was mistaken. We are not family, after all."

Not long ago I read the autobiography of British author Rumer Godden, herself divorced when she still had young children. Speaking of the marriage ceremony, she states that only then did she realize what they had just done, the solemnity of the commitment. I am sure the wisest of mankind's thinkers and poets have yet not fully explained the marital bond. Where does it come from, this shaking solemnity—the fact that your life is inextricably linked to a non-blood relative, that you have social permission to start a new biological life, that in some strange way you are a vessel for all the many ancestors behind you—and more poetically, from the merging of two souls?

Writing this, I feel pressured to write the acceptable, that once the scars healed, I went on my way just as before. But for me at least, a sense of family is hard to come by. Giving up this sense of family proved to be the hardest part of the divorce process. I suspect I will not be totally over it until I have forged new family ties elsewhere. I am perfectly ready to do so. But finding someone who provides a sense of family can be a very daunting quest.

REFERENCES

Bryant, Dorothy. *Ella Price's Journal.* Berkeley: Ata Books, 1982.

Fleming, Anne Taylor. Points west, *The New York Times*, March 1, 1989.

Martin, Teresa Castro, and Larry L. Bumpass. Recent trends in marital disruption. *Demography* 26(1): 37-51, 1989.

National Center for Health Statistics. *Remarriages and Subsequent Divorces: United States.* Vital and Health Statistics Series 21, No. 45. DHHS Pub. No. (PHS) 89-1923. Washington, DC: U.S. Public Health Service, 1989.

National Center for Health Statistics. *Vital Statistics of the United States, 1984. Vol. III, Marriage and Divorce.* DHHS Pub. No. (PHS) 88-1103. Washington, DC: U.S. Public Health Service, 1988.

Schoen, Robert, William Urton, Karen Woodrow, and John Baj. Marriage and divorce in twentieth century American cohorts. *Demography* 22(1): 101-114, 1985.

U.S. Bureau of the Census. *Current Population Reports, Series P-20, No. 433, Marital Status and Living Arrangements: March 1988.* Washington, D.C.: U.S. Government Printing Office, 1989.

Weiss, Robert. *Marital Separation.* New York: Basic Books, 1977.

Westoff, Charles F. Perspective on nuptiality and fertility, in K. Davis, M. S. Bernstam, and R. Ricardo-Campbell, eds., Below-replacement fertility in industrial societies. *Population and Development Review* 12(suppl.): 155-170, 1986.

3

Divorce in Clinical Sociological Perspective

Adrian R. Tiemann, PhD, CSW, CCS

THE PROBLEM IN CLINICAL SOCIOLOGICAL PERSPECTIVE

Everyone knows that when two people decide to marry and form a family, they embark upon a task which is entirely new to them—the creation of a family unit—inasmuch as they attained their original family status by birth. From an organizational point of view, asking two people who will come to form one of the basic building blocks of the social structure to undertake a totally new and untried task is a hell of a way to run a society. It comes as no surprise that problems might arise within systems founded upon such weak premises. But that is the way it is done, and you can't argue with tradition. However, that tradition leads, over time, to certain difficulties in social functioning, and it is *these* and their amelioration which form the purview of the clinical sociologist.

In this chapter I will examine divorce not only from the perspective of a clinician engaged in private practice, but from the wider lens of the clinical sociologist interested in helping to establish a better fit between the way in which human beings express their natural proclivities and the way in which their social environment responds to their activities. In other words, the clinical sociologist seeks to find a way in which both the individual and the society can "win."

In examining an issue like divorce, the clinical sociologist asks what social structures are involved in the process, what mechanisms each contributes, and how these mechanisms get in each other's way.

These comprise the theoretical half of the task. The therapeutic or pragmatic part of the task, addressed both to the individuals involved in the divorce process and to society regulating that process, is how to help assure that whatever change takes place is as positive in impact as possible under the circumstances. Since each mechanism was historically advanced by its proponents as an aid for perceived problems surrounding the issue, feelings tend to run high on the part of constituents regarding making any changes.

Now since both of these major issues—the theoretic and the practical—have generated volumes on their own from many fine minds, what new insights are offered here? Before answering, let me point out that we all know how solutions can sometimes become the problem themselves. Only in recent history have we had anything approaching a science of society, and its practitioners have neither been sufficiently expert nor trusted to be called upon for the task. These problems may be furthered or masked by prevailing custom, external conditions, or by the peculiarities of the people involved. Whatever outcome these problems generate—dissolution or continuance of the marital unit—they will inevitably become public and affect units beyond the original dyad. As they do, of course, they spark the interest and attention of social structures devoted to processing, helping or controlling people in crisis.

As Pittman (1987) notes, divorce, like amputation, saves lives, but it doesn't "work." It doesn't stop a battling couple from fighting, and it does not get the children out from under the conflict between their parents. Moreover, despite recent attempts at justification, it is not a normal part of the family life cycle. It is aberrant because marriage can work "only if it is treated as if it were permanent" (p.131).

While the existence of divorce may signify an advance in the ability of our values and social structure to adapt to changing times, its becoming more of a "norm" within society does not represent *success*. Like amputation, it may be the best medicine available at the time for the problem. But the victims of divorce—whose lives may have been saved by that remedy—are not restored to full functioning any more than is the wearer of a prosthesis. The clinical sociological questions, then, are what factors from which levels of the social system are facilitating divorce in society, and what meliorative actions offer the greatest opportunity for intervention? Since a full discussion of each of these topics would be beyond the scope of this chapter, I will present a framework for assessing at what *level of the system* interventions can be targeted for maximum effectiveness. Two case examples will then be provided illustrating the method. In order to begin, let us look at a simplified model of the social structure (see Table 1).

Table 1.
A Conceptual Model of Divorce

Potential Level of Marital Failure	Partner's "Causal" Characteristic	Type of Issue Raised for Departing Spouse
Biophysical	Sterility, genetic incompatibility.	Family life values and desire for children; partners' self-esteem.
	Physical characteristics: height, weight, skin color, abnormality or defect.	Esthetic values, "tribal" values, familial values. Partners' self-esteem.
	Emotional characteristics: depressiveness, mania, anger, immaturity, ability to handle stress.	Spouse's compatibility, spouse's ability to deal with partner's emotions.
	Accidental dismemberment.	Caretaking abilities.
	Stroke, heart attack, serious surgery.	Self-esteem of both.
Self	Inability to unite means and goals through action; pseudo-attempts or neurotic activities; self-estrangement.	Coping abilities, experience, flexibility.
	Rigidity in gender or other role definitions.	Spouse's competing rigidities.
	Adultery.	Trust, loyalty and intimacy.
	Sexual difficulties.	Self-esteem, intimacy, equality.
	Workaholism.	Difficulty regulating intimacy.
	Depression.	Exhaustion of resources, mental, physical and emotional.
	Alcoholism, psychosis, mania, etc.	Co-dependent patterns. Coping, being overwhelmed.

Table 1.
Continued

Potential Level of Marital Failure	Partner's "Causal" Characteristic	Type of Issue Raised for Departing Spouse
Society, social groups, family, peers, friends, reference, work and other relevant groups.	Class.	Economic powerlessness, isolation.
	Status.	Lack of social esteem, normlessness.
	Power.	Powerlessness, vulnerability in one's reference groups.
	Values.	Meaninglessness in the social network; expendability.
Culture	Cultural differences, cultural pressures.	Competing values. Conformity vs. rebellion.
	Symbolic clashes.	Ultimate meaning of life: "reality."

In this table, the first column represents *levels* of functioning which may be involved in a spouse's decision to divorce. The second column lists the kinds of *symptoms* or "causal" attributes exhibited by the "offending" partner at each of these levels which, in each level, can be provocative to the spouse. The third column lists the types of issues typically generated in the spouse by a partner's characteristics. For example, the partner may have been an unwanted child whose vulnerability is expressed in defensive suspiciousness and hostility. Under ordinary circumstances, these are held fairly well in check, but under stress, the partner's anxiety results in behaviors that are outlandish in the social context. If the spouse has difficulty dealing with the partner's maneuvers at the best of times because of his or her own competing rigidities, then any added stressor can tilt the system toward dissolution.

Some of the revolutions occurring within the mental health field represent attempts to improve the "medicine" or mechanisms available for dealing with the problem of divorce. Living together, living apart though identified as a "couple" by their friends, and commuter marriages are ad hoc mechanisms for dealing with some of the problems arising from changes in contemporary society having the potential to lead to divorce. Family therapy, divorce mediation and couples counseling are some of the mental health mechanisms striving, more often than not, to improve the fit between the problem of couples who are having trouble staying together and the personal forces, including their families and friends, who may be alternately pulling them apart and pushing them together. I say "more often than not" because divorce and separation rates for clients of practitioners treating one spouse of the pair (and presumably following individual psychodynamic models committed to self-actualization) are higher than they are for spouses seen "together" by therapists who include an interactional component in their model of family life.

But there are social forces arrayed against the marriage as well. Since our founding days this nation has celebrated an ethic of individuality and self-determination. One is made to feel inadequate if one's decisions and choices are not made from an "independent" rather than an interactional point of view (see Gilligan 1978; Kohlberg 1976; Perry 1970).

This celebration has been institutionalized in a zero-sum legal code designed to ascertain "truth" and assign blame, as well as in other sectors of society. Divorce lawyers whose practice is lodged within this rigid system often unwittingly become allied with these forces. So do those commercial interests whose sales are increased by the duplication of households at a greater rate than their profits are eroded by the decrease in disposable income of one of the divorcing pair. It may seem banal to stress the influence of these factors, but seduction in the form of what Watzlawick (1988) calls "ultra-solutions" beckon everywhere for precisely the reason many people arrive at the therapist's office in the first place. As endemic features of American life, therapists should perhaps be more charitable toward the follies of ultra-solutions that feed their clinical schedules and toward which we now turn.

THERAPEUTIC CONSIDERATIONS

Most problems which clients bring to therapists are framed in such general terms that it is almost impossible to sort it all out. The therapist must first obtain a sufficiently concrete definition of the situation to permit intervention to occur. Marital problems usually have less to do with the much proferred "communication difficulties" than they do with the couples' anger at some violation of marital norms which have breached the marital boundaries and led one or both to feel "betrayed." Because the topic of betrayal is covered explicitly elsewhere in this volume, it will not be dealt with here (see Tiemann 1986).

During the initial consultation, I find it is helpful to classify information along the lines of the model contained in Table 1. By considering the *levels* at which difficulty occurs, one can clarify and begin to scope out the tasks of therapy. A good deal of time is wasted by ascribing to intrapsychic dynamics that which is more attributable to societal or biological levels. A person does not bear responsibility for being born black and disadvantaged in our society, nor for being the object of the implicit prejudice. Nor do they necessarily bear the onus for what happens to them in the course of living. People with biochemically low stress tolerance cannot be blamed for poorly managing life's vicissitudes. The therapist has a better chance of working successfully with clients when these boundary conditions are empathically assessed and given attention. While our ability to correctly distinguish between hard-wired and learned shortcomings is admittedly limited, awareness of the differing levels lessens the rigidity of approach and facilitates taking a more holistic view.

First Case Example

When Jose and Margarita came for couples therapy, it became clear very quickly that his inability to work at housepainting in a steady manner, owing to his lack of union membership, was the major problem around which the rest of the issues were fillers. Margarita was content in a traditional role, working hard at maintaining her home while she reared three small children. She did not feel it would be right for her to take a job. She wanted to feel secure in her husband's ability to take care of his family. Jose's sporadic employment made her anxious about their future. Moreover, his depression about his "failure" was very hard for her to handle. He would mope around the house, getting underfoot and interfering with her mothering. They were fighting more and making up less. The scorecard of misdemeanors was mounting, and Margarita was at her wit's end, threatening to leave.

Despite the quarreling, there was no unusual evidence of undercutting in their relationship beyond what might be expected when people fail to live up to each other's expectations. Jose did not particularly want his wife to work; he was a good man of rather limited intelligence who just did not know how to make ends meets. He neither wanted to lose his wife nor felt she was making unfair demands upon him. He was caught in a situational bind, owing to the politics of the union he sought to join, the length of time it would take before he became accredited to work, and his own temperamental difficulties in bearing up under frustration. And Margarita was heavily invested in being a wife.

I first asked whether Jose had any objection to working on his own, if he could generate some jobs. He was agreeable but had tried earlier, finding nothing available. I asked if he minded going to other neighborhoods and working for strangers of different ethnic backgrounds. He assured me he could do that.

Since Margarita was more skilled verbally, I asked if she would help Jose in this task of generating work while he waited for his union membership. Helping *him* was not like going out of the house to work. She readily agreed. I then asked them both if they had noticed signs posted on bus shelters which advertised painting and paperhanging, moving, carpentry and so on. They had noticed, but since these were of no interest to them, they had not really paid attention. I then pointed out that Jose had skills every bit as valuable as those advertised on the shelters. Would he have any objection to taking that route of promotion? He shook his head. "Life is to work," he said.

As a task for the conclusion of the first session, I asked both spouses to make a survey of the posters on the blocks in midtown. They were to note the prices charged by each person who solicited work in interior or exterior painting and paperhanging. They were then to decide what Jose wanted to charge for his services. The only boundary condition was Jose's fee should be less than anyone else's on the market.

The second part of the assignment was to make a list of all the people whose apartments Jose had painted since he came to the United States, and to secure letters of reference from them. The purpose of this task was to get Jose out of the house and active in soliciting from people already known and therefore presumably "safe." He was to secure at least three references and Margarita was to keep the files so that when a request came in, they could be dispatched immediately.

In the second session, after pointing out Margarita's artistic talent in making her children's clothes, I asked her to help me design a poster for Jose. I would only help with the content as needed (since she was already more of an expert than I from having studied so many posters from the previous assignment). She was to design something that she felt would catch the eye. We would review her design at a "design meeting" in the following week, and if everybody agreed upon it, then she and Jose would go out to the neighborhoods I selected (we were working as a team on this problem, after all) and paste up the posters.

The third week, they brought in an eye-catching design and timidly confessed they had already posted it in some of the neighborhoods suggested. I expressed approval but some cautious concern that they might be "going too fast," and were they sure that they were ready to take this step? They laughingly asserted that they were indeed, and they wondered why they hadn't done so on their own initiative before. We spent the remainder of the session discussing how to run your own business, my pointing out that it was Jose's ability to play lion-tamer to the marketplace and Margarita's ability to manage that made them an unbeatable team. They left with appointments scheduled for two and six weeks hence to check out how the plan was working. At six months' follow-up, I learned that Jose's work was going well and that they had managed to save enough to buy a big-screen TV so they could watch the Spanish-language programs they both loved.

This case illustrates how problems of the wider system can masquerade as intrapsychic problems within the family. Had I focused on each spouse's difficulties—Margarita's prideful rigidity and Jose's shattered self-esteem—a case could have been made for more serious pathology. By accepting the inadequacies of the couple as givens rather than as points of analytic departure, a frame was found that embraced each spouse's world view. While this couple may tend to overreact to external stress, they have demonstrated the capacity to adjust, with a minimum of therapeutic help, to the exigencies of life.

Second Case Example

The Problem

The second example concerns a situation involving a never-married mother, Charlotte, a fortyish woman from middle Europe who was a children's writer. Her already consummated "divorce" from a long-ago lover had, for a variety of reasons, gotten out of hand. She was at war with the judicial and child welfare system over their decision in her case, and, having lost in those arenas not only tactically, but financially as well, was seeking to renew her psychic functioning (see Wallerstein 1989).

As a therapist I could sympathize with Charlotte's attitude that her ex-lover had contributed nothing more than his sperm to Stefan's creation. But it was clear that she had played a significant role in creating the problem, too. She claimed that after a stormy five-year relationship marked by violence and cruelty and his continuing infidelity, she had finally broken free. They did not see each other again for seven years until a chance reunion occurred. That encounter was disappointing to them both, and they had no reason to see one another again. However, when she learned of the pregnancy, she decided to continue it because of her age (40 at the time), and so informed Charles. She also called him to announce Stefan's birth, at which point he appeared with the demand for joint custody. These demands had then continued and finally erupted in a lawsuit four years later.

Charlotte had felt certain that no court of law would uphold this claim. Stefan had been born prematurely and had had developmental and social problems. For these he had been in therapy for a year from the age of three, interrupted by the mother's declining fortunes. At no time had Charles contributed to the boy's expenses. Charlotte lived with another man, Peter, who was interested in adopting Stefan.

As the battle was waged fruitlessly, however, Charlotte's increasing upset spilled over into her life with Peter. Combined with her financial fragility, the social system of this family, too, broke apart.

Although there were strong personal elements involved in this case, particularly within Charlotte herself and between the warring ex-lovers, such a view gives only a partial understanding of the tasks to be accomplished. In order to fully set out the rationale for the brief treatment undertaken in this case, we must look at Table 1. Here, under "Society" we find the level at which the "insult" actually bringing this client to treatment occurs. Had Charles been unable to pursue his claim legally, Charlotte would have had no problem. It was the decision of people acting "for" society through its legal system that Charolotte *had* to permit Stefan to spend equal amounts of time with his biological father. Against the overarching social goals relating to family life and values articulated by these spokespersons, Charlotte sought to defend herself legally in a vain attempt to authenticate her values. When this attempt collapsed, she was thoroughly demoralized.

Because of Charlotte's adamant refusal to comply with the court order, and her belief that the biological father's interference in her single-parent family would be disastrous for both her and the son, she had developed a number of incapacitating symptoms. Her major complaint was that "the parameters of my life are all in disarray." These were: her failures in work; her life with her "mate," Peter, coming to an end; her financial status declining rapidly; a frightening series of death dreams; and her day-to-day ability to cope and to be creative, upon which her income depended, dissolving.

For these difficulties she had previously been in analysis for six months, also terminating when her finances became precarious, owing to legal expenses. Charles was described as demonic, manipulative, seductive, charming, cruel and vengeful. His presence inspired the most powerful fear the client, who had until then considered herself "invincible," had ever experienced. Their relationship had been one of master and slave. Every fiber of her physical being had been violated and every shred of her mental and emotional self-respect had been destroyed. Significantly, I noted, she had never even touched on this fear in her six months of psychoanalytic treatment.

In the context of my agency, I could not challenge society, nor, given Charlotte's own role in her difficulties, would that have brought lasting relief. I could only ameliorate the situation in as expeditious a way as possible, and that included enlisting and intervening in the social system of which she was a part. Hence, at the individual level, one treatment goal was to help Charlotte to come to terms with the joint custody arrangement that had been decreed. At the societal level where divorce mediation was court-ordered, another goal was helping to select the mediator with whom a joint approach could be developed for maximal effectiveness.*

Themes and Their Relationship to Treatment Planning

The major theme underlying Charlotte's fear of Charles was his "demonic power" over her. She was helpless, being both a seducible and a violatable victim of his manipulations to which she attributed great power. He was a master strategist who would stop at nothing, partially to get even with her for leaving him, and partially because he wanted to run her and the child's life. Although the lawsuit was ostensibly over the child of their stormy union, it was really her he was after.

Given this position, Charlotte had tried to deal with Charles' actions by several tactics which proved fruitless. Appeasement enraged him further. Reason he ignored. Histrionic displays of "lioness" strength spaced him out. When he caught her, as usual, off base, she panicked.

As the situation escalated, Charlotte engaged a variety of experts to handle the matter for her. She sought analysis, legal advice and psychotherapy. The law, rather than backing her up, was forcing her to face the issue. Since the experts she consulted were unable to help her avoid the issue, and her lawyer was compromising, she began to distrust them.

---

* Fortunately, the services of a master mediator, Dr. Isolina Ricci (author of *Mom's House, Dad's House*), were secured.

Treatment Formulation and Planning

According to solution-oriented brief therapy (SBT), problems arise
when everyday difficulties are badly managed, when the solutions
attempted by the client fail to work, and when the client remains in a
rut, continuing to use them. Had Charlotte been able initially to face
matters, she would not have needed treatment because her
difficulties with Charles would never have grown to be a problem (see
Table 2).

Table 2.
Couple Dynamics

Charles' Actions	Charlotte's Responses*
Attacks	Appeases
Irrational acts	Reasons
Catches her off base	Panics
Bullies	Pleads
"Seduces"	Goes along
Files suit	Defends
Threatens	Protects
Treats her like a kid	Obeys

*Note that the responses are all reactive rather than directive actions.

Classifying the interactions that caused trouble quickly made it
apparent that Charlotte was merely *reacting* to Charles' maneuvers.
Clearly, problems in therapy would arise over getting her to enact
roles 180 degrees from those previously used, while persuading her to
remain in therapy through the process. These would amount to
getting her to face the issues on her own. Therefore, the therapist
took the role of empathic helper in a pragmatic and personal sense.
This was easy to do as Charlotte was an engaging, witty and
intelligent woman for whom I felt a genuine concern and regard.

As the main goal of therapy was to get Charlotte to *initiate* action,
Charles' behavior had to be reframed so that she was empowered to
act independently of (or, as she saw it, against) him. It was also
necessary to reframe *her* behavior in order to heighten her
motivation for action.

The clues for these reframings came from the positions Charlotte
took, melded together with an explanatory rationale that attempted
as far as possible to embody her own values. Strategic planning
centered around her self-image as a strong, self-reliant woman and
outstanding mother. Facets of her background were used to reframe

her behavior as "typical female masochism," as "the mouse" with whom this cat, Charles, was playing, but would ultimately "destroy," and as "one of a string of devastated women that he, like Wagner, had left behind." Her apparent powerlessness in standing up to Charles actually reflected her "protection of *his* inherent weakness." Given her level of concern for him, did she not still "care more for Charles than for her son, Stefan?" In this way his demonic acts were reframed as those of a paper tiger, and her paralysis as "concern."

Pragmatically, Charlotte was asked whether she was capable of acting to off-balance Charles (e.g., interdicting her customary behaviors). These tasks were given in the context of her "needing" to protect him because she was still in love with him. Among these strategies were (1) telephoning him in the middle of the night for a silly "reason," (2) giving him a nonsensical "reason" for refusing his requests, and (3) noting down in writing his attempts to bully her. It was pointed out that should he ever assault her, his case would then be lost.

Course of Treatment

When people are seen in SBT, their powerful resistances to change are hopefully met by even more powerful interventions based not upon some external theory of psychic development and functioning, but upon their very own stated and implicit values as revealed in the sessions.* Despite her self-image as an invincible woman, Charlotte experienced great conflict in changing her reactiveness to external events, especially those initiated by Charles. She felt panicky when carrying out assigned tasks of asserting herself, even though these were graded to her own anxiety levels. For example, she found it extraordinarily difficult to purchase a negligibly priced item (for which she had a use), wait a few minutes, return it to the store and ask for a refund. Although she had not thought this would be hard for her to do, she found herself shaking at the prospect. Needless to say, it took her three weeks to muster the courage to telephone Charles at 2 a.m. "merely to tell him that Stefan had enjoyed his last visit."

Once that hurdle was overcome, her feelings toward her ex-lover began to change. She began to see him less as a monster, and more as a confused, aging and rather frightened man who used the mask of bully to conceal his loneliness and terror. When this was

---

*This does not mean there is no theory; it merely means that specific developmental theories are probably irrelevant to treatment planning and execution.

accomplished, the prospect of working out a custody arrangement shrank in proportion as she felt strong enough to assert her own needs. As she became less intransigent over this matter, even finding some freedom in leaving Stefan with Charles for a weekend, he in turn felt less threatened and became more reasonable.

SUMMARY AND CONCLUSIONS

Society is built on the excitement generated by social interaction. When that excitement solidifies in a marital unit, it grows and becomes complex. Webs of affiliations are created by the mating pair. The beliefs of these webs take form in institutions, and the process adumbrates, growing to the furthest reaches of human habitation.

This chapter has examined two examples of these webs of affiliations and their associated belief systems as these affected resolution of the couple's problem, and presented a model for intervention based upon a clinical sociological perspective. It is argued that because the dissolution of a marriage has far-reaching implications not only for the social structure and the individuals involved, but for the future as well, the clinician with a holistic viewpoint does well to consider the issue not only from the level of the individual, but from all the other levels as well. This perspective may provide confusion at first, but in the long run, it will provide greater resources for solving the problem in a manner that increases the likelihood that both society and the individuals involved will have a chance to win.

When all levels of the social structure are enabled to retain the positive psychic energy embodied in their webs of affiliation, then whether divorce occurs or not, society becomes strong and capable of providing a nourishing environment for the people born into it. But when that energy becomes negative or disappears altogether in apathy and ennui, then human existence is imperiled at its very heart.

REFERENCES

Gilligan, C. *In a Different Voice: Women's Conception of the Self and of Morality.* New York: Basic Books, 1978.

Kohlberg, F. *Collected Papers on Moral Development and Moral Education.* Cambridge, MA: Harvard University Press, 1976.

Perry, W. *Forms of Intellectual and Ethical Development in the College Years.* New York: Holt, Rinehart & Winston, 1970.

Pittman, F.S. *Turning Points.* New York: W.W. Norton, 1987.

Tiemann, A.R. Betrayal in Intimate Relations. Paper presented to the

Clinical Sociology Association, Cazenovia, NY, 1986.
Wallerstein, J. *Second Chances.* New York: Ticknor & Fields, 1989.
Watzlawick, P. *Ultra-Solutions: How to Fail Most Successfully.* New York:
    W.W. Norton, 1988.

4

Betrayal:
The World in Disarray

Phelps M. Robinson, MD and Margery M. Battin, BA

Betrayal is a widely experienced phenomenon, largely unrecognized as such, that has catastrophic implications at the most basic levels of psychological functioning. For the purposes of this chapter, betrayal is defined as the violation of a significant and reasonably depended on promise.

Anyone who has experienced any of the following examples of such violations knows what betrayal is: being robbed; having one's automobile stolen or one's house burglarized; losing one's savings to a bank collapse; being let go after twenty years of loyal service because one's company is under new management; child abuse, abandonment, or being put up for adoption; being left by a lover or as the result of a suicide; or being divorced, disowned or raped.

On the basis of our clinical observations, our hypothesis regarding the betrayal experience includes the following assumptions and postulates:

1. That one's predictive capabilities have a structural basis, including the cognitive or affective organizations called basic trust, object constancy and identity.
2. That these organizational configurations of experience (data), although well established, are not static entities developed once and forever, but rather are dynamic, always evolving, always capable of growth, and therefore always vulnerable.
3. That these structures that permit one to predict what will happen are themselves dependent on predictability (that one's world stays relatively constant).

4. That the victim of betrayal has encountered information that is significantly contradictory to and at least difficult to reconcile with their previous informational base.
5. That at the structural level these contradictions and incongruencies have immense impact on basic trust, object constancy and identity.
6. That in a betrayal those structures are greatly compromised and impair the victim's ability to predict what will happen and leave the victim in a state of pronounced disequilibrium.

RAPE

A brief look at the rape experience illustrates what betrayal is all about. Far more damaging than the physical assault is the psychological legacy: never again can the victim walk through the park without anxiety, self-consciousness and hypervigilance. No longer can the easy innocence of minding one's own business suffice to give a sense of security. Self-doubt, bitterness and confusion add to the endlessly repetitive flashbacks, nightmares and obsessive ruminations, all of which are efforts to absorb and master the fact and implications of the monstrous event that was truly overwhelming and unencompassable.

We may postulate that the main locus of damage is the individual's basic trust, which we define as the gradually developing sense of relative constancy (predictability) of one's world. The terror leading to chronic apprehensiveness is a consequence of the now-demonstrated unpredictability. The confusion and self-doubt result from the disruption of a whole range of operational assumptions about the predictable conduct of oneself and one's surroundings. The rules of the game are suddenly far more complex.

Social norms are fundamental to one's self-image and world view; they are the standards for one's behavior and one's expectations of others. It is the violation of this "understanding" or tacit contract with the world that accounts for the long, complex reparative process. Structural damage has been done to the cognitive underpinnings—basic trust. A reordering of experiences and information will be required for the individual ever to achieve any semblance of "peace" or a smoothly working system. In other situations of betrayal there is the same rupture of the very sense of order and the predictability of one's world that leaves the victim with feelings of loss and grief, no longer knowing oneself, and, indeed, in utter chaos.

BEING DISOWNED

Analogous to the tacit contract one has with society are the expectations between individuals in one-to-one relationships. The more
deeply intimate a relationship is, and the more reinforced by social
norms, the more automatic and almost complacent are the expectations and the promises taken for granted. Therefore, the more devastating is the betrayal. One such type of betrayal is illustrated in the
following case of being disowned.

> A young woman raised in the semi-closed society of a fundamentalist
> sect had always been close to her father. He and the elders of the sect
> treated her with special accord because she was intellectually gifted,
> curious and challenging—the very qualities for which she later would
> be expelled. She attended schools in the "outside" community. More
> and more, she began to challenge the premises (and even some of the
> practices) of the sect, and from age 19 on she was increasingly shunned
> by the elders. When, at age 26 she divorced and went to live with
> another man, she was summarily "put away from the table"—banished
> from the sect and from her family. In the ten years since then, the
> family has rebuffed all her overtures for a reconciliation, short of her
> renouncing her worldly interests, including even her artistic career.
>   The woman sought treatment because of depression, confusion
> about "who I am," difficulty in defining and sustaining the goals in her
> career, and in making and maintaining intimate, permanent relation-
> ships. She was distressed at her restlessness in relationships and at her
> apparent need to be continually "searching." She could not accept the
> legitimate limitations in relationships (such as between a teacher and
> a student). She seemed driven to see the limits others imposed as being
> caused by their need to distance themselves from her; she imagined
> that they saw her as dangerous or undesirable. She felt constantly
> rejected, and she constantly and compulsively set up situations that
> would again confirm her certainty that she would be rejected. She
> berated herself for still thinking about her family instead of her own
> independent goals. She viewed all of this as weakness in herself, a lack
> of integrity. A constant theme in her psychotherapy has been the
> unfathomable abandonment by her once adoring family, especially her
> father.

    Imagine being deliberately denied your roots by the very people
who *are* your roots. What you are and were encouraged to be is repudiated! It is difficult enough to sustain the loss of all one's roots by
death resulting from an accident or a war in which the family is wiped
out. Actually, there is a sense of betrayal here, too—by life or God—
but in death there is at least the opportunity, reinforced by everyone,
gradually to absorb and assimilate the explanation that accidents do
occur and death is inevitable. We accept these things as the norm—
the expectable for many of us sooner and all of us later.

In banishment, however, there is no such comfort; it is not the norm. It flies in the face of everything one has learned about family, trust, loyalty, "blood kinship" and the like. The sense of betrayal from the death of one's family is at least cushioned by the awareness that if one's family were alive there would be intimacy. In exile it is the converse; intimacy is denied and one is repudiated, actively and constantly. In death there is the reality of no hope of reunion; in exile there is an ever-present and ever-driving possibility of forgiveness, reconciliation and reunion—any number of denials notwithstanding.

Surviving relatives of the deceased often feel that they have been abandoned (even though reality tells them that death is not abandonment), but in banishment, abandonment *is* the reality—one that is continually reinforced. In death the closeness, the intimacy, the history of affirmation and reaffirmation, the reciprocity, are all intact and become unquestioned memory, a part of the bereaved survivor's identity. In exile the intimacy is renounced; one even doubts its previous validity. One can no longer assume that what was once established as common ground is still common ground on any level. One's identity is cast into doubt and reappraisal becomes difficult in the face of the repudiation of all those understandings and validations that made up one's basic sense of self.

It is evident once again that violation of the reasonable depended-on premise results in catastrophic symptomatology. So it is with a variety of types of betrayal within the context of intimate relationships. For instance, two other catastrophic forms of betrayal are the unanticipated suicide and divorce.

SUICIDE AND DIVORCE

The survivor of a loved one's self-inflicted death is left with a lifetime of unanswered questions, unfinished business, irreconcilable facts and contradictory assumptions about family and other values; lifelong uncertainty about the place of suicide in the range of problem-solving options in one's life; and shame, guilt, hatred, helplessness and impotence. Above all, the survivor has need for facts or constructs with which to "understand" the act and its motives. Although the need may be quiescent at times, it always has an impact on the survivor's identity, views about life and death, interpersonal relationships and commitment. And, as is characteristic of all victims of betrayal, even though rationality demands that the victim recognize that the betrayor acted out of some peculiar motivation or need without reference to the victim, the victim nevertheless is inclined to assume that he or she somehow caused the betrayal and anguishes over it.

Again, it is the cognitive set, the entire body of intelligence, the structure of the whole experience that is violated. Until that moment of the loved one's suicide, one had certain assumptions or promises: a parent will not abandon a child; a parent recognizes that the family is more important than its problems; life is valued and to be protected, "one for all and all for one," and problems are to be solved with or without help. These assumptions were laid down by continuous exposure to the family's and society's statements and behavior and were integral to one's cognitive and affective structure. Now they are blatantly contradicted and the structure is a shambles. Chaos is the suicide's legacy to the one who is left.

An important process in the betrayal experience is reconciliation, which may be briefly defined as the healing of the breach in victims' relationships with themselves, in their relationships with their betrayors, or in their relationships with people and society at large. One may speak of breaches in cognitive or affective structure, in personal integrity (sense of self, normal narcissism), in morality and in the stability of society.

For instance, it seems clear that regaining equilibrium and reestablishing order and harmony within oneself is the basic biological force behind the great perplexity evident in the wake of the betrayal. However, it is also the basic force behind the reparative efforts of searching for motives and the scrambling for some realistic or fantasied construct to heal the cognitive breach, the narcissistic injury and the moral breach. That is, it gives the act and all of its implications a "place"—along with oneself—in some restored sense of the world as being relatively orderly and predictable.

In the betrayal of the unanticipated suicide there is no chance for reconciliation—no way to heal ruptures, to ask or answer questions, to object or rail, to state your case or hear the other's case—just no way to make peace. It is not just the finality, which marks any death, but the abrupt carrying out of a unilateral intention. One is left utterly hanging because there is no way of knowing the other's motivations, let alone of influencing them.

Divorce is another form of betrayal with the violation of all that was promised and the consequent pain, confusion, sense of failure, guilt and bitterness. Despite the many reasons why a divorce may be the logical and best solution to a bad situation, it nevertheless depicts a failure. Vows were taken and now are broken, society's institutions of marriage and family were entered into and are now forsaken, and even one's own intentions, expectations, hopes and dreams through the years are now abandoned. The complex fabric of societal norms, religious and cultural imperatives, personal expectations and interpersonal understandings is now rent.

THEORETICAL IMPLICATIONS

The implication that certain events can be grouped because of an identifiable and important common denominator and that people's reactions to these events also share a corresponding set of characteristics provides an opportunity to study the interface between external events and the internal psychological world of one who has suffered betrayal. As is evident, we tend toward a cognitive approach and use Piaget's concepts, although not exclusively. There are some major theoretical problems to be solved if our hypotheses are to hold. The chief one is the mechanism of the disequilibrium and all of its manifestations. Is there a structural (as opposed to a functional) disintegration or fragmentation of the cognitive and affective operations? Or is there regression because one is unable to cope with the new information? Or is it the extreme of a tension that always exists between the new and the old until the accommodative and assimilative process can get started (for example, great anxiety accompanying a pervasive inability to predict)? Or are anxiety and, perhaps, other affects stimulated or extravasated and left free-floating until they can be bound to appropriate new cognitive schemata?

Various theoretical schools offer answers to these questions, but if we adopt Piagetian theory to explain the cognitive aspects, then we are left with certain other problems that Piagetian theory does not address. For instance, what do we do about the question of regression? In Piagetian or related theories, is there room for an equivalent of the psychoanalytic concept of regression—a kind of regrouping, using more primitive schemata in the remodeling of the higher-order schemata? If not, how is the symptomatology to be explained?

In a related question, when is a betrayal (or any experience) considered developmental rather than traumatic? One could claim that any event that causes disequilibrium is simply a further accretion of experience in the ever-evolving structure of intelligence— intelligence forever creating intelligence—which Piaget (1960, 1970) explicitly stated is an ultimate goal in and of itself. Does the concept of regression in itself contradict the concept of a constantly unfolding development, or is there a place for regression in the service of the ego, so to speak, as a necessary part of the accommodative and assimilative process of development? In Piagetian theory, is there such a thing as traumatic experience with resultant damage (sometimes repairable and sometimes not)? Apparently trivial contradictions of intelligence simply force revised schemata, but what of grosser contradictions? Are there some from which no recovery occurs? Where does pathology fit with the biological and epistemological theory of Piaget?

Can our intelligence be shattered, as the victims of betrayal often subjectively describe? Or is there some more or less orderly process that leaves victims feeling subjectively shattered while they are really "working on it" until the process is far enough along to enable them to cope? If so, what is the nature of that affective state? And why the plethora of affects in these experiences?

Numerous authors have questioned where affect fits into Piaget's cognitive theory. Kohut's (1971, 1977) self-psychology, ostensibly a structural theory that encompasses affect, is not much clearer on this score than is traditional psychoanalysis. Trauma theory, in which one would expect greater clarity, is, instead, confusing and convoluted on what Krystal (1978) called "the role of affect in the genesis and prevention of trauma." Another major question is whether "trauma," as described by theorists from Freud (1926) to Figley (1976), is due to overwhelming affects or to actual damage done to structure, a rending of the fabric of one's cognitive and affective schemata that is manifested in disorganized behaviors, fragmented psychic operations and affective disturbances.

Thus, with so many questions and so few answers, we are at the starting point, with only empirical findings and some sketchy understanding that victims of betrayal are far more frequent than is recognized; that they suffer profound alterations of their self and world views; and that their impaired capacity for predicting seems to be the central factor in their suffering and recovery.

REFERENCES

Figley, C. R. *Stress Disorders Among Vietnam Veterans*. New York: Brunner/ Mazel, 1976.

Freud, S. *The Standard Edition of the Complete Psychological Works of Sigmund Freud, Vol. 20: Inhibitions, Symptoms and Anxiety* (James Strachey, trans.). London: Hogarth Press, 1959 (reprint of 1926 edition).

Kohut, H. *The Analysis of the Self*. New York: International Universities Press, 1971.

_____. *The Restoration of the Self*. New York: International Universities Press, 1977.

Krystal, H. Trauma and Affects. In *Psychoanalytic Study of the Child*. New Haven: Yale University Press, 1978.

Piaget, J. *Psychology of Intelligence*. Patterson, NJ: Littlefield, Adams, 1960.

_____. *Science of Education and the Psychology of the Child*. New York: Orion Press, 1970.

5

Divorce and the Expectations Offered by the Legal Process

H. Elliot Wales, JD

Practicing attorneys learn the expectations of their clients as they become professionally involved in the process of legally terminating a marriage. The degree of realism or fantasy of the expectations of the client determines in part the nature and the impact of the loss. For some clients the process is reasonably positive (or minimally negative) as they look forward to a new and better life. For others the process is essentially negative as they resist the forthcoming termination and seek to hold onto that which they perceive to be the old life. For them the loss is both real and imaginary. As such the impact of the loss is shaped by the client's perception of the marriage, by the client's perception of what the legal system supposedly offers, and by notions of what attorneys can supposedly accomplish. Therefore we are dealing with expectations. To the extent they are unrealistic, the goals of the legal process cannot be achieved, and loss will be inevitable.

For most people, the termination of a marriage is acceptable, though regrettable. Few marriages disintegrate instantly or terminate on the spur of the moment. Terminated marriages are usually the product of a long history of disappointment, disagreements and unfulfilled expectations, and the loss of caring, sharing and concern. Most divorces today are the decision of each party, after years of living together under difficulty, and perhaps living apart, to bring an end to a substantial phase of their life and to resolve issues of asset division, support and maintenance, child custody and a claim upon one another in perpetuity.

For those who approach divorce as a means of reprisal, spite and retaliation, the whole process can only be a loss. The legal system is not designed to achieve such goals. What we lawyers do best is either to maximize financial gains or minimize financial losses for clients. We can adjust the relationship between consenting parties for we know the rules of the road. We can reasonably predict what a court may do, if faced with the issue, so that we may advise our clients, with some assurance, of which expectations are legitimate, and which are unwarranted.

Let us talk about expectations and, more appropriately, "great expectations." Most clients come to a law office expecting wonders. Clients expect that as a result of our securing for them a divorce, simultaneously we will bring them happiness. Nothing can be further from the truth. We attorneys do not compete with psychiatrists and psychologists. We do not produce any of the wonders that the mental health professionals do. Clients expect that we will take their side, not only professionally, but personally, emotionally, and in every other way. Clients expect that we will not only secure for them all of the income, assets, offspring and everything else that the couple ever had, but that we will destroy the other party in the same process. Couples who struggle financially on one income now expect to live comfortably with two households to support. Wives with children make unrealistic financial demands upon husbands, and likewise husbands expect to be free of obligations that they have been meeting for years. Couples who are financially well heeled, who both have income and assets, still wish to extract a pound of flesh from one another. The female spouse may make heavy financial demands, not because she is in need of the finances, but because she wishes to express her contempt and indignation and to extract from the male spouse a penalty for the dissolution of the marriage.

The role of the attorney is to help the party accept realistic expectations of what the legal system can provide. Husbands cannot be expected to give more than 100 percent of their income, nor can children be expected to go barefoot.

The attorney must bring realism to the process, to educate his client as to what can be done and what cannot be done. Most clients come to a law firm with war stories of what supposedly happened to their friends and acquaintances. Of course they only bring the stories that they want the attorney to hear. They tell about their female friends who got everything from their spouses, and male clients will talk about their male friends who had to pay little or nothing to their spouses. In the subculture of the divorced and about-to-be divorced, the dialogue of financial expectations is a constant theme, war stories get distorted, and when the client finally comes to the law firm, his recitation of what he heard others either received or paid bears little relation to reality. Attorneys who cannot meet the expectations of their clients run the risk of losing the retainer. Attorneys who give false hope to their clients that their unrealistic expectations can be met are dooming them to eventual disappointment and dejection.

The client must be carefully educated and prepared to accept that which is a realistic result from the legal system. While first-class lawyers, brilliant litigators and hard-nosed negotiators can produce a better result than the norm for the client, there still has to be a realistic range of expectations, which limits the appetite of the client. The impact of loss or gain is measured by the realistic definition of expectations as fashioned by the attorney. We must offer both hope and realism. If we eventually achieve goals that are in line with that which we fashioned initially, loss can be minimized.

Divorce is usually the result of a decision, unlike death which is a loss that is imposed upon a person, often without warning. Divorce may be a loss that is accepted as a decision which involves both pros and cons. There may be a recognition of the inevitable or a desire to put an end to a totally unacceptable situation. Usually divorce involves a decision to accept one's loss and to terminate a difficult living arrangement, an unsatisfactory personal life style, and a no-longer-desired commitment to another person. It is an existential choice—a life style decision—a measurement of loss and gain.

For the traditional family unit divorce may involve a set of losses beyond that of the immediate relationship between the spouses. Where the children are young, the noncustodial parent may lose an effective relationship with the children. The loss may involve his status as a parent, as he becomes a mere periodic visitor. Note that I have used the male gender, which is more often the case. Young parents—with lesser income, assets and life experience—may feel totally isolated and overwhelmed by the prospect of child rearing alone. Even with respect to not-so-young children, the termination of their parents' relationship may deprive them of the opportunity to return home, and conversely deprives the parents of the type of relationship that they might have had with adult children who seek to visit or return home. The feeling of loss may be heightened, for some parents simultaneously feel the loss of their offspring who are fleeing the nest. For more mature couples who have adjusted to the adult status of their offspring, the loss of dreams for a long-awaited retirement or pre-retirement may produce a concern that it is too late to restructure their lives. However, a sound financial base may cushion the loss and permit travel and other activities that are deemed a gain.

For those who really believe in marriage, its termination may produce a sense of failure. The loss may be one of self-esteem and self-respect. In a highly traditional family, where divorce is very much the exception, dissolution of a marriage may actually involve a loss of respect and esteem in the eyes of other family members.

Divorce may result in the loss of one's own community. The couple may have to sell the marital home and move to other areas. Divorce sometimes costs one or both parties friendships with couples who do not wish to take sides, who feel uncomfortable dealing with singles, or who just do not know how to relate to a divorced couple.

Financial loss is usually a dominant factor. Today few couples really can afford divorce. The two-income household is now reduced to one. Assets that formerly were jointly owned and jointly managed are now divided and halved. The reverse of the old adage, two can live as cheaply as one, is just not applicable—one certainly can't live as cheaply as two. One income for one person does not go as far as two incomes for two people. Responsibilities that were shared now fall in their entirety upon each spouse.

With the down side so heavy, why do people separate? It is only in recent generations that we began to marry for love rather than enter into arranged marriages. With love as the glue to keep the marriage together, the loss of love usually leads to the dissolution of the marriage. With the loss of love it must be regained, if not from one partner, then from another. For some the seeking of love, or new love, is a game, a challenge, an exciting adventure; for others it is a dreary experience. For some confidence has been lost, and the singles scene does not easily restore confidence. For others long-awaited expectations or fantasies may give a positive note to the immediate future.

The fact that many persons undergo some therapy after the dissolution of their marriage is evidence that the loss factor is not uncommon. Therapists seek to cushion the loss and assist the patient in seeking to regain a positive attitude toward life. Most people survive divorce, and many survive it quite well. New relationships and new marriages attest to the vitality of people and the striving to gain affection, romance and anything else that a relationship may bring.

Surprisingly few divorced people regret having married at all. The commitment to marry survives, even though the departed spouse does not. As such, spouses become replaceable (but not fungible), and the succeeding one may prove more acceptable than the predecessor. The commitment to love easily outlives the discarded relationship and permits the formation of new relationships. And so the cycle continues—another try, another round. For most people it is indeed better to have loved and lost than never to have loved at all.

6

Death of a Divorced Spouse: The Survivor's Dilemma

Shirley Scott, RN

Several years ago, a woman was referred to me for counseling because she was depressed two months after the death of her ex-spouse, from whom she had been divorced for ten years. Her daughter was concerned about the woman's mental health, saying it was "absurd and even dangerously abnormal" for her mother to continue to be so sad over the death of a man she had not even spoken to for many years. When I talked to the woman for a short time, it was evident that she was experiencing a normal grief reaction to the death of a person for whom she still had affection. She was also grieving over the finality of the loss of the relationship and bitterly regretted never having been able to resolve some of the unfinished emotional business with her ex-spouse.

Following that referral, several similar situations came to my attention. I wondered if I had been made aware of a common occurrence or if a grief reaction to the death of a divorced spouse is, indeed, unusual. In an effort to establish the frequency, severity, cause, and other parameters of this grief reaction, I conducted a study from fall 1984 to spring 1985 on grief reactions to the death of a divorced spouse.

Eighty-two questionnaires were mailed to volunteers who responded to announcements of the project. Seventy valid responses were received and included in the final tabulations. Contrary to what might be expected, 77 percent of the respondents stated that they had experienced a grief reaction following the death of their divorced spouse. Of this 77 percent, 20 percent noted that the reaction was overwhelming or severe, 47 percent that it was moderate, and 23 percent that it was slight.

In addition to the information requested, many letters and notes were included with the completed questionnaires that mentioned dilemmas that the survivors had faced. Because there were so many of them, my curiosity was aroused. I decided to analyze the unexpected comments to see if there were some common problems among the survivors.

Four main problem areas quickly became evident. Dilemmas arose for the surviving ex-spouse during the other's final illness, at the time the death occurred, at the time of the funeral or memorial service, and during the weeks or months of the grieving process. The people who had helped create these dilemmas were the deceased ex-spouses, parents and in-laws, adult children, new spouses of the deceased and the survivors, and friends of all of the families involved.

THE FINAL ILLNESS

Some respondents who had wanted to be at the bedside of the ex-spouse at this time were discouraged from doing so by angry adult children who thought that the ex-spouse did not deserve such attention or a comforting presence. Rather than confront or alienate the adult children, the respondents had stayed away.

In some cases, the ex-spouse elected to step into the role of caregiver despite protests from other family members. Some of these situations turned out well. One woman, whose family and friends thought she was crazy, took a leave of absence from her job, moved her ex-spouse into her home and cared for him until he died. She reported that it was a peaceful, reflective time for both of them. They were able to resolve several areas of conflict, recall some of the good times they had shared and say their last good-byes. She experienced a moderate grief reaction, but felt no remorse and had no regrets.

Other situations did not turn out so well. Instead, even more dilemmas were created for the survivor. A woman reported that she cared for her ex-spouse in his apartment until he became too ill to stay there. She stated that she was relieved when he finally had to be admitted to a hospital. Being together had resurrected unresolved conflicts and reopened old emotional wounds. Tempers often flared. It was anything but a peaceful experience for either of them. When her ex-husband died, the woman was sure he felt he had "made her pay" once more for wanting the divorce years before. She reported having a slight grief reaction but stated, "It was more like grieving all over again for what might have been, if the marriage had been a good one." Four years after the death, she still harbored unresolved anger that she thought might be causing some of the problems in her second marriage.

In another family, the woman refused to visit her ex-husband during his terminal illness. Their adult children rallied around their dying father and took turns staying with him day and night for several months until he died. During that time, they berated their mother for not taking him into her home and seeing to his needs. Angry taunts were flung at her: "You never did love him"; "You're too selfish"; "Can't you see he needs you now more than ever?" She acknowledged that she had been the one who wanted to leave the marriage, but the children had forgotten or simply ignored that the divorce had occurred after years of physical abuse from the alcoholic husband. This woman realized that her ex-husband was highly manipulative. She knew that if she went back to care for him, he would revert to the old patterns. He had been successful in turning the children against her, but she hoped that in time they would see the truth of the situation. She stated that she felt no grief when he died, only relief that he could no longer hurt her physically or emotionally. After several years, she had been able to reestablish a relationship with her oldest daughter who, after a brief marriage to an abusive husband, finally understood the mother's feelings.

DEATH OF THE EX-SPOUSE

After the ex-spouse died, the survivors experienced many conflicting emotions that created feelings of guilt and remorse. One woman whose ex-husband had been found dead in his apartment wrote, "I wish I had taken care of him. I should have. There wasn't anyone else to do it. No matter what he did, no human being should die alone." She reported having only a slight grief reaction, but the strong guilt feelings stayed with her for several years.

Another woman stated, "I wouldn't let my dog live in the filth he did those last months. I know I should have just gone over there, cleaned up the place and taken care of him, but the children were adamant. Every time I mentioned it, they got angry and said not to go." She reported a severed grief reaction. Six months after her ex-spouse died, she sought counseling, on the advice of her concerned children, to resolve her conflicting feelings and dissipate her overwhelming guilt.

Many respondents reported experiencing shock, numbness, tears, and disbelief when informed of the death of an ex-spouse, particularly when the death was caused by a sudden, unexpected event, such as a heart attack, accident, suicide, or murder. According to the literature, these people experienced a normal reaction to the news of a death (Rando 1984). The survivors' dilemma arose when close friends or relations failed to understand this demonstration of grief or expressed strong feelings that were contrary to those of the survivors and that increased the survivors' emotional distress. One angry young man shocked his grieving mother by shouting, "Why are you crying? He deserved to die!"

For several people who had remarried, the current spouse's negative reactions and lack of understanding were a source of disappointment, anger and frustration that threatened the stability of the relationship. In some instances, a second divorce occurred within a year or two after the death of the ex-spouse.

THE FUNERAL

At the time of the funeral or memorial service, approximately 53 percent of the respondents reported that they felt comfortable being there and sharing their grief with family and friends. These people had maintained close relationships with their in-laws and the friends they had shared with the ex-spouse. They thought that people knew they still cared for the deceased. Some even took over the planning and execution of the services when no one else was available.

The remaining 47 percent who felt uncomfortable at the funeral or memorial services gave many reasons. The ones most frequently mentioned were fairly predictable. "I didn't know what my role should be." "I didn't know anyone there." "The new wife [or girlfriend] and their new friends made me feel unwelcome." "I felt like an outsider because the family ignored me." "Some people gave me such strange looks!" "I wasn't even acknowledged as the mother of the children!"

Another reason for discomfort was mentioned by a funeral director, who told about his experience in handling the services for a woman whose ex-husband and second husband hated each other. During the hour-long service it was necessary to call the police twice to restore order because the two men and members of their respective families started fighting.

For those who wanted to say their last good-byes without a confrontation, it was necessary to visit the funeral home during other than the scheduled visiting hours. One 70-year-old man arranged to have a second memorial service for his ex-wife, to whom he had been married for 38 years. He explained that he wanted a "decent, peaceful service" at which the children and friends could meet together without her 56-year-old second husband and his "rowdy young crowd" in attendance.

THE GRIEVING PROCESS

During the weeks and months following the death of the ex-spouse, survivors reported that they faced numerous problems that complicated the grief process. The most frequently mentioned causes of these problems were (1) continued love or affection for the deceased, (2) emotional conflicts that could no longer be resolved with the deceased, (3) family and friends who often did not understand why the survivor had feelings of grief and therefore did not offer the needed sympathy and support, (4) the reactions of children to the death, and (5) continued legal or financial problems.

Examples of continued love and affection for the deceased often appeared in the letters and notes received with the questionnaires. One woman who reported a severe grief reaction stated that she had always loved her ex-husband, but that they were both happier when living in separate apartments. Their divorce had been friendly; they saw each other at least once a week during the eight years following their divorce and they had had dinner together the night before his sudden death. She was devastated by the loss of his love, company, and friendship. She stated, "He really was my very best friend."

Another woman who reported that her divorce had been friendly said that she and her ex-spouse had planned to have lunch together the day he died of a heart attack. They were going to discuss the possibility of remarriage. She stated that she experienced an overwhelming grief reaction following his death.

Emotional conflicts that could no longer be resolved with the deceased were frequently mentioned as contributing to increased stress. A 52-year-old woman said she started having nightmares shortly after her ex-spouse died. She had been married for more than thirty years and had six children before she left her husband for another man. The nightmares were always the same. Her ex-husband appeared and berated her for leaving, for breaking up the family. She yelled back that it was his fault she left because he had betrayed her by having an affair with one of her friends. He insisted that it was not true, that she had the affair. At that point, she said, she would always wake up yelling, "No, no!" The truth was that they had both had extramarital relationships. After many bitter quarrels, she had escaped the situation through a divorce and hasty remarriage, a move she quickly realized was a mistake. She knew that she still loved her ex-husband and wanted to work out the problems with him. Before she could change this situation, her ex-spouse was killed in an automobile accident. After many months of declining physical and mental health, this woman sought counseling. She reported that she was finally beginning to rebuild her shattered life.

Unresolved anger and bitterness frequently haunted the survivors. In one family, the deceased's will was invalidated because of the ex-spouse's procrastination in having it properly executed. This caused the survivor great anger and heartache when the five children fought each other over the estate. In another family, the survivor experienced much bitterness over the irreparable damage that had been done to the family's closeness when, at the time of the divorce, the ex-spouse encouraged the children to take sides.

Several of the survivors who had remarried reported that their present spouses initially gave them support and understanding but that as the weeks went by these spouses became jealous and resentful of their repeated expressions of sorrow, anger and regret. Several people reported that they divorced their present spouses after the death of their ex-spouses. Research has shown that problems in a second marriage are frequently related to unresolved problems from the first marriage (Messinger 1982). When the ex-spouse dies before these residual problems have been resolved, it is easy to understand how the resulting conflict of emotions can exacerbate problems in the new relationship.

A lack of understanding by family and friends can also adversely affect those survivors who do not experience grief. One man wrote that his present wife thought it shocking and unnatural that he expressed *no* grief after his ex-wife died—"not even one tear." After all, they had been married for more than twenty years! As far as he was concerned, there were no unresolved feelings when the death occurred, since he had grieved the loss of the relationship five years before. He suggested that his second wife might be afraid that he would not grieve for her either. Even after a year, she could not understand his feelings on the subject.

It is easy to see the many reasons for the conflicting emotions survivors experience when other family members have different reactions to the death. One woman who reported that she had no grief reaction said that her parents were overwhelmed with grief at the death of her ex-husband. Her father "mourned him like a son." Both parents were angry and appalled by their daughter's lack of feeling. This can be a "catch-22" situation that causes the survivor to repress his or her true feelings in order to avoid confrontations with other family members.

Several people stated they had felt only great relief when their ex-spouse died. However, friends were shocked and angry when told of this lack of sorrow. One woman said that she had been on daily medication for months to control diarrhea, the result of constant harassment by her ex-husband. One month after his death, her bowel function returned to normal and she felt better than she had for years. Since she had not let family and friends know about her problems with her ex-husband, they could not fully understand her feelings. Remembering only that she had once loved him, they offered their sympathy at his death and were shocked at her expressions of great relief.

The children's reactions frequently added to the problems and grief of the survivor. One son, a college student with an A average, dropped out of school two weeks after his father died. He hitchhiked around the country for a couple of years, seldom contacting his mother, which, of course, worried her a great deal. In another family, the daughter became mentally ill and acted out her grief in inappropriate ways. Her illness was both emotionally and financially draining on her mother.

Some adult children accused their surviving parent of not ever caring what happened to the ex-spouse. One survivor's son died in a car accident six months after his father died. The young man had been inconsolable at the time of his father's death and blamed his mother for driving his father away years before. The mother was still grieving the death of her ex-husband when her son was killed. Her sorrow, plus the guilt she felt about her poor relationship with her son, led her to turn to alcohol and drugs to ease the emotional pain. After taking a drug overdose, she worked with a psychologist for several years in an effort to regain her emotional equilibrium. At the time of her letter, she felt she would now be able to lead a fairly normal life.

Several children of different ages were said to have expressed guilt about not feeling grief after their parent's death. One young adult was still angry at her deceased father for wrongs he did to her mother years before. She was reported to say that she hated her father and would never forgive him. A few months after his death, she felt guilty about her lack of sorrow and became increasingly depressed. Fortunately, she received counseling to help resolve this issue after an alert college friend recognized that the girl had suicidal tendencies. The mother was so concerned about her daughter's problems that she denied her own feelings of grief until almost two years later. At that time, she reported, she had a moderate grief reaction "which no one could understand."

Many respondents reported that their children needed more support in their grief than they did. In these cases, the survivors put their own grief, if they had any, on hold until the children had passed through the first weeks of sorrow. Some survivors stated that they could never share their grief with their children (even adult children) because it upset them too much or because the children could not believe the survivors really felt that way after being divorced for many years.

FINANCIAL AND LEGAL BURDENS

Continuing financial and legal burdens plagued many respondents for months after the death of their divorced spouses. Some of these problems were caused by the absence of a will, by a will that left everything to the second spouse and children with no mention of the children of the first marriage, or by the deceased's irresponsibility in handling business affairs. One woman reported that her ex-husband, who had been battling her for custody of their only daughter for the past ten years, had left unpaid legal fees of over two thousand dollars. Another stated that her ex-husband had left no will, owed dozens of bills, and left his business records in such a shambles that it took months to unravel them. She felt that this was his final "Gotcha!" from the grave.

Fighting for the financial rights of minor children was an exhausting and expensive process, one respondent stated. Child support that had gone unpaid for many months was not received from the estate because of prior claims filed by the ex-spouse's creditors. One year and hundreds of dollars later, the problem was still not resolved.

CONCLUSION

Grieving the death of a significant person in one's life is always traumatic. If the "emotional divorce," which is similar to the grief process (Hunt and Hunt 1977), has not been completed before the death of the ex-spouse, the survivor is likely to experience a grief reaction. Since our society does not usually recognize the severity of the grief that can be caused by such a death, the survivors frequently have multiple severe problems to cope with at a time when they are least able to do so. Additional problems arise when the death is sudden, violent, or not socially acceptable (suicide). The severity of this shock and the conflicting feelings that arise about the event can cause such a severe grief reaction that the final resolution of grief may take many years (Worden 1982).

In the United States, close to 50 percent of all marriages end in divorce, and 75 percent of the divorced persons remarry within three to five years of their divorce (Norton and Glick 1976). In studying the future of marriage, Duberman (1975) suggested that more people will be living in a second marriage than in a first marriage by the end of the century. Since there is an increasing life expectancy in this country, it is possible that a large number of people will be experiencing the death of a divorced spouse. Society needs to be made aware of this growing segment of the population whose need for understanding and emotional support is frequently not being met.

Mental health practitioners, social workers, the clergy, counselors, and other health care professionals should be aware of and recognize the special problems faced by these people. To obtain evidence of a possible grief reaction, questions about the ex-spouse must be included in the initial interview of the divorced client. In this way, the client's total needs may be fully assessed. Grief issues may be addressed, and the client can be helped to regain emotional equilibrium.

REFERENCES

Duberman, L. *The Reconstituted Family: A Study of Remarried Couples and Their Children*. Chicago: Nelson-Hall, 1975.

Hunt, M., and B. Hunt. *The Divorce Experience*. New York: McGraw-Hill, 1977.

Messinger, L. Introduction. In J. C. Hansen, ed. *Therapy with Remarriage Families: The Family Therapy Collection*. Rockville, MD: Aspen Publications, 1982.

Norton, A. J., and P. C. Glick. Marital instability: past, present and future. *J. Social Issues* 32(1):5-20, 1976.

Rando, T. *Grief, Dying and Death*. Champaign, IL: Research Press, 1984.

Worden, J. *Grief Counseling and Grief Therapy*. New York: Springer, 1982.

7

Divorcing Women: Psychological, Cultural and Clinical Considerations

Necha Cornelia Sirota, CSW

INTRODUCTION

Divorce is a turning point in a woman's life. It has a dual nature, being extremely stressful on the one hand but containing the seeds for significant growth and development on the other. A multiplicity of problems occur at once, testing a woman's coping mechanisms, while new opportunities to make positive changes present themselves.

The complexity of divorce is reflected in the observation of anthropologist Paul Bohannan (1970) that divorce has many facets: the emotional, the legal, the economic, the coparental and the communal. All these affect the individual with varying levels of intensity. The demand for change happening on so many fronts can create emotional havoc and severely strain a woman's resources.

We know that the increasing professional and economic independence of women has contributed to the rising incidence of divorce. Women now feel that they have an alternative to remaining locked into unhappy marriages. However, most of the women in their thirties and forties who have been divorcing in the last decade have been socialized in more traditional values and have only begun to alter their self-perceptions and expectations as adults. They have internalized more traditional values and conscious effort is needed to alter them. Divorce, whether initiated by the woman, mutually agreed upon by the husband and the wife, or thrust upon the woman against her will, presents a new opportunity, and also necessitates a multiplication and expansion of roles within a cultural climate where the role of women is in flux.

Western society is still ambivalent about this growing independence in women. It accepts and encourages while still resisting it. Its attitude toward divorced women is similarly ambivalent. The divorcing woman today deals with a double ambivalence: her own inner ambivalence mirrored by societal ambivalence. Happily the thrust has been toward continued personal liberation. However, increased liberation is usually accompanied by increased responsibilities.

The divorcing woman, bombarded by problems and faced with a bewildering array of decisions to make, may find herself in crisis and seek the help of a mental health professional. The challenge of psychotherapy is to provide emotional supports and facilitate choices which will lead to growth and development instead of regression and stagnation.

Much of the divorce literature relates to its effect on the family or the divorcing spouses, but most analyses fail to differentiate between its impact on men and women. Today, divorcing women who have children undergo a unique experience that deserves to be examined separately. There are unique stressors but also unique advantages.

The goal of this chapter is threefold. The first is to examine the factors within the experience that present particular difficulties or particular opportunities. The second is to look at some of the therapeutic issues that arise in the course of treatment, including those related to transference and countertransference. The third is to point to approaches and modes of intervention that can enable a woman to utilize this event for optimal growth and self-actualization.

I am writing from the professional perspective of the social worker. This means taking a holistic approach in which an individual is always viewed within the context of and in interaction with the environment. Also, the field of interaction may be intrapsychic, interpersonal or environmental. Because of this complexity, the social worker requires a repertoire of treatment modalities that includes the adoption of an active course in the mobilization of community services for the client when this is required. I choose to use the more generic term "therapist" when referring to the social worker because I believe the principles outlined here are relevant for related mental health professionals as well.

My assertions are based on a review of the literature and impressions from clinical experience with women who were divorcing after some years of marriage, mostly in their early thirties to early forties, and raising children ranging in age from early childhood to young adulthood. My own divorce added personal insight into this subject.

While some of the observations may apply to younger women, divorce after a shorter marriage span, women without children, or even men, I feel they are most applicable to the client population delineated above.

In order to understand what the divorcing woman is contending with, an overview of the salient divorce features is presented first and an examination of the specific therapeutic issues follows.

THE STRESSORS IN THE MARITAL SEPARATION OF WOMEN

Four concerns have been identified in studies of divorcing women: intrapsychic concerns regarding one's reaction to emotional separation, financial insecurity and single parenting worries, and interpersonal concerns (L'Hommedieu 1984).

The inner emotional upheaval is caused by the grieving that takes place for the loss of the marriage and separation from the spouse, and the temporary loss of identity as a woman moves from a married to a divorced state. In the midst of this emotional turmoil she must continue with her usual daily activities, and also make decisions about and perform the tasks which are part and parcel of divorce. There are legal and financial proceedings to deal with and chores to fulfill that had previously been the province of the husband. Parental responsibilities that had earlier been shared must now be shouldered alone. The children most often react to the marital separation with emotional upheaval of their own, and this will require special attention. She may also feel the need to shield them from the parental acrimony whenever possible. When there is a change of household there is a need to move, find new schools for the children, or find and begin employment.

This situation is often compounded by loss of some of a woman's environmental supports. The relationship with the husband's family is usually altered if not altogether forfeited. The relationship with a woman's own family can also become strained depending on their attitude toward the divorce. Friends of the couple often feel they must choose sides and withdraw. Often even a woman's own married friends feel threatened by the breakup and become aloof (Weiss 1975).

Just when a woman is undergoing inner crisis, facing practical difficulties and most in need, support may be less available than when she was married. Marital breakup is so difficult because a woman must engage in battle on all fronts just when her emotional and environmental resources are most depleted.

THE DIFFERENTIAL MEANING OF DIVORCE
FOR WOMEN

Various studies have shown that on the psychological level relationship is more essential for women than for men. Because female gender identity formation is linked with connectedness (unlike male gender identity formation, which is linked to separation), relationship and attachment have ongoing central importance in a woman's life (Chodorow 1978; Gilligan 1982; Josselson 1987). As a consequence, female identity is threatened by separation. Miller concurs that "for many women the threat of disruption of an affiliation is perceived not just as a loss of a relationship but as something closer to a total loss of self" (Miller 1976, p. 83).

Although both men and women experience some identity loss with divorce, this is usually greater for women than for men. In studying identity formation in women, Josselson (1987) found that a married woman's identity is often formed around the key relationship with the partner; self-definition exists in juxtaposition to this person, and "the more committed she is to the welfare of another, the less need she has to ponder the expression of her deeper self" (p. 179).

Cantor (1986) points out that even today women are expected to express their intellectual and assertive selves through their husbands. Separation will necessitate a reexamination and redefinition of who she is as an individual with the need to set individual goals.

This identity loss is also truer for women than for men because so much more of the wife's life circumstances are determined by her husband's identity. In most cases she assumes his name, the location of her residence will usually be determined by proximity to his work, and often her employment choices will be modified to accommodate and give priority to the husband's career. Thus, with marital separation many of the threads, of which her self-identity had been woven, become unraveled.

From a cultural perspective the meaning of divorce also differs for men and women. Although with the advent of the women's liberation movement women's roles have certainly expanded, the message still largely remains that ultimate fulfillment for a woman is attained through marriage. While women nowadays may be allowed or even encouraged to have careers, this option is still expected to be secondary to marriage and motherhood. Thus divorce, even when of her own choosing, means that she has failed in one of her central societal functions.

Divorced women still have a lesser social status. This is expressed by her being less creditworthy in the eyes of banks and other financial institutions, by being treated with less respect by service people, and by her children being considered fairer game for criticism and scolding by other adults (Weiss 1975). All this reduces a woman's self-esteem and makes her feel vulnerable and defensive.

A final factor that makes for a different experience is the assumption of the duties of parenting alone with the concomitant responsibilities and burdens. For psychological and cultural reasons, women have stronger ties to their children and only a small minority would even consider giving them up. Almost invariably, single parenting entails some, if not substantial, reduction of income for women because if the husbands were not the sole breadwinners, they mostly earned a higher salary than the wives.

DIVORCE AS A POTENTIAL FOR GROWTH

Divorce has most often been viewed as an expression of the individual's pathological inability to have intimate relationships. Recently some authors have begun to highlight its potential for growth and maturing. Gittelman and Markowitz (1974) maintain that divorce has been unduly stigmatized with its negative aspects overemphasized. They see divorce as a courageous act, pointing to its often liberating effect on those who dare to take the step, and note that it may mark the beginning of an important stage of emotional growth. Elizabeth Cauhape (1983) conducted a six-year study of post-divorce couples and reached similar conclusions. She observes that these people demonstrated that one can triumph over disappointment by making decisions on one's own behalf and on one's own terms.

Josselson (1987) believes that just as a career crisis can spark a burst of growth in men, a crisis in relationship will have a similar effect for women. In her research she found the most dramatic examples of growth among those young women whose first committed relationships had failed. She explains that

> losing a relationship represents more than losing a loved person. It is more deeply the loss of a precious fantasy, the belief that someone else will be there to perform psychological functions, to soothe distress, to structure time, to stabilize and to reassure, to make one feel worthwhile. Having to take over these functions for oneself seems to be growth promoting for women (p. 180).

Cantor (1986) analyzes divorce from a psychoanalytic viewpoint. She maintains that divorce can provide an opportunity to rework separation-individuation issues that were not dealt with when a woman went directly from a dependent relationship with parents to that with the husband. The initiation of divorce is often an expression of a separation-individuation thrust that cannot be achieved within the marriage.

I would also like to point out that the marital split initiates the expansion of role function. Women must of necessity learn to perform the "masculine" chores previously delegated to the husband and function in these capacities, too. Thus the divorce process means that even the most traditional women need to become more independent and versatile—liberated, if you will—in their practical functioning.

Finally, both McMahon (1980) and Jacobson (1983) deem crisis theory appropriate to the understanding and treatment of people undergoing divorce. Central to this theory is the belief that crisis contains potential for personality development and enhancement of the coping mechanisms.

THE DIRECTION OF THERAPEUTIC INTERVENTION

Given this potential for growth and development, what should the focus of therapeutic intervention be? Weiss (1975), who has conducted hundreds of workshops with people undergoing marital separation, clearly believes that the focus should be support and guidance to help people reorganize their lives and return as quickly as possible to normal functioning. He thinks people require all their energy to accomplish these tasks and do not have the energy to spare for effecting deeper change. I do not totally agree with his point of view for several reasons.

First, while it is true that this period may be overwhelming for a woman, crisis enables people to draw on reserves of strength that are not normally accessible to them. Second, during crisis there is a breakdown of the usual defenses; unresolved developmental conflicts may therefore surface and be reworked more quickly and with lesser energy expenditure than under more tranquil circumstances. Third, since divorce is a life-situational crisis during which so many changes occur in any case, it is easier to incorporate desired changes in attitude and behavior than during more stable periods of one's life.

The therapist's guide here, as at any other time, must be the motivation and inclination of the client. However, the therapist has a responsibility both to point out the opportunity divorce presents and to facilitate growth to the degree that a woman is willing and able to do so.

FORMULATION OF A THERAPEUTIC APPROACH

I will begin this section by saying that a primary prerequisite for being helpful to a woman in marital transition is a neutral stance toward divorce. Women with children are filled with trepidation when considering divorce and what they need is acceptance in dealing with these feelings and help in clarifying them. Any negative bias on the part of the therapist will be sensed and may cause them to clam up, leave therapy, or even postpone making the decision.

I have found Sarah Lynne McMahon's (1980) theoretical framework particularly helpful in formulating a therapeutic approach with my clients. McMahon based her observations on work with women in marital transition in the West Philadelphia Mental Health Consortium. She enumerates women's difficulties at this time and the stages of marital transition with the predominant concerns of each stage. The stages cited are: (1) alienation—the erosion of love and commitment, with denial and feelings of anxiety, fear and ambivalence; (2) separation—when this actually occurs on the physical level (There are feelings of guilt if the woman is the initiator, and abandonment if she is not. Anger is used to maintain the separation and deal with grief. Legal and economic issues complicate the contacts between the separating partners.); and (3) reorientation—the creation of a new identity as a single woman through changing habits, redirecting energies, taking new risks, and experimenting with and learning new behaviors.

However, the therapist must remember that as is true for most of the theoretical models of stages, these are not in actuality clear-cut and distinct. Women often move back and forth as they test their ability to contend with the new situation. Many marital breakups have several instances of separation, reunion and separation again until the final divorce.

A therapist's familiarity with process will facilitate an understanding of what is happening and enable him or her to share this knowledge with the client when appropriate. This will assist the client in gaining a more realistic perception of her situation, knowing what to expect and viewing herself as solving a life crisis similar to that faced by other women. It is also important for her to be able to differentiate between her individual problems and societal values and institutions that affect all women.

McMahon maintains that "a stereotyping of women's roles, inadequate access to economic and legal support, social isolation and certain personality traits associated with women make marital transition particularly difficult for women (p. 375)." In order to help remove these obstacles a therapist must have an unbiased perspective of women's roles and a willingness to encourage women to assume new roles and acquire new traits. These include learning new coping skills such as financial management, assertiveness, the setting of career goals and seeking job training. Emphasis should also be placed on the real and practical aspects of the divorce process. In this task a knowledge of legal divorce proceedings is useful. In addition, the therapist should be knowledgeable about community resources and be ready to take on an active role in referral when this is needed.

In working with women who are in the process of becoming single parents, knowledge of parent-child and single parenting issues is important. These women expend much of their energy in maintaining a semblance of continuity of the family in order to shield their children from the detrimental effects of the divorce. Inevitably, children will be traumatized and have some problems. Since mothering is basic to the self-identity of these women, they feel extremely guilty if they feel they have been remiss in this role. In addition, since single mothers are often overburdened, they may feel they have not been able to do as much as they should have done for their children. Women who initiate divorce proceedings are particularly prone to guilt feelings because they think they have violated social mores by placing their own needs before those of their children. Mothers often have difficulty being objective about their children's problems because they identify and experience their children's pain as their own, and this intensifies their distress. This pain is compounded for mothers who bear sole responsibility for parenting.

For these reasons, divorcing women tend to devote a significant proportion of therapy sessions to discussing concerns revolving around their children. The therapist can help in this area by assisting the mother to gain some emotional separation and objectivity. The ability to discuss parental problems with another adult also provides some measure of relief from the loneliness of the parental burden. Often practical advice is helpful. Family therapy skills are an advantage and can be utilized for occasional family sessions to deal with a particular mother-child or family problem.

THE THERAPEUTIC PROCESS

Women often enter treatment prior to the actual initiation of divorce, but being deeply unhappy with their marriage and having considered the idea of a split for some time. This is the stage of "alienation" to which McMahon (1980) refers. This may also be characterized as the turning point of "growth or regression" (Erikson 1950). There is the intense feeling of "missing out" in the marital relationship, and an erosion of love and commitment between the spouses has already occurred. However, there is still some denial of the extent of the schism and the concomitant dissatisfaction. There is great anxiety and fear of facing the situation in its full reality because this might force them to face a decision they are not yet ready to make. Women tend to be very ambivalent at this time, the soul searching being of a tentative nature because they are so fearful of the alternative—dissolution of the marriage and its consequences for themselves and their children. Often this is the first time a woman has shared her unhappiness with anyone, having maintained the facade of the "happy marriage" in front of family and friends. When this is the case, the first therapeutic step is validating the woman's experience, because within the marriage her feelings often may have been disparaged. She may have been labeled "oversensitive," "babyish," "spoiled" or even "crazy," causing her to doubt her own feelings.

The role of the therapist at this stage is to create an environment of trust where a woman can examine the source of her anxieties while verbalizing her unhappiness and explore her ambivalencies without feeling that she is being "pushed" into making a decision before she is ready to do so. This attitude should be a "truly neutral and emotionally unreactive position regarding the client's choice to change or not to change" (Lerner 1983, p. 703). I myself have sometimes had difficulty maintaining this "neutral" stance, but have learned from experience that it is detrimental to "rush" the client into any kind of decision. Several women that I have worked with have taken three to four years to pass from this stage to the actual point of physical separation.

Some women may go through the disillusionment process fully facing the rift between herself and her spouse, and yet consciously and rationally choose to remain within the marriage. They may do so for economic or social reasons, or for the children's sake. Some are able to seek "growth and generativity" (Erikson 1950) within other frameworks, such as career and outside social or even intimate attachments. For women of high self-esteem who have very clear boundaries within the marriage, this may work. Here it is important that the therapist not impose her own values on the client.

A very different group of women who may "choose" to remain within the marital relationship, even while undergoing great suffering, are battered wives. These women are sometimes hindered from changing because of unconscious conflicts—baggage they carry with them from the past. They are likely to have an early history of abuse, keeping them locked within the masochistic relationship.

To explain this puzzling loyalty, Nadelson and Sauzier (1986) point to "learned helplessness," an inability to effect change, and "learned hopefulness," by which these women delude themselves with the hope that the husband will change or that they will be able to change him. The also feel that the "Stockholm syndrome," in which victims develop positive feelings toward their aggressors based on a mix of terror, gratitude and dependence, applies here, too. Be that as it may, there are other societal and environmental issues that keep a woman from being able to break out of untenable situations, such as internalized negative values regarding divorce or the equating of the wifely role with self-esteem, and the nurturing of others as the only worthy female occupation (Martin 1983). These women have also been indoctrinated with the notion that divorce is the ultimate disgrace one can bring upon one's family. There is also a cycle of terror along with isolation, lack of financial resources or other supports that often keep these women from making a change. Validation of their experience is even more important for this group of women because of the emotional degradation that was endured along with the physical abuse.

Reframing the "failure" as not her own, but as partly a societal issue involving the inferior status of women, may help in separating familial expectations from the woman's expectations of herself. Battered women are usually in very dependent situations with very little economic resources of their own, and providing practical environmental supports is crucial along with referral to a peer support group to enable them to break out of the cycle. Continued counseling must accompany concrete assistance to help the woman gain some insight into what contributed to her situation in order to prevent it from recurring in a new relationship, and to enable her to resist regressing and returning to her spouse.

Nadelson and Sauzier (1986) highlight the frustration often experienced by the therapist because of the frequency that abused women return to their batterers. They caution against overidentification with the woman's helplessness and dependence leading to rescue attempts that may reinforce and support abusive behavior, and prevent a woman from acting on her own behalf.

It is difficult but important to maintain the delicate balance between helping the woman acknowledge and confront the actual physical danger she might be in, and refraining from causing her to feel that she is being pressured into making a decision before she is ready to do so. Such pressure might place her in a "double-bind" situation, because at the same time as she seeks to escape, she is being pulled to stay in the relationship by her husband (Lerner 1983). I have found that some women are only able to break free when they have reached a limit of endurance and reached some kind of crisis. In other instances grown children have helped a mother to finally take the necessary steps to leave.

A third category of women is those who have consciously reevaluated the worth of their marriage and are the ones initiating and actively seeking the divorce. They are reaching the end of the alienation stage and have ceased denying the problems that exist. They are still anxious and fearful of the step they are about to take and are justifiably worried about the future. However, they have reappraised the past and are disillusioned with their husbands and their relationship. These women have done a realistic reevaluation of their motives for marrying and questioned its relevance for the present. They are determined to go through with the divorce, but the ambivalence, guilt and anxiety about the future are still very much present.

Thus a woman enters the second stage of actual separation and takes on the tasks of "modifying the life structure" with much trepidation and feelings of loss, bitterness and disappointment. McMahon (1980) believes this stage of grieving, because of the loss of attachment, is the most difficult in the process.

There is a general consensus among researchers that marital separation involves grieving even when both partners agree on the dissolution (Goode 1956; Kübler-Ross 1974; Weiss 1975; Hunt and Hunt 1977; Jacobson 1983). The symptoms described are similar to those in bereavement. There is sleep disturbance, loss of appetite, poor health, memory loss, inefficiency at work and anxiety attacks. In addition there are feelings of bitterness, guilt and shame, a sense of failure, a feeling of rejection and depression, and a preoccupation with past memories and current fantasy of the spouse.

These patterns vary. Among middle-class women who had initiated divorce, shock, rage, bitterness and rejection were notable for their absence (L'Hommedieu 1984). Hunt and Hunt (1977) noted that often women will feel good immediately after the divorce, and Chiraboga and Cutler (1977) found that in women depression was more temporary than in men. McMahon (1980) emphasizes the differences between divorce and bereavement in that in divorce the husband is alive and a woman has some sense of control over the situation. Weiss (1975) believes that often the mourning will be centered more on the wasted years than on the loss of the spouse.

In my own work, I found that all women undergoing divorce had some of the symptoms of mourning and depression, particularly decreased efficiency in daily functioning. However, there was a marked difference in the degree and duration of the disturbance between the women who perceived the divorce as of their choice and those who didn't. The latter were angrier and more depressed for a longer period of time. Women who had initiated the divorce tended to feel guiltier and more ambivalent with bouts of euphoria interspersed with the depression.

These women were often baffled and ashamed about the feelings of attachment they still had to men they may not have liked or respected, who may have caused them great suffering, and from whom they sometimes needed to free themselves.

Weiss (1975) calls these baffling feelings of attachment to the estranged, often rejected and devalued spouse, "separation distress." He explains that the spouse has become an "attachment figure" and likens this to the distress often shown by an infant when separated from the parent, or to that of an abused child who still can't help pining for the abusive parent. He also describes feelings of loneliness and emotional isolation in which "the world seems desolate of potential attachment. It seems barren, silent, dead. Sometimes it is not so much the external world which seems blighted but rather the world within oneself" (p. 51).

I have found that feelings of emptiness and depression may sometimes stem from the loss of stimulation and excitement, albeit unpleasant, that the ongoing friction with the husband had provided. Its absence may leave an emotional vacuum that a woman may initially have difficulty filling in more positive ways. Understanding the source and the nature of the depression is often helpful in alleviating it.

The continued preoccupation with injuries sustained at the hands of the husband are also an expression of "separation distress" and an attempt to continue some form of attachment. The therapist must help the woman recognize the underlying longing, and the feelings of hurt and abandonment (which may be felt even when the woman is the initiator) lying at the core of the anger.

The anger and sense of betrayal may also mask a woman's unwillingness to relinquish the childish belief that there will always be someone there to care for and protect her. This fantasy is nourished by the cultural myth of the husband as a provider and protector of the wife. In therapy a woman can be given a chance to mourn the loss of this fantasy and thus become a more individuated and independently functioning adult.

Obviously, divorce is more traumatic for women when it is imposed upon them by the husband. These women were found to have the highest trauma index (Goode 1956). L'Hommedieu (1984) speaks of rejection, a sense of failure and bitterness. Women who saw their spouse as the instigator felt more hurt and were more disturbed (Weiss 1975; Jacobson 1983). Gittelman and Markowitz (1974) concur that spouses who are abandoned against their will are likely to feel a profound sense of regret and anger. These feelings are caused by separation anxiety, fear of being out of control of one's destiny, and the need to deal with ambivalent feelings toward the rejecting spouse.

Cantor (1986) distinguishes between abandoned women who have a well-established sense of self and those who don't. The former will be able to go through normal grieving processes and let go of the spouse. The less individuated woman will undergo a developmental crisis and require psychotherapy.

In my own practice, these women all need a much longer period of mourning than do other groups of women. The need to "obsessively review" (a term coined by Weiss 1975) the events leading to the marital breakup is an expression of their struggle to come to terms with the loss. Such obsessing often occupies a major portion of the therapy hour, testifying to what a difficult phase this is for them to navigate. Often the therapist feels frustrated with the seeming lack of progress at this time, and urges the client to let go and move on with her life. Such urging works more in the service of therapists' needs than those of the client. We may identify with the woman's pain echoing our own, which makes it difficult for us to be empathic and helpful in working it through.

These women feel betrayed and think they will never be able to trust anyone again. In these cases it is our task to help the client work through the grief and sense of betrayal with its concurrent loss of self-esteem, and gain a more balanced view of others. The very relationship with the therapist, with trust being a central feature, may serve as a "corrective experience" for this rebalancing to occur. Some women "tested" my trustworthiness on different occasions by arriving late and missing appointments. Here it was important to clarify the meaning of their acting out, which was to see whether I cared enough to reach out to them, thereby proving my trustworthiness. My doing so allowed the feelings to surface and to be dealt with. The countertransference issues for me as a therapist were to react not with anger nor to interpret the women's not showing up as their rejection of me or failure on my part. I also had to be wary of not "over-identifying" with the women's anger at their men because of my own disappointments in this area.

When divorcing women have been able to work through some of their grief, they can proceed to the task of redefining their identities as unmarried women. The identity transition that is triggered by marital separation takes place in the second and third stages of the divorce, beginning with the separation and continuing through the reorientation phase.

Therapy has always been considered the appropriate setting for people going through identity crises and as the ideal setting for self-examination. In the therapeutic hour a woman can sift through the pieces of the self for acceptance or rejection, and alternatives can be clarified. Some of this process also happens unconsciously. Many of the emerging changes have been simmering for a long time and are now ready to be recognized, claimed and acted upon. Others may be tried on for size and discarded. Many women welcome this opportunity to act on changes they have been wanting to make for a long time, but were prevented from doing so because of spousal or social disapproval.

The therapist may support the client in her efforts to experiment and learn new behaviors, taking new risks and creating new self-identities as a single woman. For women who viewed marriage as their only life task, this loss of self-identity is particularly difficult (Weiss 1975), and they will need more assistance at this time than those who were more versatile in their social functioning.

In a society that tends to sex-type behaviors, labeling achievement, power and mastery as masculine, and dependency, submission and nest building as feminine, divorce of necessity demands readjustment of this set of role concepts. Here the woman is partially dismantling the nest, needing to master many "masculine" skills such as financial management and career building, while giving up some of her dependent postures. Understandably, this may be more difficult for more traditional women (O'Leary 1977). However, the accumulation of a repertoire of both masculine and feminine behaviors makes for a better adjusted and healthier personality, with flexibility to choose appropriate behaviors in varying situations. This is true for both men and women. As divorcing women master "masculine" skills, their self-esteem is enhanced. The female therapist may serve as a role model in this endeavor. If she is also divorced, as I am, and this information is shared with the client, this may add validity to the therapist's supportive efforts. However, as a feminist, I have had to be careful not to impose my own values when dealing with this area, and to allow women seeking my help the freedom to choose whatever variation of emphasis they desired.

Women also have concerns about being too old to start all over again. Within a society where so much value is set on women's youth and beauty, the anxiety about competing with younger women is natural, especially around attracting men. Here, as a therapist, I again have to separate my own concerns as a single woman in midlife from the client's needs, and yet acknowledge societal realities. The challenge becomes that of retaining freshness, growth, flexibility and the excitement of new opportunities in the middle years. It is important for women to learn to value themselves at least as much for who they are and what they have accomplished as on how they look now. Most of the women I worked with initially expressed a lack of interest in beginning to date again at this stage. It was only as this was more closely examined that their anxieties were recognized. "Will I still be able to attract a man at my age?" "How do I know he will not be like my ex-husband?" "How will my children accept this?" They have to deal with these questions and relearn this social skill in an adult way very different from that of adolescence.

The issues of attachment and separateness raised by divorce force women to make new accommodations. The very act of divorce is choosing to be separate, at least for a while. This may be very difficult for some women because identity definition is connected to attachment and is so often determined in relation to others—"daughter of," "wife of" or "mother of" someone else. The task for many women is leaving this residual category and defining who they are, when they are no longer the "wife of." They have to learn to be alone, go out alone and make friends on their own rather than as part of a couple. Many women have difficulty making decisions when it is no longer in compliance with or in defiance of someone, and they may transfer this behavior pattern to the therapist/client relationship. Clearly, a "neutral" posture is important, so that the client may perceive what is happening and hopefully achieve more real independence. She may discover the freedom to make choices without having to react to others. For many women this is their first experience of being separate, and when they discover their ability to manage alone, this is a great boost to their self-esteem and may be an exhilarating venture.

SUMMARY

For effective psychotherapeutic intervention with divorcing women the complexity of the divorce process must be understood. A multiplicity of factors affect the transition from the married to the divorced state taking place within the context of cultural and personal ambivalence toward the expanding role of women in our society. The therapist must realize that he or she may be the one stable anchor for a woman when many aspects of her life are kaleidoscopically changing at this time. The therapist's role is multifaceted and includes being a provider of support, a guide, an advisor, a source of information, a role model and a catalyst for change. Allowance must be made for flexibility of the therapeutic function in order to meet the divorcing woman's evolving needs. This will maximize a woman's ability to utilize this life crisis for optimal growth and development.

REFERENCES

Bardwick, J.M. The Seasons of a Woman's Life. In D.G. McGuigan, ed., *Women's Lives: New Theory Research and Policy.* Ann Arbor: University of Michigan Center for Continuing Education of Women, 1980.

Bohannon, P., ed. *Divorce and After.* Garden City, NY: Doubleday, 1970.

Cantor, D.W. Marriage and Divorce: The Search for Adult Identity. In T. Bernay and D.W. Cantor, eds., *The Psychology of Today's Woman: New Psychoanalytic Visions.* New York: The Analytic Press, 1986.

Cauhope, E. *Fresh Starts: Men and Women After Divorce.* New York: Basic Books, 1983.

Chiraboga, D.A., and L. Cutler. Stress responses among divorcing men and women. *J. Divorce* 1:95-105, 1977.

Chodorow, N. *The Reproduction of Mothering.* Berkeley: University of California Press, 1978.

Erikson, E. *Childhood and Society.* New York: W. W. Norton, 1950.

_____. *Identity Youth and Crisis.* New York: W. W. Norton, 1968.

Fuchs, E. *The Second Season: Life, Love and Sex—Women in the Middle Years.* Garden City, NY: Anchor Press/Doubleday, 1977.

Gettleman, S., and J. Markowitz. *The Courage to Divorce.* New York: Simon & Schuster, 1974.

Gilligan, C. Restoring the Missing Text of Women's Development to Life Cycle Theories. In D. G. McGuigan, ed., *Women's Lives: New Theory Research and Policy.* Ann Arbor: University of Michigan Center for Continuing Education of Women, 1980.

_____. *In a Different Voice.* Cambridge, MA: Harvard University Press, 1982.

Hunt, M., and B. Hunt. *The Divorce Experience.* New York: McGraw-Hill, 1977.

Jacobson, G.F. *The Multiple Crises of Martial Separation and Divorce.* New York: Grune & Stratton, 1983.

Josselson, M. *Finding Herself: Pathways to Identity Development in Women.* San Francisco: Jossey-Bass, 1987.

Kübler-Ross, E. *Questions and Answers on Death and Dying.* New York: Macmillan, 1974.

Lerner, H.E. Female dependency in context: some theoretical and technical considerations. *Am. J. Orthopsychiatry* 53(4), October 1983.

L'Hommedieu, T. *The Divorce Experience of Working and Middle Class Women.* Ann Arbor: UMI Research Press, 1984.

Martin, D. *Battered Wives.* New York: Simon & Schuster, 1983.

McMahon, S.L. Women in Marital Transition. In A.M. Brodsky and R.T. Hare-Mustin, eds., *Women and Psychotherapy: An Assessment of Research and Practice.* New York: Guilford Press, 1980.

Miller, J.B. *Toward a New Psychology of Women.* Boston: Beacon Press, 1976.

Nadelson, C., and M. Sauzier. Intervention Programs for Individual Victims and Their Families. In M. Lystad, ed., *Violence in the Home: An Interdisciplinary Perspective.* New York: Brunner/Mazel, 1986.

O'Leary, V.E. *Toward Understanding Women.* Monterey, CA: Brooks/Cole, 1977.

Rubin, L.B. *Women of a Certain Age: The Midlife Search for Self.* New York: Harper & Row, 1985.

Ruderman, E.B. Creative and Reparative Uses of Countertransference by Women Psychotherapists Treating Women Patients: A Clinical Research Study. In T. Bernay and D.W. Cantor, eds., *The Psychology of Today's Woman: New Psychoanalytic Visions.* New York: The Analytic Press, 1986.

Schwartz, M.C. Helping the worker with countertransference. *Social Work.* May 1978.

Vidoni, C. Intense positive countertransference feelings. *Am. J. Nursing,* March 1975.

Weiss, R.S. *Marital Separation.* New York: Basic Books, 1975.

Whitbourne, S.K., and C.S. Weinstock. *Adult Development.* New York: Praeger, 1986.

8

Grief as a Central Component in Separation and Divorce

Madeline A. Naegle, PhD

Since divorce has become a more frequent experience in the lives of American families, it is regarded less as deviant behavior and more as a social phenomenon of concern to the society as a whole. By the mid-1990s, it is estimated that in this country more than 11 percent of children under age 18 will reside with a divorced parent. Separation and divorce change the structure of the traditional family in ways that have economic, psychological and social implications for the participants, their extended families, friends and the larger community. The processes of separation and divorce occur over time. Throughout the phases of these events, spouses and children must negotiate stressful changes and achieve emotional adjustments. Assisting them requires the mobilization of resources that are community- as well as family-based.

Separation and divorce are gradual processes that occur in phases that last from one to eight years and are accompanied by changes over time. Through these periods of change, spouses and children encounter new and potentially overwhelming stresses and must adjust their psychological and social lives. The nature of these changes will be determined largely by the psychological structure of the family before and after the decision to separate.

In clinical practice, social workers, psychiatric nurses and other mental health professionals provide support and guidance to these families. Recognizing and addressing grief and its many manifestations in these processes is a central component of treatment, but one that may be overlooked. At times, individual behaviors and concerns detract from what is occurring in the family system. Because of the pain and distress that the family is experiencing, its members and the therapist may move too quickly to reorder life and to attempt the mastery of uncomfortable feelings through a new sense of structure and a rearrangement of family members' social and emotional lives. When grief is overlooked and the necessary grieving process is suppressed or its importance minimized, its resolution may be delayed.

Grief or mourning consists of a series of emotional events that follow separation or loss. It is described as a definite syndrome with psychological signs and symptoms that may occur immediately or may be delayed (Lindemann 1944).

LOSSES

Parents and children experience multiple losses when separation occurs. These losses include the following:

1. The loss of income necessitated by the establishment of two households.
2. The loss of a life style and a familiar daily routine.
3. The loss of home through relocation, with the accompanying loss of relationships with neighbors and the community.
4. The loss of members of the extended family or modifications in relationships with them.
5. The loss of family rituals developed together.
6. The loss or modification of roles assumed by family members.

Children lose the parental unit as a protective presence and as an emotional subsystem that buffers parent-child relationships. Thus, when emotional difficulties occur with the presiding parent, a former source of support is no longer available (Hess and Camara 1979). Spouses lose the continuity of emotional closeness and sexual gratification that characterizes the marital relationship and may become estranged from friendships they had established and maintained as a couple.

As research on the impact of divorce on families has increased, the nature of the continuing instability of the family unit and the lasting changes in the family unit that occur have become clearer. Studies suggest that adjustment to divorce is more highly influenced by family interaction in response to this instability and change than by the traits of individual family members (Bowen 1978). The interaction of the spouses is of primary importance and is highly influenced by the degree of emotional attachment between them. The varying intensity of emotional attachment is felt to create an emotional balance or equilibrium in family relationships. Change or disruption in the patterns of emotional attachment help or hinder the development of each family member and result in changes in the family's patterns of emotional relationships.

Separation and divorce are anticipated or actual losses that change emotional attachments between spouses and between parents and children. Whether these events occur gradually or all at once, their impact precipitates a crisis in the emotional patterns of relationships within the family (Hoff 1978). Frequently, some or all of the family members experience loss of control, disorganization, emotional instability and a heightened sense of psychological vulnerability. The nature and intensity of these attachments influence the manner and success with which parents and children negotiate the psychological tasks that may facilitate the resolution of grief—a central process in separation. Although spousal ties and children's attachment to the ideal notion of "family" change and lessen in intensity, they are never completely broken and continue to operate at times in ways that affect both individual and family behavior. Strongly negative feelings, for example, constitute a link by virtue of their emotionally invested quality, although they are viewed as a form of resolution.

BEHAVIOR

Family members' manifestations of grief and mourning for the lost family differ, depending on the members' ages and roles. During the crisis phase of divorce, usually six weeks to three months, behaviors commonly associated with acute grief are observed. They include sleep and appetite disturbances, crying, irritability, anger, problems in concentration, and emotional distance from significant people. Children express signs and symptoms that are indicative of their developmental levels and that reflect their cognitive and emotional function. For example, sleep disturbances and regression are common in young children; aggressive behavior and inattention to schoolwork appear more frequently in latency-age youngsters (McDermott 1970). Although these reactions are intense, they are transitory, and the severity of the disturbance does not necessarily have a significant relationship to overall behavioral adjustment five years later (Wallerstein 1984).

Delayed or postponed grief responses are considered to be abnormal and occur beyond the usual time span following the divorce. Their occurrence may be an outgrowth of the individual personality or the suppression or inhibition of the expression of the normal grief response. In children, certain predominant feelings that may remain beyond a normal grieving period are identified as residual grief (Wallerstein 1984). These feelings include (1) profound sorrow, (2) anger at one or both parents, (3) concern with being unloved or unlovable, (4) intense worry about parents, (5) nostalgia for the intact family and (6) conflicts over loyalty.

Adults who experience delayed or dysfunctional grief reactions may deny that anything is wrong. They may engage in overactivity, avoid reminders of the separation or divorce, and manifest signs of preoccupation, indecision, apathy and emotional numbness. Individuals may have problems functioning at work or at home and be plagued with feelings of incompetence. Excessive reliance on alcohol or drugs can develop. The research of Bloom and coworkers (1985) suggests that such symptoms decrease or tend to be unusual 30 months after a divorce, but that circumstances related to the divorce often function to extend the grieving period. Some of these circumstances are (1) continuing adjudication procedures, (2) failed attempts at reconciliation and (3) family crises that return the couple to an interdependent state.

At times, the resolution of feelings of grief about separation and divorce is problematic because dysfunctional patterns related to the origin of these processes persist. Dysfunctional patterns that blocked the earlier fulfillment of members' needs and impinged on their growth have evolved over time and are usually chronic. These patterns then impede the therapeutic process of working through grief and include problems in communication, withdrawal and emotional distancing, and shared unreal beliefs.

Grief occurs in all divorcing families, even when family life and the marital relationship have been characterized by conflict or when conflict has been escalating for a long time. Grief reactions are complicated by long-standing and rigid dysfunctional patterns. The resolution of feelings in a climate in which painful affects have been avoided or suppressed is a formidable task for the therapist and the family members. Until such resolution takes place, however, there can be no realignment of patterns of emotional attachment between parents and children or between estranged or divorced spouses.

Adjustment after divorce, a process that includes restabilization following the disequilibrium created by the crisis, sometimes takes place in less than two years or, especially for children, may extend up to eight years. The desired outcome for all family members is the prevention of psychopathology and modifications in the psychological structure of the family that allow emotional realignment. The intensity of grief and the need for resolution will be largely determined by the degree of attachment between the spouses. This and other severely dysfunctional patterns impede the return to functional pre-divorce states. The findings of Wallerstein (1984) suggest that the more favorable outcomes of divorce are associated with the progress of the family in addressing the psychological tasks and issues elicited by it.

Wallerstein (1983) identified the following tasks of a child in a divorcing family:

1. Acknowledging the reality of the marital disruption.
2. Disengaging from parental conflict and distress and resuming customary pursuits, such as academic pace and developmental tasks.
3. Resolving the loss.
4. Resolving anger and self-blame.
5. Accepting the permanence of the divorce.
6. Achieving realistic hope regarding relationships.

Support of the children's struggles in achieving these tasks, as well as of the family's ability to deal with unresolved conflicts, appears to have a positive influence on outcomes and resolution.

Adults in the family system also face tasks that are central to change and to the modification of previous emotional patterns (see Collison and Futrell 1982; Jacobs 1982). Their tasks include these:

1. Identification and acknowledgment of the grieving process.
2. Change and modification of life roles:
    a. Social—building a social support system.
    b. Sexual—reconciling sexual needs and life styles.
    c. Economic—obtaining sufficient financial assistance.
    d. Psychological and emotional—resolving conflicts and dealing with emotional deprivations.
3. Restructuring the parent-child relationship.
4. Review of the psychological tasks of the individual's developmental life stage.

CLINICAL STRATEGIES

Separation and divorce may disrupt the normal processes of growth and development, threaten primary emotional bonds and create conflicts of loyalty for adults and children. Anticipated and real losses precipitate crises in the family. The restoration of equilibrium is dependent on the accurate identification of a crisis and on the development of strategies to address the dynamics of the family system and the psychological tasks that parents and children face.

Multiple losses, both actual and anticipated, that are experienced in the family system and by its individual members occur concurrently and in association with separation and divorce. The normal grieving response to these losses is central in efforts to adjust to these events and to activities necessary to the realignment of family patterns. Clinicians from various disciplines (see, for example, Beal 1979; Hazzard and Scheuerman 1976; Hoff 1978; Hoffman 1981; Jones and Dimond 1982; Smoyak 1975) have used various theoretical frameworks that can facilitate growth and positive adjustment. These approaches acknowledge the following:

- The interactional nature of the family system requires a relationship-centered evaluation of the separation process.
- The grieving process in separation and divorce corresponds to that experienced in relation to the loss of a loved one or a meaningfully invested life event.
- The phases of the grieving process, especially anger, require time and the guidance of the therapist to achieve resolution.
- Education regarding phases of growth and development, as well as coping mechanisms, enhances the therapeutic process.
- The successful realignment of family relationships includes continuing contact between the children and both parents.
- Therapeutic activities include the therapist's interpretation and guidance of the parent in relation to the children's resolution of their grief.

It is important that the therapist undertake advocacy activities in social support systems that are essential resources for the divorcing family.

Although loss and personal adjustment to its consequences are lifelong challenges, individuals are equipped in greater or lesser degrees to deal with such changes. For the majority of families, the damaging potential of divorce outweighs the emergency of growth-promoting opportunities. Strategies that recognize loss and use approaches to its constructive negotiation are supportive of families and the society.

REFERENCES

Beal, E. Children of divorce: a family system perspective. *J. Social Issues* 35:140-154, 1979.

Bloom, B., W. Hodges, M. Kern, and S. McFadden. A preventive intervention program for the newly separated: final evaluations. *Am. J. Orthopsychiatry* 55:9-26, 1985.

Bowen, M. *Family Therapy in Clinical Practice.* New York: Jason Aronson, 1978.

Collison, C., and J. Futrell. Family therapy for the single parent family system. *J. Psychosocial Nursing* 20(7):16-20, 1982.

Hazzard, M.E., and M. Scheuerman. Family system therapy. *Nursing* 76:22-23, 1976.

Hess, R., and K. Camara. Post-divorce family relationships as mediating factors in the consequences of divorce for children. *J. Social Issues* 35(4):79-95, 1979.

Hoff, L. *People in Crisis.* Reading, MA: Addison-Wesley, 1978.

Hoffman, L. *Foundations of Family Therapy.* New York: Basic Books, 1981.

Jacobs, J. The effect of divorce on fathers: an overview of the literature. *Am. J. Psychiatry* 139(10):1235-1241, 1982.

Jones, S., and M. Dimond. Family theory and family therapy models: comparative review with implications for nursing practice. *J. Psychosocial Nursing* 20(10):12-19, 1982.

Leahey, M. Findings from research on divorce: implications for professionals' skill development. *Am. J. Orthopsychiatry* 54(2):298-317, 1983.

Lindemann, E. Symptomatology and management of acute grief. *Am. J. Psychiatry* 101:141-148, 1944.

McDermott, J.F. Divorce and its psychiatric sequelae in children. *Arch. Gen. Psychiatry* 23:421-427, 1970.

Smoyak, S., ed. *The Psychiatric Nurse as a Family Therapist.* New York: John Wiley & Sons, 1975.

Wallerstein, J. Children of divorce: the psychological tasks of the child. *Am. J. Orthopsychiatry* 53(2):230-243, 1983.

_____. Children of divorce: preliminary report of a ten-year follow-up of young children. *Am. J. Orthopsychiatry* 54(3):444-458, 1984.

9

Divorce and the Loss of Self

Judith Haber, PhD

When a marriage dissolves because of divorce, all family members experience major physical, social and emotional losses, including the protective presence of two parents who can buffer and spell each other; the symbols, traditions and continuity of the intact family; and, perhaps, the family home, school and neighborhood. Such losses and their sequelae may be felt for years after the marital rupture (Wallerstein 1986).

In the nuclear family, the major loss occurs in the marital subsystem and involves the loss of one's spouse. This loss may contribute to the loss of the self as it was defined within the marital context. The loss of the self as a result of divorce is a significant source of distress and potential dysfunction in adult family members during and after a divorce.

From a family systems perspective, the level of differentiation of the individuals involved in a divorce is a major factor that influences their individual experience of loss as a result of the divorce (Christofori 1977). According to Bowen (1978) and Fogarty (1977), the lower the level of differentiation of self in one spouse, the greater the likelihood that the self was defined as being fused with that of the other spouse. Thus, when the fused common self is lost through divorce, one or both spouses is likely to experience a significant sense of loss, as well as dysfunction.

Clients who are devastated by the overt breaking of the fused relationship most commonly state, "I don't know who I am anymore." In a fused relationship, boundaries have been so loose and blurred that the spouses ceased to know where they ended and the other began or what they contributed to the relationship. This blending of the spouses may be manifest in overcloseness or reactive distance.

92

When the overt fused relationship is broken because of impending, ongoing or completed divorce proceedings, the result may be traumatic to either spouse or to both.

In my clinical practice, I have developed a model that helps divorced people deal with the loss of self by assisting them to define a more differentiated sense of self. The model consists of four stages that unfold over one to two years—one year being the time it takes to re-experience all of the seasons and annual events that are common to the marital relationship and to the family unit, which no longer exists in the same way.

STAGE 1: ENGAGEMENT

During this stage, clients are often in crisis, feeling out of control and helpless to manage their lives and themselves. I conduct a nuclear and multigenerational family assessment to identify significant patterns and toxic issues in the family, specifically those that relate to loss, marriage, divorce and differentiation of the self. In addition to constructing a genogram that diagrams triangles and other family data, I administer the Level of Differentiation of Self Scale (LDSS) (Haber 1984), which enables me to determine the individual client's functional level of differentiation, which in turn provides a measure of fusion and, by logical extension, the likelihood of the loss of self. The structural interventions are used to initiate grieving, decrease anxiety, and increase clients' coping and level of function.

STAGE 2: INCREASED FOCUS ON THE SELF

In this stage, clients are helped to move from a focus on the other spouse—that is, blaming the spouse for the misery he or she has caused—and to concentrate on their yearning for what the spouse contributed to the definition of self that is now missing. During this stage, it is common for clients to search frantically for another person who will fill the gap and complete them, at least in an illusory way, thus setting them up to repeat previous relationship patterns.

Therapy refocuses clients on the self, as much as they can tolerate. Clients are encouraged to take increasing responsibility for who they are and how they behave—something that many clients have never confronted—and are taught that they are in charge of how they feel. Women are particularly prone to this problem, since many went from being mommy's and daddy's little girl to being a wife without ever defining themselves as autonomous, differentiated persons who exist apart from another.

Clients are encouraged to give up their "bitterbank" of blame, hurt, resentment, anger and unmet expectations. (Wallerstein 1986). Reframing the bitterbank as a self-destructive phenomenon shifts the focus from spouse to self (Gilbert and Burden 1982). Clients must be guided back through these emotions or they will remain stuck in the past, which will limit their ability to move ahead in the present and future.

As the bitterbank, which has been their central source of self-definition, dissipates, clients are often at a loss as to how they will define themselves and manage their lives. This is the point at which they begin to define themselves. As they begin to let go of the spouse as both a savior and an enemy, they learn more about the part they have played in what happened, diminish their perception of themselves as victims, and take more responsibility for meeting their own needs. For example, Jane A realized that she had been expecting her husband to meet all of her emotional needs; she came to understand that when she pursued him in this manner, he felt overwhelmed and inadequate and became distant under stress. Her anger and hurt about his behavior arose from the part of her that was fused with him emotionally—the part that had no self-definition and was unable to gratify herself apart from what he gave her emotionally.

STAGE 3: FINDING THE MISSING PIECES

During this stage, clients embark on discovering who they are as persons. They pose such questions as "Who am I?" "What do I have?" "What don't I have as a person?" and "What do I look to others to complete in me?"

Clients are coached about how to research missing generational pieces in their families of origin. That is, they try to figure out their parents' characteristics, how relationship patterns are played out in their family of origin, how their need to fuse with another is derived from these patterns, and the role models of this phenomenon in their family of origin. Reentry into the family of origin, albeit in a different way, increases the options they perceive for relationships, as do efforts to increase their social networks.

STAGE 4: DEFINING A SELF

In the final stage of therapy, clients, equipped with a provisional sense of a solid self, work on operationalizing their emotional gains. Situations are designed to test their ability to take "I" positions and to allow others to have their own, different "I" positions. They attempt to enter relationships as autonomous persons who do not look to others for completion. The ultimate awareness of autonomy is the emptiness of knowing that all one really has in this world is oneself.

At the conclusion of therapy, the LDSS is readministered to determine whether the client's functional level of differentiation has changed. In at least 50 percent of the clients I have treated, the loss of self has been resolved, to a great extent, and a more functional, whole self has emerged. However, since the basic level of differentiation, in contrast to the functional level of differentiation, is relatively stable, clients are cautioned about the reappearance of reflex relationship patterns when stress and anxiety are high. Self-assessment and intervention strategies or checkup visits with the therapist during such times are advisable, at least during the year following the termination of therapy.

REFERENCES

Bowen, M. Theory in the Practice of Psychotherapy. In M. Bowen, ed., *Family Therapy in Clinical Practice.* New York: Jason Aronson, 1978.

Cristofori, R. Modification of loss in divorce: a report from clinical practice. *The Family* 5(1):25-30, 1977.

Fogarty, T. Fusion. *The Family* 4(2):49-58, 1977.

Gilbert, J., and S. Burden. Stage III marital conflict. *The Family* 10(1):27-39, 1982.

Haber, J. The Relationship Between Differentiation of Self, Complementary Psychological Need Patterns and Marital Conflict. *Dissert. Abstr. Int.* 45:2102B, 1984 (University Microfilms No. 800521-3042).

Wallerstein, J. Women after divorce: preliminary report from a ten-year followup. *Am. J. Orthopsychiatry* 56(1):65-77, 1986.

10

The Perfect Couple

Frank Limone, MSW, CAS

Everyone said, "John and Claire were the perfect couple." They did everything together. They went to the supermarket together, to the dry cleaner together and to all social functions together.

Everyone said, "John and Claire read each other's minds." They knew what each other needed before it was expressed.

Everyone said, "John and Claire would give their life for each other." They lived through and for each other. They did for each other what the other was afraid to do or try.

Everyone said, "John and Claire were soulmates." They were a merged personality. They were the perfect couple.

When word got around about John and Claire separating, everyone thought, "It could happen to me and I would be alone." John and Claire no longer supplied the needed illusion for everyone. And everyone kept away.

To cope with the shattering of "I thought we were forever," John and Claire opted for therapy.

Through therapy, John and Claire were able to see that they were in a symbiotic or co-dependent relationship.

John was able to see that in trying to be the perfect self he believed he should be, he married Claire so that he could live out the illusion of what he magically willed himself to be through her. When John married Claire, he divorced himself from the possibility of realizing his true self. The trauma of separation exposed John's defense structure. His compliance, poor solutions to unresolved conflicts of ego boundaries and aggression are exemplified in John's way of asking for something: "Claire, can you pick up my dry cleaning?" "Can you" is an indirect form of control that implies "you (Claire), take care of me and my needs."

Claire learned that she married John because she needed someone who needed her. John's neediness made her feel in control and in power. As Claire came to understand her need to respond to John's indirect demands, she was more able to change her response to: "You don't need me to pick up your dry cleaning. You can find the time to take care of your own needs." Claire was now aware of and confronting her defense structure, her caretaking and her unresolved feelings of powerlessness and dependency.

Each connected to a partner who would fill the neediness. Feeling powerless about their lives, they developed a defensive structure to ward off feelings of powerlessness and loss of control. For example, a compliant personality such as John obtains control by indirect manipulation, that is, under the guise of "poor me" and "I am always a nice guy." The reciprocal caretaker personality such as Claire controls and feels in power through taking charge of another's life, that is, under the guise of "I'll do that for you" and "I take care of everyone." Neediness is relieved in coming to terms with inner conflicts of dependency and hostility.

This chapter is indebted to D.W. Winicott's work in object relations, more specifically, the mother/infant relationship, and Karen Horney's work on personality types and their inner conflicts. The chapter focuses on (1) divorce and the dependent personality as poor nurturing in infancy plays itself out in a co-dependent marital relationship, and (2) the client/therapist relationship in which resolution occurs through regression in the transference.

Poor nurturing is understood as occurring when the mother or substitute caretaker is unable to respond in a major way to all the infant's physical and emotional needs. For some reason the nurturer has an abnormal inability to mirror the infant. As a result, the ego, without nurturing, remains weak and this deficit carries over into adulthood.

Poor nurturing impels the deprived person through life toward an unending search for someone to take care of his or her physical and emotional needs. The caretaking might be as basic as having a caretaker cook, do the laundry, drive, write checks and pay the bills.

The eternal quest undertaken by such people is to satisfy their needs for "merging" functions to reduce the anxiety of the feeling "I am powerless to do for and by myself."

Similarly, living as one's concept of the perfect self creates a sense of false unity with the other and with the universe. The perfect self protects one from seeing the conflicts one feels between ordinary compliance and the aggression resulting from the compliance felt to be forced when one's unspoken and unconscious wishes have been thwarted.

Through the illusion of the perfect self, compliance is seen as being always kind, always hard-working, always devoted and caring. The inner conflict between compliance and aggression arises when healthy aggression—"standing up for one's self"—is expressed. Showing any form of aggression risks rejection of self, loss of affection and separation. The perfect self diminishes the anxiety of pleasing— "being the nice guy"—to gain affection and ward off rejection.

The "nice guy" dependent partner secretly dislikes the "caretaker" partner because of being kept dependent. In turn, the caretaker also secretly resents the partner's demands but needs to be in control. The "perfect couple" is caught in the cycle of mutual neediness.

Separation and divorce occur when one of the co-dependents no longer experiences satisfying secondary gains from a defensive structure. The feelings of loss and separation intensify unresolved inner conflicts of dependency derived from poor nurturing. How does this happen?

NORMAL DEVELOPMENT

Good nurturing, enhancing the development of the ego, happens when the mother is able to merge with the infant and mirror only the infant's reflection. The infant comes to feel that all wants will be met by willing, by magic. The magic is the mother's ability, through this special merging, to satisfy nearly all the infant's needs.

Normally, the infant progresses from experiencing the mother and objects in the environment (such as a teddy bear, thumb or blanket) as a reflection of self to seeing them as separate entities. The infant then becomes aware of boundaries and learns to delay gratification.

The infant makes use of the mother and objects in the environment as a means of delaying gratification and learning how to be alone and not be alone without being lonely. The object is utilized as an intermediary between merging and separation and may take the form of breast, bottle, corner of a special blanket, the thumb or the teddy bear. The infant either physically holds an object or mentally contemplates an internal experience of the object as the *symbol* of good nurturing without needing to merge. Learning how to be separate and how to be alone in the presence of the object develops strength in the emerging ego. The symbolic use of the object marks a step forward developmentally from merging. Good nurturing by the caretaker at this stage sets up a trust, an expectation of receiving gratification.

The infant's awareness of self as separate comes through the discovery that the magic power of willing an object into and out of existence does not always work. The mother is not perfect, only "good enough" to sustain the infant's emotional growth.

NON-NURTURANCE AND ITS REMEDIATION

Poor nurturing is the mother's inability to mirror and satisfy the infant's willing it to be. Because infants are never sure what to expect, they have to look constantly into the mother's face for clues about how to act in order to receive nurturance. The infant tries to find ways to respond to the mother's look to receive gratification. This sequence promotes development of the compliant personality.

Poor nurturing drives the adult each time to choose a partner who can meet the unspoken terms of his or her neediness. This drive is unconscious, a learned behavior from infancy. Because of this fact it can be replaced with new learning. The dependent behavior can be changed to independent behavior.

Change becomes possible when there is a safe environment for practicing straightforward ways of interacting and greater rewards for noncollusive behavior. What are the rewards of being direct rather than manipulating to get what is needed? The answer, as change, comes in how the conflict between compliance and aggression is resolved. It means looking at fears of rejection, over concern about what others think and always trying to please, as well as anxiety about being angry, helpless and alone. Understanding what evokes compliance and choosing to change that pattern strengthens the ego.

Therapy is a means of re-finding and strengthening the ego, for clients, like infants, believe that they create the object and don't know that they are finding what already exists. Re-finding occurs in transference, which is the process of good nurturing through merging, mirroring and awareness of self as separate and different from the therapist and from objects in the environment. Openness to the restructuring of the ego comes through the client's trust in the predictability of the therapist.

Trust develops out of the therapist's ability to mirror the client through listening. The therapist's predictable listening, understood as merging, creates the feeling that the client only exists and the therapist exists only for the client.

When clients come to see that magically willing the therapist, the object or the environment into and out of existence doesn't work, they are ready to see that they project internal conflicts onto the environment and begin to work toward relinquishing the projections of "if only," a form of magical willing into and out of existence: "If only I had a good wife, a better job or a better home, I would be happy."

Clients can now see that the environment as the locus of fear and powerlessness and the cause of anxiety in social and new situations comes from *within* based upon their own experiences of unpredictability in early nurturing. Unpredictability creates fear, which makes for rigidity. The client only feels safe, in control and in power if he knows everything or can mind-read. Rigidity is a defense against feeling powerless and out of control.

The need to please to gain the desired outcome of an event is a compulsion that reinforces rigidity and lessens the individual's ability to take risks. In turn, rigidity as a means of warding off anxiety brought about by unpredictability diminishes the client's ability to try something new or work toward a behavioral change.

When we understand how the structure of poor nurturing works and how it effects ego development, we can develop strategies for restructuring and strengthening the ego so that the client enters the environment and relationships with less neediness and with the possibility of intimacy rather than co-dependency and symbiosis.

11

Divorce-Death Synergism and Depression

Bruce L. Danto, MD and Joan M. Danto, MSW

All too often in clinical practice some therapists develop a professional attitude of monocular vision about clinical problems. Once established this tendency flourishes into a field of specialization in monocularly defined problems like divorce counseling, bereavement counseling or therapy, child therapy, AIDS therapy and survivor therapy. Once this monocular vision becomes fixed, specializing therapists may find that they cannot see the general processes that comprise the patient or client. When this occurs it has been our experience that other problems and dynamics are overlooked much in the same fashion that a hand surgeon might be ignorant of and not interested in an unrelated cardiac disease that might kill his patient.

Because this phenomenon has been of interest to us, we want to highlight clinical material that involves two important causes of depression occurring in the same patient. We feel strongly about the need to broaden the profession's views of important events in a patient's life so that these stressors do not interfere with and possibly destroy the aims of effective treatment.

Two such stressors are *divorce* and *death* in terms of the impact they have on the depressed patient, which in some cases produces a one-two punch reinforcement of the person's depression leading to suicide.* In the suicide case discussed, it will be readily apparent that associated with the depression was a rage neither perceived nor managed by those charged with the patient's treatment.

---

*The relationship between divorce and depression has not been untangled. Some researchers contend that depression is a major cause of divorce since depression is an aversive stimulus to most people.

Clinicians who take note of the important relationship between divorce, death and depression may be able to save lives and prevent the very distraught type of death survivorship that might otherwise follow.

DIVORCE

As it seems to be with life itself, the bonds of marriage can wax with meaning and ultimately wane in terms of affective relationship. If the descent becomes progressive, then the dissolution of emotional attachments may lead to divorce. In this case, divorce becomes the end point in a process of estrangement preceded by conflict events that cause both partners hurt and loss of trust and appreciation of one another. It may occur by mutual agreement or leave one partner victimized and left out of the decision-making process by which divorce becomes a legal reality (Levinger 1979).

Marriage is a dyadic relationship, one between a pair of people. As with any group in general, cohesiveness must exist between members to make and keep it functional. Every such dyadic relationship must achieve some degree of interpersonal closeness or bonding, according to Levinger (1979), and one couple can be distinguished from another by the degree of interpersonal involvement and deeply felt mutual attachment obtaining within it. However, some pairs fail to reach any appreciable depth of involvement with each other and either persist for religious or economic reasons, or end in divorce. Similarly, some deep relationships can develop negatively and consequently end in divorce.

Once divorce is sought, regardless of the degree of pre-existing interpersonal relationship, each partner perceives a drastic and dramatic shift in personal rewards or costs. Some barriers to this shift, such as religious or cultural values, may maintain a marriage, but for those pairs who do not develop a deepening attachment, such barriers may instead create a prison for the pair. In such a case, divorce may provide a means of escape from what might seem to the spouses to be an unbearable barrier or prison.

There are over a million divorces in the United States annually. Each involves two people and more than a million or more children and in-laws. Bloom, White and Asher (1979) point out that those experiencing divorce suffer significant levels of psychosocial pathology. The divorced person is overrepresented both among psychiatric patients and among those admitted to psychiatric hospitals, attesting to the significance of divorce as a personal stressor. The divorced are overrepresented in other serious health problems as well, including

vehicular accidents, alcoholism, suicide, homicide and disease morbidity.

Greater stress from divorce is faced by older women at the time of
divorce as well as for those of any age who have been married longer.
Anxiety and depression were more common in this group, were also
higher immediately following the divorce and when the divorced person possessed low self-esteem or high anxiety. If the person had been
encouraged to file for divorce by the spouse or family and had few
economic resources, stress was greater in terms of post-divorce
adjustment (Bloom, White and Asher 1979).

Except for the economic strain of supporting their divorced families and the social strain of being lonely, men show less disturbance in
their post-divorce adjustment. Divorced women usually bear more
stress than do their ex-spouses unless the ex-husband obtained custody of the children. Women suffer economic stress, often lack work-
appropriate education and have problems trying single-handedly to
manage households and careers at the same time. Moreover, because
of societal values, women feel a greater loss of self-esteem as women,
are under greater stress rearing children as a single parent, and are
shunned socially by coupled friends as the wives of these couples
come to perceive them as threats to their own marriages.

Divorced parents usually report feeling more anxious, depressed,
angry, rejected and incompetent than married persons. For both
sexes there may be a strong change in self-concept. Men may feel a
lack of structure in their lives, a lack of roots and even a lack of
identity. Men may rush into a flurry of social and dating activity to
cope with these problems, whereas women have their children for a
sense of security. Some divorced parents may find they have difficulty parenting. This is because mothers now find they can't handle
their sons, and divorced parents may have trouble in general commu-
nicating with their children. Some cannot handle being affectionate
or administering discipline, and with these inadequacies may feel
frustrated and angry. For the parent dealing with these problems
there is no reward or satisfaction for either parent or child.

Therapists generally agree that separation or divorce brings
about a worsening in psychiatric symptomatology. Separation may
lead to the onset of symptoms, and a worsening may be more visible
during this phase than when divorce actually occurs, for by then,
some working through of feelings may have been possible. Most therapists would agree that divorce and separation are among the five top
life events reported by psychiatric patients. Other events are death,
loss of employment, arrest and personal or family problems regarding alcoholism.

Regardless of the existence of a legal divorce, spouses may still feel a sense of bonding to the departed partner. This tie resembles Bowlby's (1969) attachment bond seen in children toward their parents. Attachment as a characteristic of relationships is an element that persists for many people despite their loss of trust in the former partner or their de-idealization of him or her.

While disruption of attachment can be a major source of emotional disturbance following separation, problems are not limited to this factor alone. With separation and divorce there are changes in social roles, relationships with relatives and with one's own children. Marked ambivalence may be felt toward the departed spouse. Along with distress over separation there may be intense anger. Disturbances in appetite and sleep are common, along with a heightened sense of vigilance as if a return of the departed spouse may occur at any minute.

Not all reactions reflect immediate or intense emotional pain. Some persons react to separation and divorce by showing euphoria for varying intervals. Self-esteem and confidence in this person may appear to be increased. This heightened ego feeling can disappear easily, possibly because depression underlies the euphoria and this person attempts to deny or deflect it. Seeing through this smoke screen is especially easy if rejection or failure occurs.

Ex-partners' attempts to resolve their basic ambivalences and the problems of lingering attachment may be seen in their decisions to agree to intervals of contact, including sexual relationships. If renewed contact between the spouses does not occur and efforts are made to establish a new life style, there may be more problems associated with this than handling the divorce. Creating a new life style appears to be the most crucial element in accepting the fact of divorce and all that is entailed in breaking important emotional ties to the departing spouse. If new relationships are not established, feelings of bitterness, separation distress, regret and pining for attachment may worsen over time, leading the person to exist in a compromised drifting state.

BEREAVEMENT

In contrast to divorce, Cutter (1974) feels that when a death occurs, the daily life of a survivor is disrupted. He or she can no longer look forward to the ordinary occurrences of a shared experience. In order to carry on one must cope with the fact and emotions of the loss.

The initial and universal reaction to the fact of death is disbelief. This may be followed by an inability to accept the resulting change in a previous relationship. Although everyone knows the person is gone, it takes time to accept that absence. Memories often generate thoughts of shared activities or moments of pleasure. The internal sense of relationship continues as it fades from real to remembered as time passes.

However, continuation of these thoughts, images and fantasies may lead some to feel that the dead person is still present or soon may return. In this event, denial of death is reflected, resulting in delayed and unsuccessful or incomplete mourning.

When a loved one succumbs to a sudden unanticipated death, the shock effect is greater than if there is a terminal illness during which survivors can deal with impending loss through anticipatory grief. Where there has been pre-existing psychiatric history or neurotic dependency, the shock of loss may lead to greater psychopathology and possible frank psychosis or suicide.

Because of loss a survivor may be faced with making significant decisions alone. For one who had played a small role or no role at all in decision-making, a feeling of doom and overwhelming anxiety may occur. In this way anxiety becomes coupled with depression.

Frequently, the death of a child precipitates a breakup of the marriage. Such parents may hold onto unresolved feelings of grief that interfere with their ability to love and support one another. Guilt arising out of the parent's perceived failure to safeguard the health of a child or to produce a healthy child may create or aggravate psychopathology in the parents.

Similarly, when a parent dies there is a disruption in the parent-child relationship. This may lead the surviving parent to transfer his or her dependency needs to the child, thereby leaving the child with emotional needs unmet.

Any or all members of the family may develop physical symptoms of distress: gastrointestinal problems, weight change, headaches, chest pain, tachycardia, nightmares, sleep impairment or urinary frequency. Psychologically, one may complain of symptoms of anxiety, depression, feelings of guilt, loneliness, withdrawal from social activities, impaired decision-making, regression into dependency and feelings of helplessness and hopelessness. There may be a wish to die, and in some cases this may be accompanied by a reunion fantasy.

Phobias may occur and could involve food, geographical places or any reminder of the deceased or the events preceding the death. Relatedly, there may be an observable social phobia occurring in a previously sociable person. Social phobia is a behavior different from the social withdrawal that more commonly accompanies depression. Anhedonia, or lack of joy in living, may be associated with depression or with the social phobia that functions to help the survivor avoid another emotional attachment that might end in a similar loss.

In addition to physical and psychological problems there may be economic ones to face. For example, the deceased may not have had adequate life insurance or may have had coverage that excludes payment of benefits in the event of suicide or some other cause of death.

Support for important and special conditions may be lost. Parkes (1976) writes of the need for support that is lost through the death of a spouse and how this loss may lead to actual physical deterioration on the part of the surviving spouse, especially an elderly widow who may soon die herself. Social/emotional and financial support for important and special conditions pertaining to family members may be lost. Shared parenting or the availability of exceptional care for a handicapped survivor may be affected. Financial loss may arise out of the need to sell property in order to satisfy debts. In this type of grief situation the survivor may be compelled to leave the marital home and sell off deeply meaningful items such as the marital bed, in turn producing painful feelings. Remaining family members must then accommodate to a lesser standard of living and a changed life style.

Particularly stressful for the survivor may be intense feelings of anger when the death of the loved one appears as abandonment if it involved suicide, excessive risk-taking or carelessness about issues of health.

Feelings of loss may be aggravated if family members fail to provide support, particularly if the survivor turns to the family to gratify all emotional needs without developing new relationships and interests. This type of survivor fails to recognize that life has changed.

DIVORCE-DEATH SYNERGISM

It should be apparent from our discussion thus far that divorced and bereaved persons face similar psychodynamic challenges. Both have to come to terms with material and emotional losses, altered life styles and role changes, and the need to achieve a new personal sense of self-validation in the face of these disorienting revisions of their identities. They also have to develop a new sense of purpose and set of goals for the future. Independent rather than shared living and decision-making should be their new direction. New relationships and sources of affection should replace their loss. Children of divorce and death have similar problems, but for the bereaved child there is no more contact with the departed parent.

The task of rebuilding relationships with family and friends takes time following both death and divorce. What, then, happens to the person who experiences both types of loss? Let's take a look at some examples.

Case 1

On March 31, 1987, the *Los Angeles Times* reported that a 44-year-old woman walked into an elementary school class of fifth graders and shot herself in front of 27 students after saying, "I'm sorry I have to do it this way." She lived a quarter of a mile from the school and entered it with two handguns at about 11 a.m. when she shot herself. Later it was learned that she had had no contact or involvement with the school.

Background information revealed that her father died 10 years earlier, but had left their home when she was about 9 years old, the same age as the students in the fifth grade where she took her life. Her marriage to a man almost 25 years older had ended in divorce. In February 1986 she fell and injured her back at work and was under stress because of the pain and in trouble legally with her employer about the accident. Shortly before her death she broke out in a rash that covered much of her body, and her two sons announced their departure from home, a matter that upset her greatly. A friend advised her to be fair to her sons and let them go. This she agreed to do.

In class, before the shooting, she talked of taking an overdose of pills to "end it all." This was followed by the statement, "I have nothing else to live for." The teacher asked the woman if the kids could go outside and begged her not to commit suicide. The woman told one female student that she had been in a mental hospital where she had been tied up and that the doctor had given her acid pills. Before pulling the trigger she pointed one of her guns at a little boy, scaring him. Her first shot misfired, but the second worked when she tested the gun by firing a shot into the wall. The third shot was the fatal one. The teacher tried to instruct her students to lay their heads down on the desk as a way of not having to see the fatal shooting.

Her death was a sensational type of suicide, classically a "page one" death. She had informed others that this was her intent, to achieve recognition. It is our belief that in her lifetime there had been no such recognition, only abandonment. We feel that her sons' threatened departure was a triggering event for her suicide as it evoked a lifetime of resentment about being abandoned by loved ones, as through the separation and divorce of her parents, her father's death, her divorce from her husband and, finally, the departure of her sons. We speculate that she also felt abandoned by the mental health system, which only offered medication but no treatment relationship. In that sense the system abandoned her as well.

Case 2

In May 1987, a 41-year-old, twice-divorced woman entered psychiatric treatment because of work stress related to sexual harassment by her boss. She had accumulated impressive evidence of his motives in the form of letters, cards and actions. She revealed to the psychiatrist that her parents had been unhappily married and that her father had died of leukemia two years before. As she talked about his death she began crying. Her father was an alcoholic who was also violent, fracturing his wife's nose on one occasion; he was also self-centered and unaffectionate. Aside from sleeping in a separate room, her mother played the role of martyr and never left her husband.

In terms of the woman's two marriages, her first husband was a replay of her own father: alcoholic and physically abusive. Her three sons from that marriage have had little to do with her as they resent her divorce from their father. Her second husband was divorced by her when he was found to be involved in affairs with other women. A current boyfriend worked two jobs and had sexual contact with her, but announced that he would be unavailable for marriage because of his life style.

We believe that this is a woman whose adult relationships with men are a replay of her abandonment by her father whose death is still painful as it represents a failure to be accepted by him, a reality that will never change because of his death. In her experience, men are exploitative, insensitive, abusive, unloving and have no capacity to offer affection and commitment. The latter point has been cut in stone because of the impact of death and divorce in her life. The reason for her depression is easy to understand.

Case 3

In March 1986, a 50-year-old divorced woman entered treatment because of severe depression, obsessive levels of guilt about having divorced despite being Catholic and the feeling that she had lost grace in the Church. Associated with these guilt feelings were her beliefs that others could read her mind and that priests who had heard her confessions were talking about her.

Her parents divorced when she was 2 years of age. Her father acquired custody of her, but she was raised by a grandmother to whom she was strongly attached. When she was 12, her grandmother died in an auto accident in a car driven by her father. The father had taken his girlfriend along for the ride and had been drinking heavily.

After 20 years of marriage she divorced her alcoholic husband in 1975. He had become physically abusive and she could no longer tolerate living with him, feeling that it was time for a change as her three children were now grown. Why she felt guilt about the divorce is not clear as her husband was not Catholic and an annulment would not be necessary as the marriage was not recognized by the Church. That her relationship with her mother was now close and that her relationship with her children had always been close probably were saving graces for her.

It is apparent in this woman's case that the divorce of her parents, the death of her grandmother and her father's death one year after the divorce acted synergistically to produce significant depression with paranoid features. Having to cope with these events in childhood without receiving emotional support took its toll on this woman.

Case 4

In April 1987, a 58-year-old widow came into our office for treatment of her depression. Her second husband had died in June 1987 following an acute myocardial infarct. Their marriage had been happy and they had worked together in her husband's business. She had been the office manager and as sole owner is still working in that capacity.

Her father had left home when she was 6 years of age and had died at age 81 from a stroke. Her mother had died from the same cause at 76 years of age. As there had been no contact with her father since her childhood, she knew nothing about the date of his death, although she knew of its occurrence. Her mother, interestingly enough, died around Mother's Day, May 9, 1977. Of significance is the fact that her husband had died close on the heels of the anniversary of her mother's death.

Her first marriage had been traumatic. Her husband had been an alcoholic and was emotionally and physically abusive. Additionally, a 32-year-old daughter who had joined a cult was encouraged by it to engage in an incestuous relationship with her father, which she did. For the daughter the cult apparently provided a type of familial support lacking in her home as a child. While the affair made it possible for this daughter to establish a missing family tie, it accomplished this through the societally proscribed act of incest.

In this case we can see how parental divorce and her own, along with the loss of her second husband, combined synergistically to bring about her depression. What was different in her case as compared to the others is the fact that as an active business partner with a husband whom she loved, she acquired sufficient ego strength during the years of their marriage to avoid greater depression and decompensation.

All of these and countless other cases share in common the fact that they required antidepressant and anxiolytic medication along with psychotherapy.

CONCLUSION

It should be apparent that those of us who treat depressed persons have been trained to seek explanations and causes from the patient's history, laboratory findings, and psychological test material and scores. What is needed in addition is a window on those significant causal factors that appear in the social-psychiatric history. The clinician must search for events that reinforce one another, especially multiple losses or those occurring at or around significant events or time periods. One must take into account how loss of others and the concomitant ties of affection may be reinforced by seemingly unrelated losses occurring at the same time that make it difficult or impossible for the patient to recover from the loss without skillful psychotherapeutic intervention. Such intervention may require a longer period of time as well as greater treatment contact and a prescription of anxiolytic and antidepressant medication. If psychotic decompensation occurs, hospitalization and even electroconvulsive therapy might be necessary.

Psychotherapy must focus on a number of things. Identifying losses and working through feelings about them is essential. Exposing and dealing with the anger people feel about those who are lost to them is a must for therapeutic work.

Other areas of focus must be dealt with in treatment as well. It is important to help a patient delineate and establish ego boundaries between the self, the relationship and the image of the loved one who is lost either through divorce or death. The mourner must achieve a sense of separateness and individuality, and if abandonment is felt, the resulting anger must be appreciated by the therapist. The patient's anger may be associated with unspoken dependency needs unmet either by the therapist or by other survivors in the patient's family.

Psychotherapy must focus on practical needs concerning the patient. There may be no support system available to assist the patient in making important decisions relative to practical problems like disposing of personal property belonging to or given by the departed spouse. A home may need to be sold, jobs or training for employment may become a necessity, and some general nonpsychiatric guidance may need to be given by the therapist. Encouragement to reach out for social and recreational resources and experiences is a must both for the divorced person and for the mourning patient.

Finally, family therapy may be required to help work out problems among the survivors of either death or divorce in the family. The feelings of children are important to share with the surviving or now single parent, and the reverse is also true. Guidance in achieving this end may be necessary, and the therapist must keep service lines open and be sensitive to new modalities for handling problems for this as with any other type of patient.

Rarely but significantly, hospitalization may be necessary if the emotional reaction cannot be handled on an outpatient basis. Milieu support can be life-saving and offer valuable support for the patient who is overwhelmed by either depression or anxiety. A few days in the hospital may be life-saving and stabilizing during an acute crisis period associated with either death or divorce.

In general, the person who has experienced a divorce-death synergism is one for whom the trauma of loss and readjustment will be most severe. Psychotherapeutic and psychopharmacologic support are essential, and the therapist will have to meet the challenge of offering a sophisticated array of supportive services.

Both patient and therapist must strive for the goal of independence and self-responsibility on the part of the patient. But creating an atmosphere where feelings can be shared and accepted is the task of the therapist. If the patient is to move in the direction of establishing new relationships and affectional ties or utilizing those with other survivors, the treatment relationship must serve as the paradigm for seeking the comfort of intimatos and froodom from foar of loss.

Family therapy can be employed to assist the primary survivor as well as survivors in the family unit. A new leader for the family group can be identified and helped to take over the function for the lost member.

REFERENCES

Bloom, B.L., S.W. White, and S.J. Asher. Marital Disruption as a Stressful Life Event. In G. Levinger and O.C. Moles, eds., *Divorce and Separation: Context, Causes and Consequences.* New York: Basic Books, 1979.

Bowlby, J. *Attachment and Loss, Vol. I: Attachment.* New York: Basic Books, 1969.

Cutter, F. *Coming to Terms with Death.* Chicago: Nelson-Hall, 1974.
Levinger, G. A Social Psychological Perspective on Marital Dissolution. In G.
    Levinger and O.C. Moles, eds., *Divorce and Separation: Context, Causes,
    and Consequences.* New York: Basic Books, 1979.
Parkes, C.M. The Broken Heart. In E.S. Shneidman, ed., *Death: Current Per-
    spectives.* Palo Alto, CA: Mayfield, 1976.
Woman commits suicide in front of fifth-grade class, *Los Angeles Times,* part
    II, pp. 1, 4-5, March 31, 1987.

12

Love Shock:
Therapy and Management in
Loss of a Love Relationship

Stephen Viton Gullo, PhD
with Henry Berger, MD, PhD

In this chapter I would like to give you a brief overview of a deeply personal journey, a journey from life to death, that began in the New York Hospital-Cornell Medical Center over 10 years ago. In 1972, as a graduate student in psychology at Columbia University, I had received a grant from the National Cancer Institute to study what happened to each of 16 women from the point at which they learned that their husband had a terminal illness to the point at which he died. The work that began a decade ago studying death, loss and grief on the terminal wards, has led me away from the study of death back into the mainstream of life.

Specifically, my work with bereaved people has taught me not only about the dynamics of loss and grief, but more importantly, about how we, as men and women, cope with the loss of love relationships. And I would like to share with you some of the work that Dr. Henry Berger and I have conducted during the past four years on a very universal and unique aspect of human loss: loss of a loved person, not by death, but by separation and divorce.

The study of the grief experience was pioneered by Erich Lindemann (1965), Avery Weissman (1972), Colin Murray Parkes (1972) and others. They have probed deeply into the experience of losing a loved one through death, but I would turn your attention to another phenomenon: the experience of loss when the loved one lives on, perhaps to choose another.

This chapter examines the circumstances of "loved but lost," an experience which has probably touched each of us at some point in our lives. What are the emotional and physical costs of personal loss? How do people cope with it? How can we, as professional interveners, help clients to overcome its pain and, despite it, facilitate their growth?

There are other issues as well. There are significant differences between losing someone through the termination of a relationship by divorce or separation and losing them through death. First of all, when we are divorced or separated, the person lost to us remains in the sphere of our reality. On a daily basis we are forced to confront both the fact of her existence and the impact that existence has upon our self in the personal rejection that it implies. And it matters not whether one is the person who has been rejected or the one who has decided to terminate a love relationship. One still has to live with feelings, not only of loss, but of failure, rejection and guilt. Moreover, a great deal of one's reaction to loss may be colored by what the other person is doing.

As children we heard the expression that misery loves company. It is not true. Misery does not love company. Misery only loves company that is also in misery, and if your ex-partner is on Sutton Place or on the Côte d'Azur partying with a new person and you are sitting at home feeling rejected and "empty," this will dramatically affect your response to this loss.

A final point about loss of a love relationship through divorce or separation takes us completely out of the field of grief research into the concept of addiction. One of my colleagues, Dr. Daniel Carr at the Harvard Medical School, made an enormous contribution to my thinking by relating much of the love experience to the production of certain neurochemicals in the human brain. The work of Michael Liebowitz and Donald Klein at Columbia University also suggests that there may be a specific chemical in the brain associated with being in love, possibly phenylethylamine, a compound related to amphetamine.

This means that when we are in the state of love or falling in love, there is evidence that the production of these neurochemicals appears to dramatically increase, and when we are withdrawing ourselves from a love relationship, there may not only be a psychological component, but probably there is also a physiological component which contributes to our feeling of distress. High levels of these neurochemicals appear to be correlated with feelings of well-being, elation, or what some would call the "love high." Correspondingly, their presumably dramatic decrease under conditions of loss may contribute to feelings of emotional pain and depression.

THE LOVE SHOCK EXPERIENCE

As I studied women who had lost a husband, I heard again and again certain statements such as, "I knew he was dying. I knew the end was near, but when it happened, I was in shock. I couldn't believe it— never again to hear his voice, to see his face or to touch him. The finality was difficult to comprehend." Working with people who had come through a divorce and with lovers who had decided to separate, I heard again and again the same expression of disbelief and numbness, a sense of "loss and wondering" when a significant relationship finally came to an end.

As I studied the phenomena of emotional disorientation that arise when someone loses a lover, it became increasingly apparent that there is a striking parallel with soldiers in combat who have experienced shell shock. Once again, there is the sense of disorientation and withdrawal—the hesitancy to come close to others for fear of losing them. There are sleep and eating disorders, grief, and most of all, the feeling of emotional numbness over what has happened to them. It is almost as if they have experienced a near loss of life itself.

From these similarities of experience between people's responses to love lost and shell shock, the concept of *love shock* emerges. Technically defined, it is the state of psychological disorientation and numbness characterized by feelings of profound loss and emptiness and yearning precipitated by the termination of a significant relationship. Since first identifying this phenomenon (Gullo 1979), I have become increasingly sensitive to its existence in my work with patients suffering from the proverbial "broken heart."

As Dr. Berger and I studied love relationships it became clear that many people initiated breakups they did not desire because of profound dissatisfaction with the relationship or the pain it caused. But we also found that some people who ended the relationship did so both in anticipation of being rejected by the partner *and* in order to foreclose that possibility. In these cases the person initiating the breakup has been found to suffer love shock as strongly as, or even more strongly than, the person who is rejected.

THE STAGES OF LOVE SHOCK

The experience of love shock appears to follow a definite emotional course. The patterns identified with this loss are, sequentially, shock, grief, blame, magnification, resignation, renewal and "goodbye."

The *first* stage is one of shock. There is a sense of numbness, of wondering, a sense of void, a sense that you have lost part of yourself. I can give you countless adjectives or words to describe it more accu-

rately. More poignantly, I can give you the words of some of the
women who went through the experience. One of our patients was at
home when she received a phone call from her husband saying that he
had been thinking of their relationship and had been re-evaluating
the relationship in light of some of the talks they had about separating and divorce, and he had decided that it was right for them to
divorce and was leaving tomorrow. This woman, at that moment,
described a sense of "numbness . . . a feeling of time stopped," and
the only vivid picture she has in her mind to this day, five years later,
was that of the open window, and wanting to jump. This was the only
man who had ever been in her life since she was 14 and for 30 years
this man had been her life. Perhaps he was a painful and often disappointing part of life that she often wished to be rid of, but at the
moment when he stated "it's over," she felt as if part of her own body
had been "ripped away."

The *second* stage is one of grief or despairing sadness. The loss of
someone you love, whether through death, divorce or separation, represents a significant part of your internal world. And regardless of
whether that part was all you desired or not, important losses have a
profound effect upon our psyches. It is normal to expect a period of
mourning, to expect a desire or a yearning to be reunited in some way
with this person. In cases where the relationship was a dissatisfying
one, the person's mourning may take a more intricate course. They
may mourn for all the time and psychic energy they've invested fruitlessly, or for the lost hopes and dreams, or for the promise of what
could have been. They may mourn for the "role loss" rather than the
person; for example, no longer being married and now being a widow
or a single person alone in the world again.

Indeed, some of the most "grief stricken" individuals I've worked
with had very unsatisfactory relationships. Perhaps this is what Congreve had in mind when he wrote that "Heaven hath no rage like love
to hatred turned, nor Hell a fury like a woman scorned."* The widow
throwing herself on the casket or the brokenhearted's hysteria may
be more related to the feelings of personal loss and insecurity, rather
than to the passions of love. Nevertheless, there are still elements of
emotional void, numbness and shock, even in these cases.

In our studies of love shock victims, in addition to the sense of loss
and mourning, there are other significant symptoms in the second
stage. Victims often experience obsessional thinking about their
lover or former lover, constantly wondering what they were doing,
constantly longing in some way to have this relationship again.

---

*William Congreve, *The Mourning Bride*, Act III, Scene 8.

The next stage we have identified is *magnification*. This term represents an emotional form of the grass being greener on the other side of the fence. When a love relationship has broken up, the loser frequently magnifies the positive aspects of what he or she imagines the lost lover's situation to be. "He must be having such a great time." "She must be with a new partner who is so handsome, dramatic and rewarding to be with, whereas I am here feeling all this pain and rejection." Magnification produces idealization of the life of the lost person: "his life is sailing along smoothly while mine is shattered and scarred." And finally, it also extends to the former partner's personality, which unrealistically, is either remembered as unbelievably wonderful (they can never find such a "catch" again) or, conversely, is unbelievably bad and to blame for all the loser's difficulties.

The *third* stage we see is that of *blame*. Most frequently people blame the loss of a love relationship on one of three factors: the other person, themselves, or circumstances (including another involvement). Sometimes it's a career, or the demands of traveling, or just growing separately and apart.

One of the things that has amazed me is how little anger some people feel. In spite of the hurt, in spite of the sense of failure, a deep caring for the other person has continued. I recently had the opportunity to work with the wife of one of America's leading personalities. They were going through a divorce, and there was so much that she could have said in terms of destroying his career. There was so much she could have used as a bargaining chip in terms of the financial settlement. But her own conscience would not permit her to do this, in spite of his frequent infidelities and trysts reported endlessly in the media. As a matter of fact her own conscience would not even permit her to continue with his name. She felt that he had worked a lifetime for his name recognition, and that his name was part of his assets. She did not wish to retain it as she continued with her life as a single person.

The next stage we see in the love shock phenomenon is one of *resignation*. Although some writers have conceived of it as "acceptance," I specifically reject this notion as inaccurate. When people have made a deep commitment to each other and have worked at this commitment, they simply do not part with it easily. The commitment remains even if the emotion upon which it was originally based has attenuated. Consequently they resign themselves to the failure of the love relationship rather than to acceptance of it. The implications of resignation have a bearing upon their future actions, for they admit reality to consideration. After a person goes through the stages of shock, mourning and magnification, resignation takes over as it becomes increasingly clear that the relationship is indeed over and that it can never be again.

The penultimate stage is identified as *renewal.* In this stage the divorced begin to pull together the shattered pieces of their life and their ego. They begin once again to be interested in dating and in reentering that world engage in "comparison dating." If you have ever gone through the breakup of a love relationship that mattered deeply to you, one of the first things you would find yourself doing when you start dating is comparing your current date with your former partner. This may not be entirely fair to your companion, but it is entirely normal in the process of love shock.

Part of the renewal stage is the re-emergence of risk-taking behavior. It may seem strange to think of risk-taking in terms of loving, but Rollo May had understood it correctly when he said that "to love takes courage." After you have been hurt or scarred, after you have lived with a sense of failure, to once again open yourself to this vulnerability does take courage. It may be far easier to isolate yourself. We can pull a nail out of a wall, but it is far more difficult to repair the scarring, and so it is with the human psyche in terms of love.

The final stage is described as the "goodbye" stage. If resignation was the stage wherein the person intellectually recognized that the love relationship had come to an end, then the goodbye stage represents the emotional recognition and acceptance of finality. "Goodbye" can only occur after the person has let go his or her internal emotional ties to the past relationship. This includes having resumed a normal social life and dating, and being able to have let go without suffering severe psychic pain.

The goodbye stage represents an emotional experience of the psyche, a "closing of the door," so to speak, on all that has happened. The person no longer has that intense interest in what the former lover or mate is doing, or desires to see that person. He or she has, in the words of Freud, been emotionally "decathected," so that psychic energy had been withdrawn from the former lover and freed for investment in another. Perhaps the Hebrew concept of *Kaddish,* the prayers said for a deceased loved one, is appropriate here. In the goodbye stage, the person is finally able to "say Kaddish" for the relationship and close the door on what has been most significant. They can now go forward without the impairment, the sense of bondage and loss.

One of the questions arising from contemplating the love shock experience is whether one can intervene to anesthetize a sufferer to some of the psychic pain of his or her loss. Certainly there is tragedy in human life, and all the therapy and drugs in the world cannot remove this pain of living. But through love shock therapy we can help people to cope better, give them support and bolster their egos. Dr. Berger and I have been particularly interested in these issues because they are critical in two therapeutic dimensions. First, can we reduce the *intensity* of this pain, and second, can we *accelerate* the painful process of withdrawal from a love relationship?

The answer to both of these questions for most people is "yes" with an exclamation point! Let me give you a brief peak into the process of loveshock therapy that we have developed to take people through this crisis period in life. My greatest teachers in this work as a researcher and as a therapist have been the women who have come forth to share their experiences, to be open about it, and not to be afraid to say "I hurt," whereas men often have a hesitation both to admit the feelings and to share them.

CASSETTE THERAPY

A key element in love shock therapy is the use of cassettes specifically geared to the experience at each stage of love shock. The goal of these cassettes is systematic desensitization, slowly and gradually to bring the love shock victim to a confrontation with the painful memories of the experience of the lost love relationship, to facilitate their grief work, and minimize the pain they have endured. In this way they can rebuild their own sense of themselves and help themselves in the process of withdrawing without pathological symptoms, without inhibiting the normal process.

The use of cassettes is particularly helpful in the mechanics of therapy in four ways: it enables us to *intensify* the therapy since the person can hear the therapeutic message and suggestions again and again to facilitate insight and healing. Second, they enable therapists to *place the therapy* concurrent with *situations of greatest pain* and stress, such as at night and on weekends, when the person may be feeling lonely and rejected. Third, they increase the *time efficiency* of therapy. The ability of patients to "bring home" with them therapeutic insights and review them minimizes the "forgetting" of painful material and corrective suggestions. It also serves as a *spur to motivation* and a *reminder* that the pain will pass.

Those of you who have been students of history know that the Victorian Age was an era of unresolved mourning, with a queen, imprisoned by her grief, who disappeared from the public view and civic functions for over two decades. It was only during the Golden

Jubilee of her coronation, in 1887, that the "Widow of Windsor" reluctantly agreed to reappear. We do not wish our patients to be the new "Queen Victorias" who carry with them through their lives emotional scars that create a phobia, a fear of their own love. One of the principal characteristics of schizoid or schizophrenic behavior is the fear of intimacy, a fear of one's capacity to need another human being. Often, when persons have been hurt in a love relationship, they go through a period of such uncompleted mourning, and it is most critical to overcome this fear—to immunize, so to speak, the person to the love phobia that could easily develop.

Through the use of these audio cassettes, one additional goal is facilitated—*education*. Our work is truly a teaching therapy, not a psychotherapy for psychopathology. The experience of love shock is a normal and almost universal experience. We are dealing with a normal process by trying to mitigate its pain and facilitate its course. Love shock is not a pathological state. Indeed, it is not the shock and grief upon the breakup of a love relationship that is pathological, but the absence of it that bodes ill for the person's mental and physical welfare. And so the cassette serves as a continuing teacher, encouraging the person to talk of the lost love as well as teaching what has gone wrong in the love relationship, so that the person can take from this a positive experience rather than a negative and painful one.

THE PROCESS OF LOVE SHOCK THERAPY

Proceeding now to the specifics of this therapy, in the opening session with the patient, we violate all the advice of the love columnists. We insist that they *do not* throw out the pictures, the love notes, and the gifts. These things can truly be called "linking objects." In the women we have studied they create a link between the sufferer and the lost person. We do not want them to throw out this link until they have dealt cognitively and affectively with several issues: first, that the relationship has ended, second, why it has ended, and third, what needs to be done to complete the unfinished business of loving the lost person. Frequently when a love relationship ends there is much that the sufferer would like to say to the departing partner that ego, pride and anger block. Consequently, we often play the role of the other partner to recreate the environment for them to express these suppressed emotions. We insist that they finish the unfinished business of loving, however painful it may be. They begin by saying to us what they would have liked to say to that partner. This is not an end in itself but a bridge that hopefully will enable them to speak more freely of the person they have lost as well as to the next person with whom they share an intimate relationship. We insist that they bring with them a personal statement about why they loved this person, and why the love relationship came to an end. We insist that they also include any pictures or mementos of the relationship.

As the therapy progresses, the tapes are changed to coincide with the different stages through which the person is going. One element we emphasize is the role of idealization. People have a great capacity for self-delusion about others, especially in love relationships. Often women spoke of their ex-husbands as being very loving and caring. Therefore they felt forgiving and placed blame upon themselves when it simply was not true that they were at fault.

The human psyche is very kind. It suffers from its own form of amnesia. It blocks out pain and helps us to hold onto and retain that which is positive. I don't object to this quality unless it interferes with our functioning. The "Eleventh Commandment" given on Mount Sinai was not "thou shalt confront reality." I have no particular fondness for reality. I often tell my patients it really doesn't matter if they are "normal," it only matters if they are happy! However, in the breakup of love relationships there is often a peculiar form of amnesia to block out the negative and to suppress its pain. We are human. We run from pain and perhaps we should not before we have learned from it. Pain is a teacher. As Proust said in *The Sweet Cheat Gone:* "We are healed of a suffering only by experiencing it to the fullest."

As the process continues we go into a period of rebuilding. It is one thing to suffer a loss and to cope with it; it is another thing to resume the act of living and loving! As clients progress, we focus on their building new social relationships, building a sense of confidence and renewal. In my work I have seen a drive in bereaved people to become whole again, to heal, to live again. We encourage this natural drive in the person. Where anger is appropriate, we also use it to help them separate from the lost person.

In the final phase of our work we ask clients to draw up a balance sheet of what they took from the relationship that was positive and what it cost them emotionally. There are few things in life that are free, including our emotional lives. Hence the balance sheet provides a final reckoning of what the relationship both gave and took from their lives.

Readings in thanatology teach us how critical it is for the dying patients and their loved ones to be able to complete the business of living and to say goodbye, to be able to tell loved ones how much they meant to us and what they gave to our lives. Having written about this topic for many years, I had thought that I understood it. But later I came to realize that I did not. My grandmother, who had made a major contribution to my life, became terminally ill, and her time was extremely limited. I knew when I saw her that this might be the final time that I would ever do so. And in that moment, in all honesty, I searched for the words to say how much I loved her, how much she gave to my life. I began to understand also what Robert Frost had in mind when he wrote, "sometimes one moment can last for all eternity."

And so it is in our love relationships; we must be able to see not only the negative, not only the costs, but to see whatever positive elements there may have been. We must recognize that as in the case of death, a failed relationship requires us to let go—not because our ex-partner had died, but because we have resigned ourselves to the fact that it cannot be. In the final statement on the balance sheet, one of my patients wrote as if she were writing to her husband: "I have not failed you, and you have not failed me. We are children of two different worlds and we must find in those worlds the love, the support, the companionship that we could never give to one another." More than anything, these lines summarize the psychological process of letting go—becoming able to see the person that you loved not just with anger, or hatred (where appropriate), but also with caring and positive feelings—and to be able to separate yourself from that part of your life. And you may ask why. Freud was correct in his notion of object decathexis. He maintained that psychic energy is limited rather than infinite, and that before we can go on to a new love relationship, we must first withdraw our commitment to the old one (decathect the old object). Only then are we free once again to invest in another alliance.

A FINAL PERSPECTIVE

Beatrice Meize (in Kübler Ross 1974) wrote regarding the death of her son that when it finally happened, she was filled with numbness, pain, void and a sense of wandering. A decade of clinical research with the victims of loss has shown the same phenomena we have termed "love shock" whose dynamics we have outlined and attempted to explain in this chapter.

The final message that I would give you is something that applies to each of our lives as we work with the victims of loss, whether it be death, separation or divorce, or even someone who has lost a part of their body through illness or accident. The profound lesson for the health professional is the emerging recognition that there is no experience in the human life that is more central and universal than loss.

It began with the loss of our pets, of our grandparents, of our youth, and as we get older, our loved ones, our health and ultimately our own lives. I have been fascinated by this topic of the loss of love, not only as a scientist and therapist, but also because I realize how universal the experience of loss is.

Undoubtedly you have heard the statement that there are only two certainties in life—death and taxes. Both of them, regrettably, involve the loss of something we value. And when you think about it, the only certainty in life is loss. How we cope with this fact is critical not only for our patients, but also for our own growth as professionals. For in the final analysis the greatest lesson is that all of us are the children of loss. To study this phenomenon is to probe more deeply into one of the germinal forces shaping all our lives.

REFERENCES

Blackwell, R. *The Fighter's Guide to Divorce.* Chicago: Regnery, 1977.

Bohannon, P., ed. *Divorce and After: An Analysis of the Emotional and Social Problems of Divorce.* Garden City, N.Y.: Doubleday, 1971.

Bowlby, J. *Attachment and Loss. Vol. 1: Attachment.* New York: Basic Books, 1969.

Gullo, S. Games Children Play in Coping and Facing Death. Keynote address presented at the Symposium on the Child and Death, sponsored by The Foundation of Thanatology. New York: Columbia-Presbyterian Medical Center, January 1979.

Jones, E. *Raising Your Child in a Fatherless Home.* London: Collier-Macmillan, 1963.

Kübler-Ross, E. *On Death and Dying.* New York: Macmillan, 1974.

Lindemann, E. Symptomology and Management of Acute Grief. In H.J. Parad, ed., *Crisis Intervention: Selected Readings.* New York: Family Service Association of America, 1965.

Marris, P. *Loss and Change.* New York: Pantheon, 1974.

Martin, J. *Divorce and Remarriage: A Perspective of Counseling.* Scottdale, PA: Herald Press, 1974.

Parkes, C.M. *Bereavement: Studies of Grief in Adult Life.* New York: International Universities Press, 1972.

Weisman, A. *On Dying and Denying.* New York: Behavioral Publications, 1972.

13

Love, Loss and Divorce: The Risk of Suicide

David Lester, PhD

Suicide is a puzzling event because it is so rare. Of the roughly 2,000,000 deaths in the United States in 1980, for example, only about 27,000 were from suicide. For every 100,000 living people, about twelve committed suicide. The problem of predicting which people will commit suicide and of explaining why any one particular person killed himself is as difficult as explaining why one particular uranium atom decayed at one particular instant.

Physicists are good at predicting how long it will take for half of the uranium atoms to decay, but bad at predicting which particular atom will decay next. If we use this as an analogy for our problem in suicidology, we can predict that the sociologist will find it easier to study the suicide rates of societies, while the psychologist will find it hard to understand the life of an individual suicide.

PRECIPITATING CAUSES

Researchers typically list the precipitating causes for a group of suicides that they have studied. Often divorce, or some other interpersonal conflict with a lover, is listed as a precipitant. However, in the United States in 1980, there were 1,200,000 divorces and 11,000,000 divorced people in an adult population of 175,000,000. Yet only 4000 divorced people killed themselves. As readers of this chapter can readily observe, the majority of us are divorced, but surviving, often quite happily.

The problem is true for other precipitants. Cancer patients do have an increased risk of suicide (Lester 1983), but the vast majority die from their cancer. No matter how bad life is, whether the individual is in a concentration camp or dying of starvation in an arid part of the world, most people cling to life and fight to survive for as long as possible.

Therefore, when we observe that a suicide has recently been divorced and perhaps read their suicide note to their ex-spouse, we ask ourselves why this individual felt that suicide was an appropriate choice.

MARILYN MONROE

Recently, I have been studying suicides of famous people for whom there are detailed biographies that dissect their lives in great detail. The suicide of Marilyn Monroe in August 1962 provides some information that enables us to answer the question raised above at least partially (see Guiles 1984).

A Predisposition to Psychiatric Illness

Marilyn's maternal grandmother and grandfather were both diagnosed as psychiatrically ill. When Marilyn was seven, her mother, with whom she had been living for just six months, was hospitalized for depression and spent much of the remainder of her life in psychiatric hospitals.

Thus, Marilyn may have had a genetic predisposition to psychiatric illness, and she certainly feared that she would eventually end up psychiatrically disturbed like her grandmother and mother. Later in life, she would be hospitalized in a psychiatric clinic, and she would have psychiatrists available daily for therapy both in Los Angeles and in New York City.

Early Loss

Lester and Beck (1976) found that women who had attempted suicide in response to a recent interpersonal loss were more likely to have lost both parents before the age of ten.

Marilyn's life was full of loss. Her mother decided not to raise her, but boarded her with a family across the street, the Bolenders. Her mother did, however, visit her regularly. At the age of seven, Marilyn's mother decided to live with Marilyn, but she was taken away to a psychiatric hospital after just six months. Marilyn stayed with the couple who were boarding with her mother. After a year this couple moved away, and Marilyn moved in with neighbors, the Giffens.

When Marilyn was 11, the Giffens moved away, and Marilyn was placed in a boarding home for 21 months. After that, Marilyn was placed in two foster homes before living with friends of her mother, the Goddards. When Marilyn was 16, the Goddards planned to move, and a convenient marriage was arranged between Marilyn and the boy next door.

Marilyn never met her father, Stanley Gifford. She knew who he was, though she would fantasize that her real father was Clark Gable. When she was grown up, she made two attempts to meet her father, but he refused to meet her.

Thus, Marilyn's early life was full of loss. She had a father who was never present and a mother who was only sometimes present, usually unpredictably. She experienced getting close to the people in a family and soon afterward losing them—again and again.

Husbands and Lovers

Marilyn was married three times: to Jim Dougherty, Joe DiMaggio and Arthur Miller. Each marriage ended in divorce, and the last two divorces were especially traumatic for Marilyn. (She had psychologically disengaged from her first husband during his absences for Navy service and already had replacement lovers.) She killed herself two years after her break with Arthur Miller.

Marilyn's early suicide attempts were in response to the loss of her lover/agent, Johnny Hyde, and after the early deterioration of her marriage to Arthur Miller (though the marriage lasted four years).

It is possible that her final and lethal suicidal act was in response to the loss of her lover, Robert Kennedy, who had made it clear that he would have nothing more to do with her.*

The Final Deterioration

At the time of her suicide, Marilyn was living alone, recently fired from the movie she was making, heavily addicted to the drugs she was taking, and in fear that her depression and psychological problems would result in further psychiatric hospitalizations. The basis for her success was her beauty, but at age 36 this was proving to be difficult to hold onto.

---

*There is speculation that Marilyn was murdered, but it is likelier that she was embarked on a suicidal course that could only have ended with her death.

Marilyn was at the end of her life as she defined it. She had arrived at an existential choice point—to create a new existence or to end the old one. She chose to end the old one.

CONCLUSIONS

Our analysis of the suicide of Marilyn Monroe has suggested three risk factors for the person experiencing a separation or divorce.

Persons at risk for suicide may have a genetic or experientially caused psychological disturbance that renders them more susceptible to the loss. Such persons may also have experienced early loss that sensitized them to the later loss. This later loss then re-arouses all of the old pain and conflict surrounding the early loss and makes this later loss so much more difficult to cope with.

Finally, these persons may also be in the midst of a life crisis of which the separation and divorce may be but one component. Often a spouse or lover can help their mates through the crises of life, but in this situation they only add to the crisis. Abandonment accompanies the crisis, and suicide seems the ideal solution.

REFERENCES

Guiles, F. L. *Legend.* New York: Stein & Day, 1984.

Lester, D. *Why People Kill Themselves.* Springfield, IL: Charles C Thomas, 1983.

Lester, D., and A. T. Beck. Early loss as a possible sensitizer to later loss in attempted suicides. *Psychological Reports* 39:121-122, 1976.

14

Divorce as Betrayal:
When "To Love" is "To Be"

Adrian R. Tiemann, PhD, CSW, CCS

Among the varieties of human affairs in which betrayal can be perceived, divorce captures the imagination with a power that until recently led most societies to erect formidable barriers against its employment. Despite the importance of betrayal in this context, it has not received serious attention from social scientists. This chapter addresses this anomaly by examining the situation where divorce is perceived as or felt to be betrayal by one partner. We will first disentangle the meaning of betrayal as recursive exchanges between spouses akin to the category of actions known as "double binds." Focusing on marriage, we will examine the effects of betrayal by deceit upon the self-system of both partners. Because not all divorces are so conceived or executed, we will examine divorce in the context of the marital self as a socially constructed reality and the divorced self as betrayed. We will use the perspectives of sociological theory and self psychology to develop a preliminary model in which to frame clinical interventions. Finally, we will provide some applications of the method which emphasize that therapy is interactional, too.

Elsewhere, I have pointed out:

> At first glance, society's foundations appear firm and substantial—that is, materially real. But sociology teaches that the mortar of the social world is actually human emotion hardened upon expression through the give and take of personal interaction. In this process, the building blocks of society are lathered with the cement of human obligation. They are then set by fulfillment of the contract, that mutual exchange of resources in which each participant construes advantages. The quality of the resulting edifice is thus a function of how well each participant has performed the duties enumerated by the contract.

Nowhere is this insight truer than in the realm of relationship epito-
mized by marriage. While all behavior, even the withdrawal of the
schizophrenic, is essentially interactional—since it is not possible to
not communicate—the fact that marriage intersects wider levels of
functioning evokes elemental aspects of being more deeply than do
other forms of association. A business partnership can indeed plumb
our depths in many ways, as Donald Trump has shown, yet its
achievements are mere analogs for that more primitive achievement
of connubial union.

Moreover, every transaction between people forms a context for
learning. As the fundamental unit of *sociation* from which society (in
the form of new members) and all other social forms derive, marriage
as progenitor of the family shapes our ideas of what society is like.
The way in which our parents and siblings were treated and treated
each other model for us from the very beginning how the wider world
works. If you stop to consider it, the very fabric of society is woven of
feelings—of human bonds: bonds of affection, of respect, of affiliation
and responsibility. When we love another, we love the other in ourselves and the self in the other. Love is unifying, symbolically and
physically.

For these reasons, the self with which an individual cognizes,
feels and acts is not only a construction, but is also a learning context.
Aphoristically, the statement "to live is to learn" is equatable with
"to love is to be." Created by social exchanges identifying an "objective" definition of subjective experience (the context), the "self" that
the person comes to identify as the "me" of experience is successively
shaped through negotiation (see Bateson 1972; Goffman 1972; Greenberg and Mitchell 1983; Marx 1972; Mead 1934; Simmel 1955). The
"power" that we exercise over others, and they over us—as in any
relationship—is *embodied in the parameters of that relationship*. This
fact is important in considering how divorce as betrayal comes to
effect its damage.

While anyone with whom a person interacts during the lifespan
has some impact on that person's social self, those people who come to
play roles of significant others in the subject's life, such as spouses,
are disproportionately important in this regard. Through their emotional and transactional significance to the subject, these people
develop the *power* to create, add to, or make basic changes in that
panoply of cognitions, feelings and remembered actions that comprise the subject's identified self—as they themselves are similarly
affected by the subject. Exchanges within intimate relationships
therefore have the potential for both providing the most benefit to the
self and, in the case of betrayal, for wreaking the most havoc upon a
person's identity.[1]

Being joined in marriage (conventional or otherwise), people are unified in the eyes of the state, establishing power centers of action from which they can pool resources and further their dreams and destinies according as their *feelings* move them. Having accomplished a major human task, that of repaying life's debt by undertaking the progenitive role, they are free to investigate whether those objects of desire that titillated them will in fact help them to fulfill themselves.

CONCEPTIONS OF BETRAYAL

While betrayal is inevitable, it is always unexpected. At the macro-level it occurs because the behavior of people pursuing their unique interests on a finite planet follows laws independent of human needs, hearkening instead to the dynamics of change inherent in all open systems.

At the micro-level, accordingly, a rich array of definitions of betrayal have arisen. Webster's Unabridged defines betrayal as (1) to mislead, as by leading astray *and* into danger, or by leading astray *and* abandoning, as in seduction; (2) to violate another's trust *and* deliver into enemy hands by treachery or fraud; (3) to break faith *and* to fail or desert in time of need; (4) to have shared a confidence *and* to then reveal, perhaps unwittingly, something not obvious, or to disclose something in violation of trust.

Betrayal represents (1) a "set up" of the victim, (2) his or her subsequent letdown by the betrayer, with (3) the implicit involvement of an external party or element *hitherto unknown to the victim.* It is a form of "con" like three-card monte, which is based on the hidden inequity or asymmetry in the exchange between shark and pigeon.

Suddenly, victims face a monumental discrepancy between their expectations and the other's performance along three dimensions: (1) the future, regarding some envisioned situation or ideal; (2) the present, or breach of contract; and (3) the past, as in violations of trust to another person or entity. Under these headings can be arrayed such particulars as deception, fraud, misrepresentation, disappointment, violation, treachery, disclosure/exposure, invalidation and dishonor. Unlike some other forms of betrayal, all three are involved in divorce because marriage is a convention transcending time.

Betrayer (B) and victim (V) originally lie on the same plane of power. The contractual nature of betrayal emerges most clearly in considering outcomes. Through B's deceit, unilaterally taken and at no perceptible cost to himself, and/or V's lack of understanding, V has been deprived, has suffered a loss, or has been dispossessed. V is unconsentingly moved by B from parallel/equal status to demoted/ object status while O is elevated. By taking matters into his own hands vis-à-vis V, B rescinds his obligations toward V previously defined in the marriage vows.

Thus betrayal is always a violation of a relationship, a unilateral action by B involving the formerly peripheral element O.[2] V's loss is doubled: V loses not only the quid pro quo with B, but indefinably in terms of O as well. This partially perceived and partially material loss is in turn reflected in V's self-system.

In turn, O, formerly nonexistent or peripheral to the marriage, comes to represent a standard of worth along some dimension against which V is found wanting and which B values enough to warrant violating the contract with V.[3] Note that O may be a person or social entity, or exist only in the mind of B. Regardless of how betrayal originates, our *feelings* of it reside within ourselves. It is the self that feels betrayed. Hence it is to the self's perceptions that we must turn for answers.

IMPACT OF DIVORCE AS BETRAYAL UPON THE SELF

Since everyone is unique, people are bound to have different ideas and disagreement to be an inherent element in social relations. How then, does disconfirmation come to threaten the integrity of the self? As said at the outset, reality is socially constructed by a self operating as a feeling-thinking schema that eases or biases the processing of information on the basis of past experience.[4] In every bit of self, therefore, there is assimilated a bit of external reality, or other. We are biophysical organisms permeated by the sum of our experiences and relationships, taking in and transforming "social nutrition" into self in the same way that our muscles and bones absorb and assimilate food nutrients we consume, transforming them into muscle and bone tissue. Popular songs are right: somebody *is* "in our bones."

As a result, betrayal affects V's cognitive-affective schema, her self, proportionate to the importance, intensity and intimacy of the preexisting relationship that has been violated. In intimate relationships such as marriage, V mentally associates herself with B as B's wife.

> Repeated associations of the self with other concepts and structures for example, *his wife* will lead to stronger and more certain links. Eventually there may be a virtual overlapping of the self and some other concept. This occurs when a large number of representations . . .

become self-relevant and when an increasingly larger share of the representations comprising the self-system are associated with this structure. Once there is an overlapping of the self and another concept, a self-schema may be said to emerge. *This structure is now part of the self* and is automatically activated when the self-structure is activated. These structures become the ones most salient, central, or important in organizing information about the self, and, perhaps, the social world in general (Kegan 1975).

The confusion evoked by disconfirmation is very upsetting to V and will arouse anxiety in proportion to the violation of her expectancies. Anxiety is that powerful harbinger of readiness to change in which the organism is hypervigilant and alert to every cue. In the case of deceit, anxiety paves the way for a change in V's mental map of the shared marital territory as her existing construction is shaken by revelations regarding B's behavior. Tapping into these nodes of anxiety provides therapeutic leverage for helping the client deal with betrayal.

In response, the self is forced to initiate a major restructuring of that mapping along whatever relevant dimensions have been cast into doubt by the betrayal. The shock, pain, disorganization and denial experienced by clients who have been betrayed signify both the necessity of restructuring as well as its difficulty.[5]

The contents of this structure are not only shaken and rearranged by betrayal, but they may be emptied of its major contents by divorce. The remainder-self then exists in a state of suspension, of rootless wandering, alienated in the original sense of the term—of being bereft of full-self through having transferred ownership of one's self to another. For desire and yielding expresses one's inner self, that most personal aspect of being in which authenticity itself takes form.[6]

Loss is not the only wound left by betrayal. Even without marriage a pair form a socioeconomic unit. Everyone "knows" this and apologizes for taking one member "away" for an evening. The couple's sharing of gains and losses, social position and esteem, joys and sorrows, attest to their trust of each other. Because trust is the earliest element incorporated by the developing child (Erikson 1963), its violation represents a profound injury to the structure and functioning of the self (see Lingis 1977). Sexual access signifies *emotional* access and commitment expressed in loyalty and affirmation of the other's adequacy as a partner, concern for the other's well-being, and honoring of each other within a context of warmth and caring. These are the elements cast in doubt by betrayal.[7]

Social Exchange and Relationship Schema

Relationships form through mutual exchanges and persist as results of these transactions embodied in feelings (see Tiemann 1986). A general case displayed as X and Y in a table will show how the many pathways to betrayal might relate to divorce. Because of the current ascendance of the biological sciences, and my wish not to confuse the reader with different nomenclature, I will use the X to refer to the female and Y to relate to the male.

Cell entries represent the point of view of X as subject with Y as object. They depict X's view of possible relationships between them, or feelings resulting from evaluating or making attributions about Y, their quality of their potential interactions, or X's expectancies about Y's actions. This point is crucial to unraveling the phenomenon of betrayal for therapeutic purposes.

We start with a couple who are dating. What potential relationships does X perceive between herself and Y based upon the amount of agreement they share relative to means and goals? (See Table 1.)

Table 1.
X's Perception of Potential Relationship with Y

Perceived Agreement on Means		Perceived Agreement on Goals		
		Disagreement	*Neutrality*	*Agreement*
Agreement	+	"Unfriendly" competition 1	Distance 2	Possible marriage 3
Neutrality	0	Dislike; they never joined together 4	No relationship at all 5	Liking 6
Disagreement	−	Hatred; probable enemies 7	Distance 8	"Friendly" competition 9

Where means and goals are shared, close friendship or intimacy is seen as possible (cell 3). Other things being equal, congruence in attitudes and values tends to promote liking, which in turn promotes the desire for further sharing and perhaps, ultimately, intimacy. This assumes, of course, that no competing and intimacy-relevant discrepancies exist between participants, such as appearance, age, sex, and social class, although popular literature records many such violations where partners construe affiliative advantages to outweigh normative disadvantages (the prince and the pauper, beauty and the beast, May and September romances). In the case study that follows, the discrepancy is ethnic.

Interestingly enough, Table 1 shows that outcomes differ depending upon whether means or goals are primary. If people agree on goals, then competition, shading into betrayal under certain circumstances, is possible. For instance, it might occur when competitors who disagree on means perform "end runs" on each other (cell 9). This highlights the implicit element of power underlying relationships.

Along the means-neutral continuum, agreement on goals fosters feelings ranging from dislike to liking (cells 4-6). Along the goals-neutral continuum, however, differing preferences for means generally seem to preclude relationship (cells 2, 5, 8).

Let us presume that all went well with the pair depicted in cell 3 of this table, and X and Y joined in holy matrimony. Realistically, we have to allow for negative outcomes in various areas of functioning because life is rarely idyllic. From time to time both partners might reconsider their earlier decision to wed. As therapists know, anger and animosity are passions no less binding than love and esteem. We are woven together by the threads of our individual and group animosities as tightly as we are by its and our own affiliations.

In Table 2 let us examine the situation of the couple a few years after marriage, in which X's attitudes toward the marriage and her expectancies about Y's attitudes toward it are arrayed.

Table 2.
X's Expectancies About Y's Behavior

X's Attitudes toward the Marriage		X's Beliefs about Y's Attitudes		
		Negative	Neutral	Positive
Positive	+	Expect Y to oppose the marriage 1	Expect Y to compromise re marriage 2	Agreement: enjoy the marriage 3
Neutral	0	Expect Y to propose ending marriage 4	Renegotiate relationship: end or redo 5	Expect Y to propose saving marriage 6
Negative	–	Agreement: end the marriage 7	Expect Y to compromise re divorce 8	Expect opposition by Y to divorce 9

Here the row descriptors show X's attitudes toward marriage, while the column descriptors depict X's *beliefs* about Y's attitudes toward it. The cell entries then depict X's *expectancies* regarding how Y will act, based upon these suppositions. If these perceptions are correct, there is little basis for betrayal because X has correctly predicted Y's overt actions and understood his underlying feelings in relation to her own. There may be competition between them, antipathy over certain issues, or even feelings as strong as hatred, but both parties are clear about the other's motives and behaviors, and their interactions can be equitably "symmetrical," even if complementary in a functional sense.

Predispositions to Betrayal

The previous section has described betrayal from the victim's perspective. As the title suggests, divorce as betrayal is a complex matter with not necessarily definable devils. Psychodynamic theory points to specific omissions, contaminations and interactional difficulties in upbringing as having far-reaching consequences on our developing outlooks, our hopes and fears, as, for instance, *learning* not to trust, or that love is dangerous. These are said to affect our psyche and all of our life choices, especially those of intimates and marital partners, as well as how we will relate to those partners after the bloom has faded and our underlying weaknesses or anxieties come to the fore. Some writers refer to the "false self" that develops under adverse conditions.

In a less pathology-oriented vein, it is obvious that something like betrayal has to be a common human issue because all of us are vulnerable and inadequately prepared for the first semblance of its occurrence as *discrepancy* or deviation from some norm. And that deviation is itself a major motivator of learning since its opposite, sameness, lulls us into boredom.[8] Fascinating research with infants (Stern 1985) demonstrated that so long as its world is predictable, a baby will happily venture forth to explore it. When mothers played with their babies by jiggling their backs in rhythm to their crawl, the infants seemed to feel no "discrepancy" and continued to explore. But when the mother's rhythm went out of step, it produced concern sufficient to cause the infants to stop, turn around and look anxiously at the mother, as if to say "What's wrong?"

This was no betrayal situation, but the infant's upset attests to the power of simple deviation to engage our interest. And, given the limited nature of the young child's response repertoire, it is inevitable that occasions will arise in which a parent or caregiver will be unable to meet the child's expectations, and may also be unable to provide comfort. When they are serious enough disappointments, these events are probably experienced as betrayals by the child. The point is that discrepancy shades into betrayal when expectancies have become established—on the basis of pre-existing attention-getting deviations—and we do not know how to cope with it or feel hurt by it.

We can diagram this sequence as follows:

1		2A	
Predictable environment	→	Learn trust and begin to develop ability to relate to family	→

3A		4A		5A	
Construe others rightly	→	Make friends readily	→	Develop healthy self	→

versus

		2B	
Unpredictable environment	→	Distrust others; retarded in ability to relate to family	→

3B		4B		5B	
Misconstrue others	→	Difficulty with making friends	→	Develop false self	→

As you can see from the diagram, analytic theory suggests that people whose development has been faulty in some way are left with learning deficits that affect not only their selves, but interfere with the healthy bonding through which they are to get their needs met.

As the process continues over the lifespan, these difficulties in functioning accumulate and betrayal becomes increasingly likely:

1-5		6A	
Success in negotiating stages	→	Form intimate relationship based on true self and healthy loving	→

7A		8A		9A
Construe others rightly	→	Healthy intimacy possible	→	Loss possible, betrayal unlikely

versus

		6B	
Failure in negotiating stages	→	Form intimate relationship based on false self and "unfinished business"	→

7B		8B		9B
Misconstrue others	→	Difficulty with intimacy	→	Betrayal

Regardless of the details, all theories of human behavior recognize that people act in the present on the basis of past learning, a little bit like scientists seeking to make sense out of a vast universe of experience (Kelly 1955). Now let us turn to betrayal in marriage, where for clarity's sake we replace X with V (victim) and Y with B (betrayer).

Betrayal and Expectancy in Marriage

We describe as betrayal those actions on B's part which preempt, in a way V perceives as hurtful, some crucial element of their "normal" transactions. They are not only actions in the present, but a comment upon the nature of the relationship V presumed they had in the past, discrediting what went before.* Added to this duality is V's difficulty in "leaving the field" by the hold of her formerly valid expectancies— their shared positive experiences in the past and her "love" for her betrayer. Mapped in her mind, heart, and motor nerves (as feelings always are), her emotions lead her to experience these revelations as a double-bind in retrospect.[9]

By definition, relationships are interactional. Because betrayal has an effect *meta* to V's expectations, it not only arises from B's actions, but it also arises from a failure on V's part to assess her environment correctly; specifically it arises from her inability to "read" B's status or intentions and thereby to conceive his willingness to take asymmetrical action. Although this evaluation sounds harsh and "victim-blaming," it is objectively accurate.

What conditions give rise to this inability on V's part? In feats of magic or a true con game, B purposely miscues the audience/victim to distract them from his trick. But there is a big difference between a con or trick and a marriage. This difference is the intimacy of the partners, through which, presumably, they get to *know* each other in all the rich variety of their vagaries and gain the ability to predict with fair accuracy how the other will respond to the many situations that develop in the course of a life together.

The next question then becomes how it is possible for two people to live side by side and *not* know the other's feelings. Or, how is it possible to know another's feelings and continue to ignore the impact they might have on one's life?

Consider *deception* in marriage. Let us look not at the grand pas-

---

*The discrediting of one's past is tantamount to disavowing the part of self bound to other. The challenge to V's existing self-definition paves the way for revision. Depending upon circumstances, it ranges in intensity of feeling from wearily discarding something outgrown to traumatic amputation.

sions about which tragic novels are written, but at the ordinary daily deceptions that partners practice on each other regarding mundane issues such as taking out the garbage, repairing the window, getting the car greased, watching the kids, or calling the roofer. Here V's beliefs about B's actions and attitudes toward V (presumably based upon B's previous claims to V about their relationship) are revealed as false, implicitly with reference to some party or element external to the marriage. As shown in cell 1 of Table 3, inauthenticity in the relationship is made explicit through an act of deceit on B's part.[10]

Table 3.
V's Feelings

| V's prior beliefs re B's actions for V's sake | | Revelations about B's Behavior to V | | |
		Negative (commission) Preemptive act does ($-A$)	Neutral (omission) Non-action does nothing (0)	Positive (commission) Positive act does (A)
Would do "A" (A)	+	Deceived A/ $-$ A	Disappointed A/0	Affirmed A/A
Might do "A" (A?)	0	Annoyed or irritated A?/ $-$ A	Unconcerned or indifferent A?/0	Pleased A?/A
Would not do "A" $-$(A)	$-$	Enmity or fury $-$(A)/ $-$ A	Distant $-$(A)/0	Suspicious or manipulated $-$(A)/A

If V believed that B would perform some task and he not only did not do it but did something that would impede or preclude his later doing it, she would feel duped. The intensity of her response would depend on the extent to which the action comprised a disavowal of her self—how crucial the element was to her identity.

The next question is how to use this information therapeutically. If relationships are contexts for learning, then new relationships can moderate or transform old learning.

INTERVENTION WITH DIVORCING SPOUSES

In working with people who may be heading for divorce, I use a combination of dynamic, behavioral and strategic techniques. This is because each has certain strengths that keep therapy moving. The strategic approaches are system-oriented and help me to keep in focus the multiply triadic nature of pair-bonding in which shadowy dancers often play significant roles in a divorce ballet that ends with the emotional morbidity of one or both principals. Being alert to their existence helps me to consider that the strange movements of my client in the session may be *responses* to whispered cues and unseen steps, as well as to the off-stage gesturing of the battling partner. It also helps me identify ways of directing the dancers in using their own momentum so that they perform with greater ease and the ending becomes less tragic.

An important goal of therapy is helping the client "get over" her ex-spouse. But melioration aimed solely at resolving loss through retraining (the strict behavioral approach) is insufficient because it incompletely maps what happens to a victim.[11, 12] The clinician must discover what components of the self/schema (roles or part-roles) exist and how they have been affected by the betrayal—what remains intact, what is bound to the loss, and what has been shattered.[13, 14] The rationales for these roles must then be explored in the client's present and past to clarify patterns that caused difficulty and sensitize the patient to interactional traps. These issues are usually best understood from a psychodynamic perspective.[15]

Since roles find existence only through ongoing or imagined interaction, changes in roles are effectively developed through alliance with the therapist.[16] The difficulties associated with them are usually reenacted and refelt in the transference. By responding differently through offering the client a more benign introject, the therapist can provide a "corrective emotional experience" (see Freud 1963; Simmel 1955; Lederer and Jackson 1968). In the language of change, the therapist reframes the client's past by redoing it in the present. With this more benign "past" internalized as a guide, the client is better able to confront the present and the future.[17]

Consequently, when I ask the client how betrayal is a problem to her, and what about it creates that problem, the client provides me with a map of her reality as well as observations on the road conditions prevailing there—those emotional markers of the path. Is it sleeplessness, inability to work, or inability to manage financially? Whatever element is selected as the key, change efforts are directed to reframing this element in ways the client can manage,[18] and in initiating client *action* based upon the reframed elements.*

Generic Model

A generic model shows that although each approach postulates different primary factors having different weightings, all are variants of the same schema built upon the theory of development presented earlier. The following diagram extends those given earlier and may help readers place their treatment strategies within a broader context.

1-5		6A	
Developmental stage(s) negotiation: success	→	Form intimate relationship based on true self and healthy loving	→
		6B	
Developmental stage(s) negotiation: failure	→	Form intimate relationship based on false self and "unfinished business"	→

7A		8A	9A	
Intimacy possible	→	Construe others rightly	Loss possible, betrayal unlikely	→
7B		**8B**	**9B**	
Difficulties with intimacy	→	Misconstrue others	Betrayal	→

---

*The simplicity and elegance of natural phenomena—physical, biological and social—is shown in the parallel with Prigogine's analysis of discontinuous change within chemical structures whose processes exist far from equilibrium where there is "motivation," if you will, for the structure to jump to a higher level of organization to "escape" its dissipativeness. (This is analogous to the frantic searching of victims for retreat, escape, explanation and understanding of their "fate" that precedes the reorientation and reorganization of their psychic structure.) Here a small but certain perturbation of the system will generate increasingly larger effects until the system convulses and begins to reorganize itself at a new and higher level of functioning. Once such a level is attained, change can reverberate throughout the system, domino-like, generating modifications in all the elements touched in some way by the reorganization.

Behaviorist and Strategic assumptions and scope of examination:

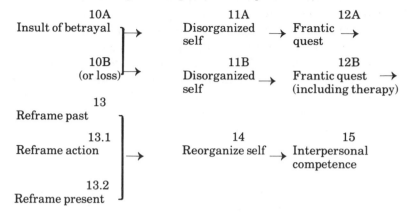

In the diagram above, the numbers refer to the elements considered by the treatment approach. Psychoanalysis focuses on all elements of the patient's social functioning, going back to the initiating events in early childhood (number 0) and continuing with a relational history through the present (numbers 1 to 15) as revealed by and enacted in the transference. The A and B of each stage refer to outcomes expected to occur based on developmental success or failure, the A referring to success, and B referring to failure. Behaviorist and strategic therapy, by contrast, focus on the precipitating event (number 10) and subsequent actions by the client within and outside the therapy situation. Reframing (insight/positive introjection: steps 13 and 14) permits transformation of those actions into "healthy" responses.

Rather than examining these treatment strategies more specifically, let us look at a case where brief therapy helped to reveal that a couple was moving toward divorce through a series of steps that escalated elements of their implicit emotional contract past its boundaries into the betrayal zone.

The MacDonalds

Stewart and Sybil were an interracial couple who married 28 years ago when he was stationed in Germany. The match was approved by the wife's family since Sybil's older sister had also wed a black man. With certain compromises, the marriage had been satisfactory to both for many years. He worked at a bank and made good money despite his lack of a college education for he was bright. She worked behind the scenes in the entertainment industry. Together they enjoyed visiting on weekends with both sets of relatives (some of her brothers and cousins had emigrated, too), and they loved travel. Since there were no children they could indulge these interests.

Sybil took the position that Stewart came first; he could not be wrong. Even with company present she would serve him first. She didn't care if this was considered rude; that was the way it should be in a family. The wife was her husband's handmaiden, accommodating her needs to his demands. In return, the husband provided a home that was secure financially and emotionally.

As the baby of a family of 12 sharecroppers who had been catered to by his older sisters after his parents' deaths when he was six, this attitude suited Stewart very well. He believed that men had needs which must be fulfilled. At six foot seven, one of Stewart's needs was being the star basketball player on the local team. The other of these needs was women. The couple had ultimately agreed that Stewart could have girlfriends if he remained loyal to Sybil. She would not pry and he would not leave her.

In terms of Table 3, the MacDonalds' contract had overlapping elements. So long as Stewart enacted the good provider role, Sybil would grant him time off to be the basketball star and to have girlfriends. However, her demand implicit in this arrangement was that Stewart would not take so much time from their shared life playing ball that she became an "athletic widow," nor elevate any girlfriend to special status at her expense.

While Stewart did in fact earn good money in a bank, Sybil also took a job. Thus she performed dual roles: wage-earner and homemaker. It is not clear what implications this change in the ground rules had upon the marriage. For 24 years there seemed to be no problems.

The trouble arose four years ago when both lost their jobs within months of each other. Note that this event caused Stewart to violate his role as provider, which was important to Sybil at several levels of meaning and probably touched upon deep intrapsychic vulnerabilities.

Moreover, the way in which this event had occurred gave Sybil the kind of pause that would fit into cell 1 or 7. Stewart had always been a work situation manipulator, using his considerable good looks and charm to get by. Insofar as Sybil was inclined to hold back, his forwardness in this regard must have been very exciting for her. Contributing to the daredevil image was his practice of snorting cocaine. He did this for years without being too obvious about it, and pursued the prettier office employees. In the climate of the 1970s, employers were reluctant to call him on it as long as he maintained a reasonable level of productivity. It was when he became careless about his behavior that it became offensive and he was fired after failing to heed warnings.

From her position, Sybil had contracted for the financial and emotional security that she believed only a good provider could offer. In the meantime, she had unknowingly contributed to his downfall, giving him extra money which he used to buy the drugs that enabled him to jeopardize and ultimately lose that role. By realizing her money was used this way, she felt deceived. Stewart's act revealed his contempt for her wishes and his selfishness regarding his own desires. The meta statement of this action is "regardless of what I tell you, our relationship is one in which your opinion counts for little with me." The victim (V) is then left wondering "Is this *really* one of the many ways in which love is expressed?"*

Although one might have predicted that Sybil would "do" something to reinstitute Stewart's job supremacy, she did not have to. It turned out that her work unexpectedly succumbed to changing technology. She "undid" the violation by acquiescing to Stewart's demand that they take the generous severance pay they had both received and spend it on a lengthy world cruise without putting any of it away for the future. Their (symbiotic) dreams of nurturance fulfilled, they returned home virtually penniless. In Sybil's unconscious fantasy, Stewart would now *have* to get a job and act the manly provider role.

It was when he did not that Sybil became a cleaning lady and Stewart responded by increasing his drug use. For a year she continued waiting for him to "find" the right position. His failure to do so might not have affected the marriage except that he indulged in drugs mainly in the company of a younger woman with whom he had actually developed a more serious relationship than he admitted. Sybil felt threatened by this woman, who was also black and in her thirties. In contrast to Sybil, who was a plump 50-year-old Hummel figurine, Sareena was the lithe seductress on the black velvet canvas.

In effect, Stewart implied that he would job hunt (return to his old role), but then he failed to make the necessary attempts, or made the attempts in so half-hearted a style that he lost the opportunity. That Sybil tolerated this state of affairs for a year indicates that she was mainly disappointed (cell 2): he was not the dashing protector of her

---

*Note that fraud is a close companion to deceit, differing only in time frame: while deception looks to the past, fraud looks to the future. When B's presenting self is someone other than the "real" B (as subsequently determined by B's actions), this establishes a relationship and expectancy about role obligations on V's part which B violates by the commission of an "inauthentic" act.

dreams, but a sluggish laggard immobilized by indecision.[19] Incidentally, I say "mainly" because as the ante goes up, so does the potential for betrayal.†

Before all this started, if Stewart had fulfilled her expectations of obtaining a new job (cell 3), she would have been pleased by the affirmation. Were she unsure of his response because of his insecurity about finding employment in midlife, she would not quite know how to respond if he took no action at all (cell 5). This is what seems to have happened for the first year after their return from the cruise when she worked and waited. Later on, when it became clear that he was not only *not* actively seeking work, but was "wasting" time with Sareena in self-destructive behaviors, she got irritated (cell 4) as her commitment to their joint future (by her working) was disavowed by his continued lethargy.

This was when their battles—and the motivation for therapy—began. The precipitating causes were a series of paranoid hallucinations suffered by Stewart that followed their escalating fights in the third year, when Sybil "found out" about the liaison. As she explained to me, Stewart had "hid" Sareena's existence from her for years, but she consoled herself with the thought that "He still comes home to *me*!" (I put the words in quotes because unconscious collusion is almost always involved in unexpected revelations: both partners receive advantages from such arrangements, usually with the aim of regulating intimacy.)

One evening during a period when their German nephew, a young man in his early twenties, was staying with them, Sybil had gone to bed. Stewart had been staying with Sareena and on this evening had come home unexpectedly early. He had been with Sareena and was sitting in the living room when Sybil got out of bed to get a glass of water. Not knowing the nephew was in the apartment at the time, she was nude. At that moment, Stewart felt forced to conclude that she been "with" the nephew. Enraged, he attacked her, throw-

---

†Consider what happens if a couple are hiking and V slips, grabbing a branch overhanging a thousand-foot gorge as she does so. Now should B fail to throw her a tethering rope he holds in hand, she is assuredly betrayed if she falls to her death below. But there are elements of doubt about B's lack of action: was there a mitigating element of which V was unaware that framed his decision? Did he perceive a graver danger, perhaps that the tree to which she clung was itself ready to release its hold upon the cliff, and thus thrust the two of them into the abyss? Did he see a rescue team hard by? Or is he so caught in the moment of panic that his will is frozen in terror? Should she manage to extricate herself and clamber back up the slope, will these lingering doubts not chip away incessantly at her previous romantic beliefs about the inviolability of their union?

ing her down on the bed and giving her the third degree about her "affair."

Her terror at his behavior made her freeze. As a child she had undergone the relentless bombing of Munich and was paralyzed by threat. The one act she could not tolerate was being hit. For his part, the more mute Sybil became, the more uncontrollable Stewart grew as memories flooded him of racially motivated interrogations he had suffered. Because the one thing he could not tolerate in anyone was a refusal to answer him, he believed that her silence justified his punishment.

Until then, Sybil's position had been that Stewart simply had a drug problem. It was normal to have a home and know that you could put your head on a pillow at night and go to sleep. Stewart was changed by his addiction; he had never accused her before of anything and there had never been a hand raised in the household. Now he was accusing her of paying someone to create the shadow figures and drive him crazy. It was impossible for her to understand how he could believe that, or accuse her of having an affair with her nephew. Even her snoring at night was supposedly a signal to someone.

These violations of her expectations happened more and more frequently until one night, after he had quieted down and gone to sleep, Sybil called police. When they came he was a wild man, and somehow during the tussle, he wrenched a knee tendon which required surgery and left him lame.

These events left both of them feeling betrayed and those parts of their identities committed to the other, shaken. Stewart's behavior fits into cell 1 of Sybil's map where she believed Stewart would protect her and instead he beat her, and cell 7, where she unconsciously expected he would not find a job, and he spends his time with Sareena, which indeed threatens their marriage. This action devalues and dismisses her as a person, and she responds with fury to the perceived attack.

Increasingly, Sybil saw Stewart as being unwilling to "help out" and by confirming her prediction this led her to say "I thought so!" and to feel justified in distancing herself from such an unwilling partner (cell 8). But Stewart could not recognize these signs of disaffection in her precisely because he was invested in a contract calling for "endless love."

Following the last battle, Sybil pressed charges and, while Stewart was jailed and hospitalized, went into hiding. He returned to an empty home, and panic. He began to see shadows of male figures under the bed, creeping along. These hallucinations led to his psychiatric referral to the clinic where I was working. They had now been separated for some months, but she was still paying the bills for the apartment out of her salary as a domestic and Stewart was getting disability.

Using the logic of Table 3, Stewart's behavior was interpreted by Sybil as various combinations of

A/ – A (deceiving):
He used "their" money for himself and his girlfriends.

A/O (disappointing):
He failed to follow through on financial tasks.
He failed to act the manly provider role.

A?/ – A (irritating):
He disqualified much of what she said.

– (A)/ – A (infuriating):
He betrayed his loyalty to her by pairing with Sareena.
He broke his (implicit) promise never physically to abuse her.

From Stewart's point of view, the situation had emerged as a violation of his unconscious expectation that Sybil would "mother" him as had his sisters so that he could continue to play the darling child (cell 1). "I don't want to believe she's doing this to me, but I can't help it. She's trying to hurt me back. I told her I'd put her in jail for false arrest." So long as his demands for caregiving fell within the time limitations imposed by his job and he had enough money to indulge his passions, he felt safe. But when he lost his job under degrading circumstances, his anxiety (masked until then by his "success") shot sky-high. These terrors were then only mollifiable by acting out his grandiose fantasies of success with women under the sway of the drug. In turn, Sybil's decreasing confidence in him as time dragged on was reflected in her increasing provocativeness toward him, leading to the physical battles.

All of this had happened before I even knew of their existence. The referral came from the hospital where Stewart had been treated for his injury and detoxified. Outpatient treatment was not maintaining his gains, and it was hoped that marital therapy might bring greater leverage to bear. It was clearly a situation ripe for crisis, which determined my decision to choose strategic and behavioral tactics to start, with the plan in mind of using dynamic techniques if later they were warranted.

When I saw the two of them together, Stewart took the dominant role in answering questions, while Sybil remained relatively quiet.

Whenever she did speak, he challenged what she said. They had not traveled together to the appointment: she was still in hiding. But they both *seemed* to want to continue the marriage; at least each asserted so in private to me. While reserving judgment on whether they did or not, I first worked as if they did want to stay together. Hence the immediate task was to block the accusation process that led to the escalating physical fights. This was done by telling Sybil in Stewart's presence that whether she were having an affair or not, she should admit to it whenever he asked.

The other pragmatic problem was finances. While Sybil was earning money, she was working below her capacity and wanted to obtain more prestige and a higher salary. Stewart, hobbling on his crutches, was thoroughly demoralized and convinced that he could not work: I'm not mentally or physically able to work," he said. Thus I sought to move both of them forward on this front.

I agreed with Stewart that he might not be able to work *now*, but that to prepare for the time when he *would* be able to work, as well as to get over those interview jitters that he complained of suffering, he was to select three job postings that he *knew* were unsuitable. He was to go on the interviews and do what he knew had to be done to *fail* them. Stewart liked this assignment; its play-acting elements appealed to his sense of fun and aligned with his deeply held belief that he was unemployable. It also served to get him out of the apartment with its shadow figures. Sybil was asked to place an ad in the newspaper in the fields she wanted to try, and to post notices in places where people might hire her. Both were to report back after doing these tasks.

In the next session two weeks later, I applauded Stewart's "failures" and learned that he had an interview to do office work. The remainder of the session was devoted to asking each one how the other generally succeeded in doing tasks, and how they might coach each other on their failures. It turned out that Sybil's approach was "technical," whereas Stewart's was "personal." I asked them to switch roles so that they could better help each other to "fail" in getting the jobs they wanted. Sybil was to teach Stewart the technical approach and then point out how he could do it badly, and Stewart was to help Sybil be more personal, showing her how to do that badly. This intervention had two purposes, the first being to provide a suitable rationale for failure, and the second to bring them closer by putting them in each other's skin.

In the third session with Stewart alone he was ecstatic. He was seeing the shadows less, his energy had returned, and he was being physically active once more. He had been hired by a contractor for

part-time work, the Department of Social Services had agreed to send
him to computer school, and Sybil had invited him to the annual
family Easter gathering, which they had not attended for two years.
He was going to cook for it and was eagerly planning his part of the
menu.

When the day arrived, however, Sybil was less enthusiastic and
warm than he had hoped she would be. She seemed distant and
refused to come home with him. We can understand this behavior on
the basis that her image of Stewart has been changing over the
months of their separation. Her position is now more likely to be
doubt that he can act responsibly (or she believes he will not do so). If
he surprises this negative expectation (cell 9), she is likely to wonder
what is going on. Is he manipulating her or has he really changed?

Verification of this attitude arrived in the form of a letter from
Sybil. She chose this method to tell her side of the story. The relevant
extracts assert her desire to be free of him:

> I feel that you really only heard one half of the truth of what is going on.
> Stewart has made me look like a lying Persian in your eyes, and I feel I
> was not given a fair chance to defend myself properly.

> Until Stewart got fired from his job I did not know that we had nothing
> because he had put us into debts beyond my imagination. I begged him
> to go and file for bankruptcy, but he didn't finish it. The bills we had he
> made. All I was ever told was "Sign here!"

> Sounds ignorant, doesn't it! But I did a lot of things in my marriage just
> to keep peace! So now we have inherited $3000 from my aunt, but it was
> just a curse for me! Stewart insisted there is more. And his girlfriend
> called me to tell me that I owe her $2000 plus half my inheritance for
> helping her drive Stewart crazy!

> Please, if you can, see that Stewart gets some help. I cannot help him
> anymore! I have lost everything in my life! My husband! My name! And
> my self-respect!

The question is what moved this marital system to the level of disruption, given the unconscious compact between them. Table 3 shows
that the potential for change in a relationship occurs at the outermost
points where the emotional impact is greatest (cells 1, 3, 7 and 9). In
cells 3 and 6 the effect is positive, leading to greater closeness of the
couple. Most of the rest are negative in various degrees, including
those along the axes of neutrality/inaction radiating from a central
core of disinterest or negotiability, to confirm the pessimistic dictum
that there are more ways to go wrong than there are to go right in the
world.

His dream of an easy reconciliation vaporized, Stewart returned alone to his empty apartment in deep despair. His was a fragile self that could little tolerate challenge. Two days later, he was holding Sareena hostage at the apartment, convinced now that she was two-timing him as well. Sareena had managed to call Sybil who then called me. By the time I called Stewart, he had let Sareena leave. He then told me, "Sybil won't give me the idea that I'm doing what she wants. If she'd be straight with me about not wanting me, then I could deal with it; I would let her go." In short, he felt betrayed as well:

A/ – A (deceiving):
Easter was like old times, but Sybil wasn't straight with me.

A/O (disappointing):
She won't live up to her part of the bargain.
It hurts me that she tells me she cares for me when she doesn't.
She knows that I need her and so her staying away means she doesn't want me.
She should come back home and show an effort.

A?/ – A (irritating):
Her reactions really don't pan out.
She is hurting me.

– (A)/ – A (infuriating):
She led me to believe we had made up when she called the cops and had me arrested.

Was Stewart telling the truth about giving up Sybil? Did he know the truth about how he would feel if she "really" went through with divorce? What about Sybil? Both had played cat-and-mouse games with me, missing appointments, being late for appointments and doing 180-degree turns. My intuition said that Sybil had been silently chafing for years under the ignominy of Stewart's high-flying life and had built up enough resentment to last a lifetime. That attitude did not augur well for the continuation of the marriage, and I didn't see how I could change it without major reconstructive therapy, an out-of-the-question option in the low-income clinic where I worked.

I began to focus on helping Stewart come to terms with his loss and to make alternative plans for his future, for Sybil indicated by her physical absence a lack of desire to mend the rift. This work was more dynamically oriented, and it and the task of mourning were not easy for him. But tentatively he began it, greatly helped in this endeavor by the supportive existence of those ten loving sisters who had raised him.

SUMMARY AND CONCLUSIONS

The concept of divorce as betrayal has been examined in terms of a biopsychosocial model having implications for therapeutic interventions. The role of social interaction in developing a self and in learning has been stressed. In addition, it was noted that deviation from a norm is the paradigm underlying betrayal. This knowledge not only places betrayal in perspective, but yields a clear framework from which to develop meliorative techniques.

More specifically, betrayal represents the *perception of a relationship status change* by the victim. Given that perception in the context of marriage, actions by the betrayer become "double-binding" for the victim: he or she cannot "leave the field" because of prior romantic commitment. Thus the element of emotional investment on the part of the victim is a sine qua non for betrayal in intimate relations to take place. Where one experiences no threat, loss or damage from violation of one's romantic expectations, even though other persons might so construe it, there is no betrayal. For betrayal is ultimately a *private* affair. Hence it is possible and even probable that many betrayers are "innocent perpetrators." When it comes to crimes of the heart involving two people (if we take seriously Freud's dictum that there are no psychic accidents), it is clear that neither partner acts without reasons that the other "knows."

This chapter, therefore, has proposed a model that sets the therapeutic process into bold relief so that in the future it may be accomplished more efficiently and effectively in order to lessen the human and social toll exacted by the defective transactions which betrayal represents as solutions to the problems of everyday living.

NOTES

1. Psychoanalysts and sociologists, as well as research psychologists and anthropologists attest to the unique importance of significant others in a person's life (Allport 1937; Balint 1965; Bowlby 1969; Cannon 1942; Erikson 1963; Fairbairn 1952; Freud 1963; Kohut 1971; Lee and Noam 1983; Levine 1962; Mahler 1962; Scarf 1980; and Sullivan 1953). Even in comparison with the usual variables of social analysis, family factors reign supreme (Wilensky 1964). As Bowlby points out, personal autonomy requires trust, and even minor disappointments by significant others are often seen by a person as forms of betrayal (Weiss 1975).
2. Szasz (1965) asserts rightly that when autonomous beings interact, the exchange is equitable. This is true even if the transactions take complementary forms. In couples, roles are sequentially exchanged (Lederer and Jackson 1968). In betrayal, this flexibility is lost when the betrayer arrogates responsibility for action to himself, and assigns reaction to the

other, the victim, violating the quid pro quo of the relationship.

3. As Goffman (1972) points out, "It is probably impossible for interaction to continue among three persons for any length of time without collusion occurring, for the tacit betrayal of the third person is one of the main ways in which [they] express the specialness of their own relation to each other" (p. 339).

4. Allport (1937) points to the centrality of the self in trait organization. And Bachrach (1962) notes how a person's values change as a consequence of dissonance-reducing decisions. In fact, dissonance reduction and classical defense mechanisms are similar (see also Cantor and Kihlstrom 1981; Kuiper and Derry 1981; Mischel 1981; and Mead 1934).

5. The deadly effects of social stress are vividly portrayed in Cannon (1942). As Wallace asserts, "A relationship, a status and a way of being are lost when someone goes out of our lives. The . . . person lost also takes with him or her that part of our selves that they alone maintained—our self which was a son, our self which was a mother, our self which was a spouse" (p. 231).

    In suicide, as Everstine and Everstine (1983) indicate, "significant in accounts of the retrospective thoughts of widows . . . is that each woman was herself *diminished* by the suicidal death of her spouse" (p. 210). For men, one would expect that violation of expectancy involving work roles and career would generate the most stress. For women, on the other hand, it is personal betrayal because culturally, women build their lives around intimate relations: "[Woman] lives in a culture which provides no security for her except in a permanent "love" relationship . . . The neurotic need of love is a mechanism for establishing security . . . in a cultural situation producing dependency. Being loved not only is part of a woman's natural life . . . but it also becomes, of necessity, her profession" (Thompson 1964, p. 263).

    Research by Pearlin and Johnson (1977) attest to the importance of intimate relations for both sexes. Symptoms are inversely ranked in the order: married, never married, widowed, divorced, separated. In regression analysis, social isolation, economic strain, marital status times social isolation, and marital status times economic strain, were all significant at the .001 level (see also Horney 1934; Mahler 1962; Ramsay and Noorberger 1981; Scarf 1980; Schneider 1984; Weiss 1975; and Winnicott 1965).

6. See Note 4.

7. The quote is from Markus and Smith (1981, p. 244). A role is, as Sarbin (1954) indicated, a part/structure of the social self, with an internal organization that is subject to the constancy principle (see also Kelly 1955; and Sullivan 1940, 1953a).

8. Czichsentmihalyi (1976) studied creative people in different arenas (such as music, chess, mountain climbing and dancing) to ascertain what interested them about their vocations and what their experience of it was. All of them described "flow"—that point at which they are in complete harmony with what they are doing and the world—as lying exactly midway between feeling entirely bored with the activity because it is too easy and being terrified that they would fail, fall and lose it.

9. In order to be "double-binding" (Bateson et al. 1956, 1962; Weakland

1960), a message must contain three elements: (1) a statement paired with a primary negative injunction (e.g., a statement containing a threat of punishment for noncompliance); (2) a secondary injunction conflicting with the first at a more abstract level (say, a comment upon the first statement) and like the first, enforced by punishments or signals which threaten survival; (3) a third injunction prohibiting the victim from escaping the field, such as the implication that the perpetrator "loves" the victim (and therefore, the victim should somehow acquiesce to the previous two messages *and* be grateful). These three messages also represent conflicting logical types (see also Sluzki and Ransom 1974).

A person loses the ability to discriminate between logical types whenever (1) that person is involved in an intense relationship where it is crucial to make correct distinctions; (2) the other person is expressing two orders of message, one of which *denies* the other; and (3) the person is unable to *comment* upon the messages being sent in order to ascertain what order of message to respond to.

Betrayal is just such a situation in an expanded time frame. A typical set of messages might take the following form. The first message is from the past shared experience: I love and want only you; you're perfect. Moreover, I'm very needy (e.g., devote yourself to me or else!). The second message, in the present, constitutes a comment upon the first: I am leaving you because I "have to," since although I love you, I've realized I want something more than we could ever have, and I will give you up if necessary (e.g., I will "punish" you by withdrawing what love I have left). The third message, also in the present, is an implicit injunction against leaving the field: I still love you, even though I no longer wish to be intimate, and hope we can continue to be friends (if you do as I say).

The victim in this situation is not only bound by her affectional ties to the betrayer—whose unilateral action has preempted options she might have taken. She is also bound by his now contradictory comment upon the nature of *their* relationship, that it was lacking. And because the situation caught her unawares, she is still projecting their couplehood into the future, and still loving. He is, perhaps, loving, as he says, but is either "in love" with another, or not "in love" with *her*. His words, "I still love you," comprise an implicit, provocative demand that she remain bound in hopes of reconciliation with him while it simultaneously denies that possibility.

10. Definitions of an individual are "accorded" by society, and constitute the individual's "person." Corresponding to them are "acted" definitions, projected through social interpretations of the person's conduct. These assumptions constitute the individual's "self." Person and self are portraits of the same individual, the first encoded for the actions of others, the second in the actions of the subject himself (Goffman 1972, pp. 340-341). In general, when a rule of conduct is broken, as by the betrayal of deception, two individuals risk becoming discredited: one with an obligation, who should have governed himself by the rule; the other with an expectation, who should have been treated in a particular way because of this governance. Thus rules of conduct are fundamental to definitions of self and society (Goffman 1972, p. 343).

11. The behaviorist school views all varieties of inadequate responses to social stimuli ("neuroses") as learned habits undergirded by anxiety. Since anxiety is autonomic, it can only be unlearned through involving primitive subcortical levels, as by pairing deep relaxation with systematic desensitization to the stimuli causing difficulty. The betrayal situation is conceived as one of loss magnified by depression and obsession. In part the depression is a reaction created by the victim's learned helplessness (conditioned submissiveness) toward the betrayer. But associated with the loss are obsessive thoughts, evoked by memories of the past and forgone images of the future. In all of these, the inhibiting and synergistic effects of anxiety—about one's own self-worth, about one's options—may be operating either as a predominant agent or secondarily to the helplessness. Treatment is therefore directed to correcting the obsession and restoring the victim's interactional power.

12. Wolpe's systematic desensitization attacks the affect connected with the cognition of loss. Raimy attacks cognitions (misunderstandings of the self) as a more direct way of breaking these bonds.

13. A person's initial reaction to betrayal is one of shock, disorganization and often morbidity. There is denial, with searching, pining, despair, guilt, anxiety, jealousy, shame, protest and aggression. These conflicting emotions reflect the pain of letting go versus lingering hopes of reconciliation. Victims often lose the support of friends. In addition there may be no sanctioned social structures and processes to meliorate the loss because it is not "legitimate" or not seen as a loss by society.

14. Kegan (1983) has a six-stage model of self-in-balance-with-the-other. A person moves from incorporating to impulsive, to imperial, to interpersonal, to institutional and on to interindividual stages through life in a pattern continually "weaving" between individuation and integration. The first two years of life are not primary because the task of becoming one's self is lifelong; current interactions outweigh past object relations. (Analysts would assert their isomorphism.) And "separation anxiety" revolves more around the experience of transformation from one stage of development to another than from the loss of objects. Fourth, he sees the overwhelming motive for a person's action as *subsuming* both cognition and affect in the task of figuring out how to create a *coherent* self. Fifth he decries the "masculine" emphasis on differentiation being favored with the language of growth and development, while the "feminine" emphasis on integration is spoken of in terms of dependency and immaturity. In fact, there is a continual oscillation between the two throughout life.

   Factors influencing vulnerability of the victim include these: sustained a loss before age 10, lacks resources or friendships, lacks a solid sense of identity or meaning in life (as when one has lost a job or role), has had multiple losses within a short span of time, or suffers a loss while undergoing stress from other causes. Change and conflict represent additional stressors: there is a cumulative effect over 1 to 2 years on cancer morbidity, and loss is more difficult to adjust to when it is unexpected. Among other factors influencing adjustment is isolation—simply the deprivation of intimate touch is hurtful.

   In losing the predictability of one's everyday life, victims beat a strategic retreat and become hypervigilant. Additionally, they lose their intimate predictability (sense of self); they have trouble orienting themselves and doubt their past abilities can carry them through.

15. Overdetermined items are always systematically related. A child who loses first his mother and then the nursemaid upon whom he came to depend in his mother's absence, identifies with both partners of a lost relationship; he is the nurse and he is the baby whom she likes to tend. In mourning we become the lost person *and* we become again the person we were when the relationship was at its prime. This makes for much seemingly contradictory symptomatology. Perhaps taking the role of the other helps us conduct an "inner conversation" to integrate our loss as it creates a new self in the process (Erikson 1963, p. 58).

16. Erikson (1963) believes that females suffer particular trauma from loss. "The fear of remaining empty (oral) or of being emptied (anal) has a special quality in a girl, since her body image (even before she 'knows' her inner anatomic arrangements) includes a valuable inside on which depends her fulfillment as an organism, a person, and as a role bearer. This fear of being left empty, and more simply, that of being left, seems to be the most basic feminine fear, extending over the whole of a woman's existence (p. 410). Taking this position further, Dowling believes that cultural training results, in girls, in the development of excessive "affiliative needs," by which is meant the need to experience relationship above all else. I would instead affirm the importance of balancing the affiliative needs within both gender roles as a way of lessening the stress in society wrought by the battles of the sexes over the primacy of love or work.

17. The MRI group (Bateson, Jackson, Watzlawick, Weakland and Fisch) asserts that people bring to therapists those problems that they have mishandled and are continuing to mishandle through their own and their intimates' behavior. Therapy helps them to change or eliminate it, thereby resolving the problem. And the behaviorist Wolpe notes that depression seems to arise only when victims' conditioned submissiveness leads to their domination. The victim becomes unable to handle the other effectively because of habituated anxiety to the thought of self-assertiveness, or to how other might respond. This is like the double-bind situation, and there are strong cultural aspects of such conditioning for women.

18. Regarding loss in women, Marguerite Duras, in *The War*, writes of the interplay between fidelity, memory and obsession in the lives of women. She says that the power of our obsessions vastly supersedes our fidelity to the remembered object of our obsessions. Her characteristic heroine is driven to neurosis by her obsessive memory of a lost love (usually a feckless, inconsequential man) who might return to offer her some form of liberation, and for whom she is willing to wait indefinitely. One recalls *Hiroshima Mon Amour, The Ravishing of Loi Stein, 10:30 on a Summer Night, Moderato Contabile, The Sailor from Gibraltar* and *The Lover,* whose motif of love unto death pertains equally to the male protagonist. Her women identify so totally with the male object of their obsessions that their loyalty is ultimately a form of fidelity to the self. Their fixations far transcend any erotic longing, are almost mystical in their irrationality and fervor. And their hallucinatory, faithful waiting embodies the author's ambiguous feminist vision of woman as both pas-

sive victim and active redeemer, woman as sanctuary of mythic memory and principal interpreter of human suffering.
19. In Kegan's schema, betrayal represents the limits of self-development of stage 2 attainment, the "Imperial/I." One who functions at this level can understand how his victim might feel about being betrayed. But how the victim feels is simply not part of the source of his meaning-making (1983, p. 285).

REFERENCES

Allport, G. *Personality, A Psychological Interpretation.* New York: Holt, 1937.

Bachrach, A.J. In Conclusion. In A. J. Bachrach, ed., *Experimental Foundations of Clinical Psychology.* New York: Basic Books, 1962.

Balint, M. *Primary Love and Psycho-Analytic Technique.* New York: Liveright, 1965.

Bateson, G. *Steps to an Ecology of Mind.* New York: Ballantine Books, 1972.

Bowlby, J. *Attachment and Loss* (Vols. 1 and 2). New York: Basic Books, 1969.

Cannon, W.B. Voodoo death. *Am. Anthropologist* 44:169-181, 1942.

Cantor, N., and J.F. Kihlstrom, eds. *Personality, Cognition, and Social Interaction.* Hillsdale, NJ: Lawrence Erlbaum Associates, 1981.

Czicsentmihalyi, O. *Between Boredom and Anxiety.* New York: Basic Books, 1976.

Erikson, E.H. *Childhood and Society,* 2nd Ed. New York: W.W. Norton, 1963.

Fairbairn, W.R.D. *An Object Relations Theory of the Personality.* New York: Basic Books, 1952.

Everstine, D.S., and L. Everstine. *People in Crisis. Strategic Therapeutic Interventions.* New York: Brunner/Mazel, 1983.

Fisch, R., J.H. Weakland, and L. Segal. *The Tactics of Change: Doing Therapy Briefly.* San Francisco: Jossey-Bass, 1983.

Freud, S. *General Psychological Theory: Papers on Metapsychology.* New York: Collier Books, 1963.

Goffman, E. *Relations in Public.* New York: Harper/Colophon, 1972.

Greenberg, J.R., and S.A. Mitchell. *Object Relations in Psychoanalytic Theory.* Cambridge, MA: Harvard University Press, 1983.

Horney, K. The overvaluation of love: a study of a common present-day feminine type. *Psychoanal. Q.* 3: 1934.

Kantor, D., and M.I. Vickers. Divorce Along the Family Life Cycle. In J.C. Hansen and H.A. Liddle, eds., *Clinical Implications of the Family Life Cycle.* Rockville, MD: Aspen Publications, 1983.

Kegan, R. A Neo-Piagetian Approach to Object Relations. In B. Lee and G. Noam, eds., *Developmental Approaches to the Self.* New York: Plenum, 1983.

Kelly, G.A. *The Psychology of Personal Constructs* (Vols. 1 and 2). New York: W.W. Norton, 1955.

Kohut, H. *The Analysis of the Self.* New York: International Universities Press, 1971.

Kuiper, N.A., and P.A. Derry. The Self as a Cognitive Prototype: An Application to Person Perception and Depression. In N. Cantor and J.F. Kihlstrom, eds., *Personality, Cognition, and Social Interaction.* Hillsdale, NJ: Lawrence Erlbaum Associates, 1981.

Lederer, W.J., and D.D. Jackson. Reciprocal Behavior. In W.J. Lederer and D.D. Jackson, eds., *The Mirages of Marriage*. New York: W.W. Norton, 1968.

Lee, B., and G.G. Noam, eds. *Developmental Approaches to the Self*. New York: Plenum, 1983.

Levine, S. The Effects of Infantile Experience on Adult Behavior. In A.J. Bachrach, ed., *Experimental Foundations of Clinical Psychology*. New York: Basic Books, 1962.

Lingis, A.F. Sense and non-sense in the sexed body. *Cultural Hermeneutics* (4)4:345-365, 1977.

Marx, K. The German Ideology. In R.C. Tucker, ed., *The Marx-Engels Reader*. New York: W.W. Norton, 1972.

Mahler, M.S. On the Significance of the Normal Separation-Individuation Phase: With Reference to Research in Symbiotic Child Psychosis. In M. Schur, ed., *Drives, Affects, Behavior*, Vol. 2. New York: International Universities Press, 1962.

Marcus, H., and J. Smith. The Influence of Self-Schemata on the Perception of Others. In N. Cantor and J.F. Kihlstrom, eds., *Personality, Cognition, and Social Interaction*. Hillsdale, NJ: Lawrence Erlbaum Associates, 1981.

Mead, G.H. *Mind, Self and Society*. Chicago, University of Chicago Press, 1934.

Mischel, W. Personality and Cognition: Something Borrowed, Something New? In N. Cantor and J.F. Kihlstrom, eds., *Personality, Cognition, and Social Interaction*. Hillsdale, NJ: Lawrence Erlbaum Associates, 1981.

Odier, C. *Anxiety and Magical Thinking*. (Tr. by Marie-Louise Schoelly and Mary Jane Sherfey.) New York: International Universities Press, 1956.

Pearlin, L.I., and J.S. Johnson. Marital status, life strains and depression. *Am. Sociol. Rev.* (42)5:704-715, 1977.

Piaget, J. Relations Between Affectivity and Intelligence in the Mental Development of the Child. In *Sorbonne Courses*. Paris: University Documentation Center, 1964.

Pine, F. On the Development of the "Borderline Child-to-Be." *Am. J. Orthopsychiatry* 56(3):450-457, 1986.

Prigogine, I. *From Being to Becoming*. San Francisco: W.H. Freeman, 1980.

Ramsay, D.W., and R. Noorberger. *Living with Loss*. New York: William Morrow, 1981.

Sarbin, T.R. Role Theory. In G. Lindzey, ed., *Handbook of Social Psychology*. Cambridge, MA: Addison-Wesley, 1954.

Scarf, M. *Unfinished Business*. New York: Doubleday, 1980.

Schneider, J. *Stress, Loss, and Grief*. Baltimore: University Park Press, 1984.

Simmel, G. *Conflict and the Web of Group Affiliations*. (Tr. by Kurt Wolff.) Glencoe, IL: Free Press, 1955.

Sluzki, C.E., and D.C. Ransom. *Double Bind: The Foundation of the Communicational Approach to the Family*. New York: Grune & Stratton, 1974.

Stern, D. *The Interpersonal World of the Infant*. New York: Basic Books, 1985.

Sullivan, H.S. *The Interpersonal Theory of Psychiatry*. New York: W.W. Norton, 1953a.

_____. *Conceptions of Modern Psychiatry*. New York: W.W. Norton, 1953b.

Szasz, T.S. *The Ethics of Psychoanalysis*. New York: Basic Books, 1974.
Thompson, C.M. *On Women*. New York: Basic Books, 1964.
Watzlawick, P., J.H. Weakland, and R. Fisch. *Change: Principles of Problem Formation and Problem Resolution*. New York: W.W. Norton, 1974.
Watzlawick, P. *The Language of Change*. New York: Basic Books, 1978.
Weiss, R.S. *Marital Separation*. New York: Basic Books, 1975.
Wilensky, H. Mass society and mass culture: interdependence or independence? *Am. Sociol. Rev.* 29:173-197, 1964.
Winnicott, D.W. *The Maturational Process and the Facilitating Environment*. New York: International Universities Press, 1965.

15

Divorce and the Dissolution of "Love as Oneness"

Juerg Willi, MD

THE PROBLEM

Just as no life is without pleasure, so, too, is no life without some pain. The vicissitudes of daily living affect us all, forcing us to recognize our vulnerabilities and oftentimes to make distressing adaptations that we never foresaw and that lead to our having to readjust our self-assessment. We find ourselves not as strong as we thought, not as brave, more "irrational" than we hoped to be, and less attractive, less intelligent, or less good-natured; the list of possibilities is endless. At the same time, these encounters inform us of resources we may not have realized we possessed. Life becomes a progression through various challenges, some of which we will surmount, and others of which will defeat us.

In the same way, every marriage progresses through periodic crises specific to each stage of its growth; hence conflict at these points can be expected. Is there a way for the helping professional to distinguish between conflicts that are irremediable and those which are not? Can one know when divorce is an appropriate solution to a marital problem and when it is not?

This chapter examines the issue by looking at the potential for working with couples involved in relationships of a kind increasingly seen in today's society of statesmanship by show and presidency by performer in a "culture of narcissism."[1] These relationships are those obtaining between narcissists and their partners. And the framework of "collusion" offers a guide to working with such couples. By

---

This chapter was edited for publication by Adrian R. Tiemann.

identifying the kinds of transactions occurring between them, it suggests when, where and how intervention is likely to help, or when it is futile. In order to develop this concept further, let us first look at relationships in general.

THE REQUIREMENTS OF NORMAL RELATIONSHIPS

Each person has needs that are often hard enough to meet in ordinary life. When two people form a relationship, the difficulties each faces are multiplied, for there are now two separate identities as well as a third, that of the couple as a unit, whose needs must be met.[2] Healthy relationships require each partner to feel at ease in assuming progressive (independent, assertive) and regressive (dependent, passive) roles vis-à-vis the other depending upon circumstances. The health of every human being requires the free interplay of progressive and regressive fantasies and conflicts. This flexibility indexes a person's *intrapsychic balance.* When interacting with others, a flexible person is able to act freely without arousing unmanageable unconscious conflicts about being strong or weak that then tend to promote a negative self-image.

For example, all of us have times when we need to be cared for by someone, abandoning ourselves to dependence without feeling guilty or ashamed about it. On the other hand, we just as fiercely desire recognition of our autonomy—again, without disparaging ourselves for enjoying confirmation.

In addition to the *intrapsychic* balance in which marital behavior is determined by each person's inner dynamics, there is the *dyadic* balance in which the marital relationship is determined by the interaction between the partners.

Again, the same principles apply. If the couple as a system can exchange roles and support each other in doing so, then they will have greater flexibility in dealing with external challenge than will a more rigid system. They will be able to exchange complementary roles as needed: the more active the one is, the more passive the other; the more selfish the one is, the more altruistic the other. At income tax time, A, the accountant wife, will take the lead, while B, her artist husband, follows, even if he is usually the more "dominant."

Note that each partner sets the limits on what the other can do: A can lead only so far as B will follow, and B can only follow so long as A is willing to lead. A can give only so much as B will take and B can take no more than A gives him. The couple comprise a structure that must function as a unit. They do so by adjusting their behaviors homeostatically to each other to balance extreme deviations. When A is despondent, B is determined; when B is upset, A is soothing.

Finally, the couple, again as a unit, are open to the environment without being permeated by it, and are flexible in altering that boundary as necessary. In this way they can meet the external conditions they face as a couple. For instance, as neighborhood residents, the couple may take the lead (vis-à-vis the community) in promoting a tree-planting effort. But when their home is ravaged by fire, they are able to open themselves to their neighbors and work through the loss as well as to accept help.

MARITAL DIFFICULTIES AND
THE CONCEPT OF COLLUSION

Lack of flexibility in these ways promotes conflict and indexes difficulties in the marital relationship. The conflict then degenerates into a destructive (because it is irrational) search for solutions. Such failure usually derives from conflicts each has left unresolved from childhood that may have drawn them to each other in the first place. Under this stress, then, a normal stage of their maturing as a couple becomes paralyzed, inhibiting the individual development of both partners. Neither can be objective in evaluating and resolving their differences. Fighting becomes a formalized ritual that bars both solution and escape from the trap. They become rigidly committed to certain roles in their relationship.

This rigidity usually encompasses one of four basic themes that form the basis for the concept of "patterns of collusion." What makes it collusive is that roles are chosen for irrational reasons originating in unresolved traumatic childhood experiences. Moreover, the choice does not lead to a free interplay between the partners but, instead, forces each into the role that the other needs.

The four main themes (and their related roles) around which relational conflict typically arise are (1) narcissistic, (2) oral, (3) anal-sadistic and (4) phallic-oedipal, derived from the childhood developmental stages posited by psychoanalysis. This chapter focuses on narcissistic relationships by exploring their genesis, relational "styles" and typical patterns of collusion.[3]

On the positive side, since the unrealized personal potential of each partner fuels the fascination they hold for each other, it motivates them to adjust to each other in developing the common self of the couple. It also motivates them to solve their problems in realistic ways, aware that there are no simple solutions other than cooperating in the process of maturing and enduring the long search for a way out of the crises.

The Couple's Unconscious and the Various Balances

The easy interplay of progressive and regressive roles between partners depends not only upon their flexibility, but also on their willingness to compensate for each other behaviorally. Such willingness is
self-motivated: the active partner is drawn to behave in this way, just
as the passive partner seeks someone to recognize and assume
responsibility for playing the active role. Each feels not only that his
behavior is needed by the partner, but also that there is no pressure
on him to assume the opposite role that he dreads, since the partner is
already motivated to assume this role. Psychodynamics describes
this process in terms of *projection*.[4]

For instance, if A uses defensive passivity to protect himself, then
B must assume protective activity in order for the couple to maintain
a stable relationship. Their dyadic balance then reinforces the intrapsychic balances of both since A embodies the regressive passivity
that B tries to repress in herself. Projections do not occur in a vacuum;
B seeks out her partner's projections for her own use since A's social
behavior corresponds to B's repressed potential.

From Common Unconscious and Balance to Conflict

Marriage is a mutual endeavor binding partners together in obvious
ways and at deep levels. When people fall in love, each modifies his or
her self to unite with that of the partner in creating a harmonious
mutual self. Partners also find in their mates a substitute for their
own repressed potential. As long as both partners feel committed to
the couple as a unit, they find it interesting to act as extensions of
each other.

But this sharing of images and unconscious fantasies creates as
much basis for mutual attraction and passionate attachment as it
does for conflict within the couple. Under the routine of everyday life
they increasingly differentiate from each other through their roles.
As each retreats to the self, hitherto submerged parts of the self
spring to life and undermine the stability of the couple. Their connectedness then becomes very restricting while the couple-self loses
value. The larger the behavioral territory one partner seizes for use
while the other shares it in fantasy only, the greater the threat to the
relationship on both dyadic and intrapsychic levels. In this way the
shared unconscious agreement lying at the core of the couple's relationship may become the basis for collusion.

For example, the active wife may force her mate into a dependent
role without allowing him that regressive satisfaction which she
denies her self. As he increasingly delegates initiative because he is

unwilling to take responsibility, he comes to despise her progressive-
ness because being dependent makes him feel weak. Indeed, he may
go so far as to undermine all her efforts. Even so, he despises himself
for it, knowing that it promotes the cycle. In turn, the wife, while
critical of his passivity, cannot accept his desire for independence. In
thus limiting her husband she has frustrated herself because her
leadership is not fully recognized.

The problem can only be solved when the husband assumes
responsibility for himself and the wife admits the falseness of her
strength and enterprise. But this extremely difficult task destroys
the vicarious transference which once made marriage seem so attractive to them both.

In the collusive relationship, then, one or both of the partners
clutch tightly to the mutual self while struggling to reinforce the
original contract by keeping the partner bound to a set of complementary reactions. Collusion arises when one or both partners refuse to
change this pattern. At the same time, the emphasis on their own role
defends against the disowned aspects of their own personality.[5]

The fundamental conflict, therefore, lies in each partner's reluc-
tance to confront repressed aspects of self, whether their own or the
partner's. Such refusal creates guilt which, projected onto the other,
makes them appear responsible for one's own failure: "I am how I am
because you are like you are. If you were different, I would be, too."
Characteristic of collusion is an implicit agreement between the partners concerning their mutual disinterest in the unconscious. Accusa-
tions from both sides are merely rituals; any real attempt to alter the
partners' collusive roles and involve them in their own repressed
shares of the conflict is immediately undermined.

Collusive Stalemate

As times passes, collusion further entraps the couple, binding them to
their original fears with little chance of escape. Far from fulfilling all
infantile needs, marriage brings a partner more frustration than
anyone else. An observer would marvel that rational people could
hurt and victimize each other so incessantly, oblivious to the futility
of their attacks. Why can't the wife be a little more tolerant and
flexible, and allow her husband to go out by himself once in a while
without interrogating him afterwards? Is this too much to ask?

The trivialities that are fought over usually show a rigidity arising from countless past frustrations that make all changes in behavior appear doomed. Inflexibility in trivial conflicts attests to the
partner's inhibited interaction and betrays the unconscious

dynamics of the dyad. A husband who refuses to bring his wife flowers assumes that if he did so and failed to come up with caramels the next day, his wife might say, "You don't love me anymore." Thus, in reality the cause does not lie in the trivia.

THE "LOVE AS ONENESS" PATTERN

The *narcissistic relationship* centers on the question: How much must I sacrifice myself for my partner, and how much can I be myself? How far can we set limits for each other, and to what degree can we become one with each other? How much should my partner live for me and confirm my self-concept, and to what extent can I assume a better self under my partner's influence?

The problem posed by the narcissistic theme is finding a solution acceptable to both partners. Its existence signifies the workings of unresolved conflicts, sabotaging their efforts at accommodation. As is true of our relations throughout life, the child must negotiate the problem of relating to its parents in terms of "love as oneness." If this conflict cannot be acceptably resolved but remains linked with feelings of fear, shame and guilt, it is understandable that in adulthood the quest would continue in marriage.

Unfortunately, this hope is rarely met since narcissists encounter conflicts in the partner-relationship that correspond to those that earlier blocked them in relating to the parents. Both partners get caught in a paralyzing fixation, and growth is stifled.

NARCISSISTIC DEVELOPMENT PATTERNS

Concerning the development of self in relation to others, Freud distinguished two forms of narcissism. *Primary* narcissism corresponds to the first months of life when the child confuses himself with his surroundings. Adults with a primary narcissistic disturbance lack a sense of basic security, have an extremely fragile self, and usually become psychotic. Interpersonally, they find it difficult to differentiate between their own self and that of the other. In their fantasies they see themselves as grandiose and omnipotent.

Secondary narcissism arises when previously established relationships (as with parents and siblings) are given up because they are alien and frustrating. Investment in others is then put aside because it is too painful and one's energies become totally directed toward the self. As adults such people are insecure and easily wounded, and strongly dependent upon the confirmation of others.

From these two basic developmental paths arise two types of narcissistic characters: the schizoid narcissists, who have a primary narcissistic disturbance, and phallic-exhibitionist narcissists, who suffer from secondary narcissistic disturbance.

Mother-Child Experiences of the Narcissist

Narcissists derive from a family matrix of disavowal. Either their mothers barely recognized their existence, or they failed to perceive them as separate beings.

In the first case, the child's existence was basically ignored. They rarely had a stable relationship in which their worth and feelings were valued, in which somebody sincerely cared for them. Never having had anyone take *their* feelings into account, they failed to learn how to empathize with *others'* feelings and hence developed a feeble moral capacity. To compensate for this lack, they withdraw into a world of wish-fulfillment and fantasy belonging only to them. Never having been avowed, they too deny the reality of the partner as someone of independent initiative by merely giving them a script from their fantasy world.

In the second case, the symbiotic relationship is breached when the child begins to develop physically, act on his own, and seek separation. This angers the mother, who reacts to prevent the child from experiencing himself as a separate being. Her language reflects this: "We slept late this morning and wouldn't go to school, would we?" One strategy is to assign characteristics to the child that correspond to *her* ideal, believing that *she* knows what he should think and how he should feel. Any deviation from *her* image will be punished. The child is then forced into the paradox: "I am only myself when I am the image my mother creates. When I am how *I* feel, I am not myself."

When attempts to establish an identity are disparaged, the development of autonomy is precluded. Without being able to exercise responsibility, to acquire and test his own ethical standard, the child cannot develop a mature superego. Such personalities are consequently characterized by self-doubt, vague ego-boundaries, and inferiority complexes. Values and standards are felt as impositions. Moreover, because this child may be the mother's prized possession, he or she must fulfill the mother's dreams. This makes separation from her extremely difficult. Magically imbued, she is an invisible worker, omnipotent and omnipresent, the giver of life of whom one can never be rid. Love comes to be seen as a tactic of exploitation and manipulation.

Hence the child becomes deeply disillusioned with "love," rejecting any form of it, and as a narcissist sees intimate, enduring relationships as very dangerous. Although the partner may not act like the withdrawn or narcissistic mother, he will be experienced as someone wanting to manipulate for his own ends or to shape his partner as an extension of himself.

The end result is that both profiles produce the same narcissistic disturbances in partner relationships: the over-idealized prince or princess is no more "real" than the disavowed child.

The Schizoid Narcissist Character

Schizoid narcissists (SNs) are socially inhibited and empathetic. They do not impose themselves upon the environment, but are introverted and wait quietly for others to discover their worth. They have the ability to create a feeling of happiness, of primal unity. Their modesty and reserve impress companions, and SNs are often extraordinarily perceptive, rapidly becoming trusted confidants. Their companions tend to idealize them, feeling an inner oceanic understanding with SNs that transcends normal discourse.

In this idealized harmony, much is left unsaid. In his impression of union, the narcissist assumes that the other agrees with all his feelings, endeavors and fantasies, and is often surprised and hurt when the therapist, for example, asks questions. He feels alienated if the therapist does not know everything about him already since he is in constant internal dialogue with the therapist.

The therapist then faces a dilemma: either to dispute such "knowledge" and destroy the only fragile relationship possible with the narcissist—idealized symbiosis—or accept the assumption, be idealized as omniscient and leave the patient's intimations in doubt.

While therapists can bear such uncertainty, love partners cannot. They demand the clarity that the narcissist wants to avoid. The narcissist must always have an exit available. Consequently, the partner does not feel confirmed as a separate being, but only as the narcissist's fantasy of her. Neither partner can express demands to the other. This undemonstrativeness so attenuates the relationship that it becomes sterile and leaves the partners doubting that it actually still exists.

The Phallic-Exhibitionist Narcissist Character

The social relations of *phallic-exhibitionist narcissists* (PENs) are geared toward raising their self-worth. Men of this type gravitate to the business world where the prevailing ideology confirms their personality structure—dynamic, ruthless, selfish and successful.

Females of this character are generally found in the performing arts.

PENs have a way of immediately letting others know how remarkable they are: a fantastic sports car, a yacht with an indoor swimming pool, or an eccentric hobby. Inquiries about their companion's attributes are made only to establish their hopelessly inferior status. Should the latter be an unusual and interesting person, he or she will be appropriated like a jewel. PENs like to hear that you are a really crazy guy or a revolutionary, a pervert or a genius. At the next party they can say, "Do you know my friend Bill, the famous so-and-so, he's really a weird guy . . . ." Generally, however, you are assigned the role of astonished listener dazzled by their talents, or of critic questioning their boasts and opposing them.

This example sums up the structure of the relationship. While PENs need social contact because they depend on the admiration of others, their friends are generally insignificant as individuals. Their role is only to mirror the PEN's brilliance. If friends reject this structure, signifying their autonomy, the relationship loses its basis and they cease to exist. Similarly, PENs can only accept a partner as a "narcissistic object," an extension of their own self heightening their self-esteem.

Basically, narcissists long for a primal existence of fusion between self and other. Since this is now impossible, they idealize their partners—accepting only those aspects of the partner that accord with their imagination and expectations. In this illusion they *feel* united; after all, it is *their* projection to which they are responding. When this illusion is shattered, as it must be in daily life, they react with anger to the discrepancy.

Narcissists divide people into black and white, friends and enemies. Perpetually disappointed in their hope for total harmony with the other, they become resigned and cynical, and fantasize retribution. Deeply mistrustful, they believe neither in love nor in any values in general, and dare not embrace their deeper feelings as these contain only the danger of more deception. Often they suffer from feelings of emptiness and meaninglessness. Recurrent depressions are avoided through hypomanic activity or concealed behind constant theatrical and social exertion.

Narcissists are intelligent social critics or cynical satirists, totally unshockable because they have nothing to lose, having lost it all long ago. In their bitterness they seek to destroy others' illusions of goodness, idealism and nobility. The discrepancy between their verbal nihilism and reticent longing for tenderness has a strong effect on persons relating to them, who would like to restore their faith in love, envelop them in utter comprehension and support them in their frailty.

As direct and uncompromising as the narcissist is in critiquing others, he himself reacts oversensitively to every criticism or refusal to admire and idealize him. If a companion does not support him unconditionally, he or she is blacklisted and dropped, and the break is radical and absolute. The narcissist's motto is "Either for me or against me." Because he cannot conceive of an honest difference of opinion, he will do nothing to bring about reconciliation.

The narcissist's radical methods, his resolute stance and fearless struggle against enemies is experienced by many as strength and independence. The narcissist is a leader whom they can idolize and follow, for whom sacrifice is meaningful. Throughout history, entire nations have become victims of narcissistic leaders.

The Complementary Narcissist Partner

In intimate relationships, the narcissist faces a dilemma and a paradox. Believing that love requires sacrifice (of oneself for the partner or vice versa), differences of opinion are seen as inevitably jeopardizing the love bond. An intense love relationship should be a fusion with the other in perfect harmony. The narcissist hopes to find a partner who, making no demands of her own, will adore and idealize him.

But such fusion poses a terrible threat for someone so insecure. He feels overwhelmed and engulfed by a stable relationship with a partner and is terrified that his fragile ego-boundaries will be penetrated. As a consequence, many narcissists remain single or fail if they do marry.

The complementary narcissist provides a way out of this dilemma because her narcissism works in reverse. This seeming difference masks her own grandiosity, lack of autonomy and weakness in self-esteem. While he seeks admiration, she seeks sacrifice; while he dreads engulfment, she seeks merger. He elevates himself through her adoration as she basks in the reflected glory of identifying with and appropriating an idealized self from the partner.

The Narcissistic Marriage

The narcissist dreads marriage. He prefers life with someone where his freedom to exit is maintained and delays marriage as long as possible until, under pressure from the partner or circumstances, he finally agrees. If married, he often prefers to remain childless, fearing that a child would take advantage of him.

The narcissist maintains sovereignty by choosing someone who will make no demands upon him. She may be inferior in character or in intelligence, much older or younger, or have some other characteristic that prevents her from being judged on an equal basis. The narcissist experiences the adulation of the complementary partner as self-development and can feel grandiose. No threat of loss of self, engulfment or false definition of self exists for him because the partner idealizes him and sacrifices herself for him.

The complementary narcissist interprets these expectations in light of her own weak self-image: seeking growth through adoration of the narcissist, she finds an idealized substitute for her self through projecting an idealized image upon him with which she identifies. Her feelings of inferiority are at last ended as the narcissist will now fulfil these demands in her place.

Both feel sure of their defenses. The narcissists say to each other: "I can be so grandiose because of *you* —Because I adore you so effusively—You adore me because I am so grandiose—because you are so grandiose for *me*."

Narcissistic Couple Conflict

While only a very diluted relationship would be possible for the narcissist, the complementary narcissist will tolerate only an ideal and refuses all compromises in a relationship. In each case, partners are repressing and projecting onto each other what they seek for themselves.

But as the couple spends more time together the confidence and freedom of the narcissist begins to prove false for his subordinate partner. Since the complementary partner can live only through empathy with the narcissist, she lives out every fantasy through him. She merges with him and exercises control over him paradoxically by forfeiting her own image. In the end it is no longer clear whose self-worth is being enhanced and who is borrowing a self-image from whom.

In sacrificing herself for him, the complementary partner claims the self of the narcissist and confines him to her idealized image of him. Since he thrives on admiration, he succumbs to this projection, too late feeling the sting in its sweetness.

As the relationship increasingly comes to resemble that which the narcissist had with his mother, he becomes terrified. The complementary partner's idealization, once a source of prestige, becomes his prison as it buries his demand for autonomy. In revolt, he seeks to destroy the partner for getting so close to him. He becomes petty, ruthless and cold. He cannot free himself because she lives and breathes the ideal he wants to be. But all is to no avail; his cruelty is interpreted as his false self. "I know you too well. Deep down you really don't mean it." Now the narcissist is lost; withdrawal from the partner requires divorce, or a crime repaid by years in prison, or mental illness—but nothing will change. She will continue to live for him in almost magical ways, regarding the separation as a temporary break before their ultimate reunion.

The complementary narcissist is also truly desperate. Having sacrificed herself completely for this relationship, she has lived only for her partner. She trusted him completely and now feels cheated out of her deepest dreams: "I loved you so much! Nothing has any meaning for me without you, and now you have betrayed me." The vicious circle now becomes: "I am so malicious and ruthless because you trap me and fence me in," and she replies: "I trap you and fence you in because you are so malicious and ruthless."

By definition, the complementary narcissist must protect the embodiment of her ideal self in the partner. No disappointments can modify her expectations for she never let herself see and accept him as he really is. Like his mother, she created in him the self *she* wanted to be.

The linkage between partner choice and conflict becomes more evident as time passes. The partners live together in cold disillusionment, each hewing to their own interests and having their own lovers. They seem to remain together only for the children's sake or for material advantage. However, beneath the icy facade wild passions seethe. Each watches and controls the other in all their thoughts and actions. Studied indifference is one desperate defense against overwhelming intimacy.

Another is divorce. Although it may separate the narcissistic couple, their collusion remains until they have each worked through the loss. If the departing spouse is the narcissist, he can cut himself off from his feelings most easily by starting a new relationship. This enables him to assign to the old partner all that negativity, stupidity and insensitivity from which he sought to free himself.

The complementary partner often attenuates the pain of the loss by continuing to remain faithful to the departed partner, even if they never see each other again, fantasizing that she is indispensable to him and that no one can ever know him as she did.

On the other hand, desertion by the complementary partner creates a severe crisis for the narcissist, for without the ego-inflation of mirroring, his self collapses like an emptied balloon.

Divorce and the Resolution of Collusion

Basically, narcissistic collusion represents an escalating alternation of extreme positions taken by the two partners. In this feedback loop the more extreme their behaviors become, the more persistent will be parallel unconscious fantasies. The more these fantasies are repressed, the more extreme the behaviors, and so on. Each person becomes trapped into greater and greater rigidity by the other. Clashes will continue as long as the progressive narcissist is unwilling to support or acknowledge his partner's individuality, or as long as the regressive narcissist refuses to be responsible for her own development.

THERAPY OF COLLUSIVE PAIRINGS

The fundamental conflict lies in both partners' unwillingness to confront repressed layers of the personality. This refusal creates a sense of guilt which, projected upon the other, makes *them* appear responsible for one's own failure. The other's actions become an alibi for the one's own poor performance.

Characteristically, neither is interested in the unconscious, and any attempt to alter the collusion and involve them in their own repressed share of the conflict is immediately undermined. They will lapse into renewed collusion through stronger attachment to each other—or withdraw, both going their own ways.

The following section presents a synopsis of a couples therapy in which the idea of divorce paradoxically permitted a narcissistic couple to come together as best they could. Over a 13-month period, Heidi and Andy (H and A) were seen by the therapist (T) in 31 sessions. They were a couple in their early thirties, married seven years with two sons, aged six and two. The problem they identified was their being stuck in a pattern in which Heidi responded to threat with overblown behavior: too big, too loud, too strong. Andy, quieter and more reserved, withdrew from her at these times, increasing her unease, and ultimately devastating quarrels broke out.

H: (to A) When I get very aggressive, you simply withdraw. You've always done that. I used to think: "He's a kind father, calm and benevolent." I always admired him for that, but he really wasn't being tolerant at all. He just didn't say anything about it. So we got further and further apart.

T: How do you feel when he shouts?

H: Then I'm glad! Then I have something to hold on to.

T: How do you feel when you get so aggressive?

H: I'd feel better if I felt some resistance.

T: You can't feel any limits?

H: Yes, I'm very emotional.

In this couple, Heidi represents emotion and wants Andy to serve as a sort of vessel into which she can pour herself and by which she can feel herself limited and contained. Andy, on the other hand, sits as if he were curled up inside himself, his arms folded. When he feels attacked by Heidi, he places his hand protectively on the cheek turned toward her, and often glances at her suspiciously, from the side.

T: (to A) How did you two meet?

A: We met at a ski party. Already that first evening I wanted to be alone with her. Strangely enough, what attracted me to her was the same thing that bothers me now: her way of dominating everything, of being the center of everything, having everybody admire her.

T: (to H) Do you remember your first impression of Andy?

H: I liked you, but I don't know how I felt. It wasn't clear to me for a long time.

A: I think I liked you.

T: (to H) You felt accepted by him?

H: For me that's a basic requirement, even the crucial thing.

The precondition of a relationship for Heidi is that she feel admired and accepted. In the beginning, Andy fully met this condition, but now his lack of response signifies rejection to her. In this typical reversal of attitude, the qualities that first drew the couple together are now driving them apart. At first each felt the other made up for his own deficiencies. But then Heidi's trust in Andy as an ideal father figure was destroyed by the necessity of an abortion brought on by his "carelessness." This required Heidi to invest more in the relationship than Andy, forcing him into the position of debtor.

T: How did it happen that you went on to get married anyway?

A: It was more or less that once people are engaged they ought to get married. I was afraid of it, but I thought, "This feeling won't last; it can't get any worse."

H: Naturally, that made me furious when it came out. I was
        under the illusion that he was marrying me because he loved
        me. I felt intuitively he was the partner for me. I had a com-
        pletely false image of Andy then. I thought he accepted me so
        completely because he never said anything.

T: (To A) Is that the way you see it too?

A: Not exactly. After things changed—it didn't happen
        overnight—it bothered me. When I said something she didn't
        like, critical or not, she got so aggressive I preferred to say
        nothing at all. And then I just closed off and shut things off.

T: Why was it that the very qualities that had attracted you at
        first annoyed you later on?

A: I don't know whether they really did attract me. One factor
        definitely was that everyone admired her so much and I was
        the one who got her. Whenever I thought that she wasn't
        seeing me as I am, I didn't say anything so that I wouldn't
        destroy the image she had of me.

T: Would you have liked to be a calm, peaceful man?

A: Yes, I think everyone would like that.

When Heidi asks Andy why he married her, his reaction is evasive:
he only did so because he was afraid to withdraw his proposal. This
remark strikes at Heidi's most vulnerable spot, his acceptance of her.
There is a clear intermeshing of their behavior: Heidi's insistent
questions lead Andy to return evasive and hurtful answers. His withdrawal leads her to even greater emotionality than is natural to her.
The behavior of each determines that of the other. This sequence
occurs particularly with regard to what Andy does on his own. The
more Heidi demands that he account for his time, the more evasive he
becomes. Her life is determined by his behavior. She cannot bear to
have him feel anything that deviates from her expectations. She thus
places him in an emotional trap in which he gets caught no matter
what he does. In addressing what the partners have in common, that
neither feels accepted by the other, I make clear to the couple that I
will not take sides.

T: (To H) Probably you feel you wouldn't be like that at all if he
        didn't withdraw from you so. The more he pulls away, the
        more you pursue. (To A) And apparently you think "I pull
        away because she crowds me so."

A: Of course, if I could accept her and love her as she is, it would be a lot easier.

T: But you can't accept her because you don't feel accepted by her.

A: Yes, that may play a part, but I have very little feeling for her, and naturally she sees that. I really have to make an effort.

H: And for me, I don't feel accepted, I don't have an orgasm. I feel like a prostitute.

T: Do you both really want therapy?

H: I'd say yes.

A: I don't know. You should tell us what is the right thing. It might be a lot of effort for nothing. The only thing she wants is for me to love her.

Andy is afraid that therapy might obligate him to love Heidi and that he might disappoint her in this hope.

T: One cannot be obligated to love someone. Divorce can be a legitimate goal of therapy—you should be free to love Heidi or not.

A: Then I'd have to watch out that these feelings of obligation didn't develop in me, so that I'd notice them in time if they came.

T: You seem to feel that you are running the risk of having those feelings without noticing them.

A: Or that I might notice them too late, mostly because I know she expects me to love her.

This encouraging sign evinces Andy's urge to commit himself. This clarifies that Heidi, with her ideal of absolute love, is acting out an aspect of Andy that Andy has delegated to her but that he resists in himself as he does in her.

It turns out that both partners had attempted through extramarital affairs to validate their ability to have relationships and to define themselves as separate beings. Giving these up would imperil their efforts to put some space between them. It is difficult to gauge Andy's motivation for therapy, and the question for Heidi is whether she is willing to modify her model of marriage.

Andy's conflicts are like Heidi's: he, too, yearns for an exclusive love, for a wife who accepts him absolutely and unconditionally. While disliking Heidi's violent outbursts and demands for absolute loyalty, these fascinate him as proofs of her ardent love. His extramarital relationships serve as cushions should Heidi sooner or later leave him. He has to keep several women—substitute mothers—in reserve. On the other hand, he is deeply hurt by her affairs. He also makes contradictory claims: that she be completely loyal to him while expecting nothing in return.

T: I'm just thinking how you, Heidi, said you'd like to know where you stand with Andy, and that's just the problem one has with you, Andy, which I'm also feeling now.

My interpretation is important to Heidi in serving as a model of how to deal successfully with couple conflict. I show her that although I react much as she does to his wavering, I accept him as he is without trying to make him live up to my ideal image.

A: Often I don't know where I stand. I have no relationship to Heidi as a woman. To make up for that, I have a girlfriend.

H: On our trip, things were wonderful between us and I naturally thought, well . . . not that I went into raptures straight off, I just hoped to keep a spark alive between us, and then Andy started up again with another woman. And I thought, "Well, nothing's changed!"

T: These other relationships that you two have; do you each want to prove yourselves to the other?

H: Of course. Before I had Peter I wondered if I were still a woman.

A: Peter as such doesn't bother me. But because of him, I always have the feeling that Heidi isn't sincere in what she says.

T: Both of you get certain advantages and disadvantages from your affairs.

I believe at this point in time that each needs these other relationships as a barrier against the stress they feel as a result of the excessive intimacy of their marriage. Moreover, I am cautious about encouraging premature changes in therapy because it is futile to try to deal with underlying factors in a marital problem if these factors have already been eliminated.

Not until later sessions does it become clear that Andy's reserve arises from Heidi's tendency to approach him with open arms and then subsequently to create a distance between them by discovering in him something that enables her to feel frustrated and rejected and that confirms her suspicions.

A: I find it really hard to tell you about my feelings because you immediately smother them in sarcasm. I feel inhibited because you take advantage of it.

H: I do it in self-defense, out of hurt.

T: React directly then, show the hurt! (To A) I wonder, does it make sense for you to tell Heidi all these things? Doesn't it keep adding fuel to the fire? Isn't it important for you both to talk about *your* relationship? How do you feel about each other? This is where you should try to be really frank. You both hurt each other by having lovers.

H: He claims it doesn't matter to him at all. If it doesn't, then that is a rejection of me.

T: But apparently it does matter to him.

A: My feelings vary. Sometimes it bothers me and sometimes I feel nothing. Sometimes I have told her it didn't matter to me when it did.

T: But is it hard to admit that because you're afraid that she will then get the better of you?

A: No, it only bothers me indirectly.

T: Because you interpret it as meaning that her feelings for you are not genuine?

A: Yes, that's it.

H: And that makes me feel: what's the point! He doesn't care what I do anyway!

T: So it's like this: He doesn't show his feelings, so then you wonder, "Well, if it doesn't matter to him, what must I do now in order to get through to him?" You continually face the question, "Can I touch him at all, or will nothing I do reach him?"

H: Yes, he didn't react at all, and then I went too far. Then he withdrew more and more. It wasn't helpful when you took up with Susie because you could always think about her and not have to make any effort with me. You could withdraw into your world and our problems never got solved. Then I was left high and dry. Maybe things would have been different if you could have told me it hurt you.

A: Back then I couldn't do that. I don't know why. I just couldn't.

H: Last fall, Helga was sitting around in tears, I was sitting around in tears and Andy was gaily off with his *other* girlfriend.

Heidi had hoped that her affair would provoke Andy so that she could reach his emotions. However, he simply withdrew further and intensified his own extramarital relationships.

After several good therapy sessions, Heidi announced that she was breaking off her relationship with Andy, and indirectly, also with me as therapist. Here the divorce symbolizes the couple's inner divorce, the need of each to establish his separateness from the other and to accept the fact that in their love they must remain two separate people.

H: Because of the therapy, I've been thinking and realizing that Andy doesn't want to come back to me. At night I couldn't sleep, and it's been like that all year. So I said to myself, "No more, I don't want to be dependent any more on Andy's moods. I'd like to take charge of my own life." And what Andy said was, "I don't want any liberated wife. I want a wife who will spoil me." But I don't want to be pulled this way and that all the time. It takes too much out of me. And I think it's asking too much of Andy to expect him to give a clear yes or no. But it's destroying me. I feel attracted to him and he pushes me away again. Even if it is the worst choice and even if it scares me, I'd like us to simply split up. When Andy isn't there, I feel relieved. I don't want to go on waiting and waiting. I'd like to get more involved in my work again, but I can't pull myself together. If I separate from him, then I know that I can get along a lot better. I don't know how I can become independent of Andy except by a divorce.

T: It strikes me that you see living with him exclusively in terms of possible dependency.

H: And it makes me furious. I get nothing from him anyway and yet I'm dependent!

T: Do you feel that he'd like to keep you dependent? That he doesn't allow you any other kind of relationship?

H: Probably he allows me others, but I don't know whether I can.

T: And how do you see all this, Andy?

A: I think I could allow her to be independent, but she can tolerate only the extremes. It's too bad there's no middle ground for her.

H: Oh come on! After all, you're the one saying you don't feel anything for me at all. When I try to draw the logical conclusion from that, you start talking just as sweet as can be about how we could do this or that, and what we had once upon a time. When I see a clear path, I can follow it. But I have to figure out how to get myself out of this mess of yes-no, yes-no. Whenever I see him I react strongly to him and don't know how to change that. I have the feeling that if I'm to find myself again, I have to separate from him.

Heidi's problem is that she cannot separate herself from Andy either emotionally or externally. She defines herself through him and so is handicapped in her own development thereby. As a therapist, my job is to probe into the deeper experiential content of what goes on between the partners, and then to help them make their own decisions—perhaps even the decision to get a divorce.

A: It's only with me that Heidi can't be herself. Otherwise, she can. She thinks if we get a divorce we'll never meet again and she wants to get free of me.

H: I used to be self-sufficient.

T: (To H) When you say that do you have the feeling that you've lost your identity?

H: It wasn't deliberate; it just happened.

T: It strikes me again how much alike the two of you are. Both of you find it hard to be yourselves within the confines of such a close relationship. You, Andy, have the feeling that Heidi gets too close to you and you have to struggle to keep hold of your own space and you, Heidi, are so absorbed in him that you can't find yourself either. Both of you find it hard to be yourselves in an intimate relationship.

A: It's the same with my girlfriends. It's not so much that I'm
        scared of their getting mad. It's more difficult for me when
        they get sad.

H: Yes, you're scared of all emotions.

A: Maybe so.

T: I think you two ought to separate. (Both partners stare at the
        therapist in shock.) The only question is, In what way? As I
        see it, the crucial thing is that you have to separate your-
        selves more clearly from each other. I think that's a more
        internal process.

A: Heidi sees physical separation as a necessary precondition
        for this process.

T: I don't know. Maybe it would be easier if you separated out-
        wardly, too. But the problem is that you can't separate
        inwardly, you can't define your boundaries. Heidi, you are
        too absorbed in him, and Andy, you feel full of her. There is no
        clear boundary between the two of you. With no clear bounda-
        ries, a relationship is always threatening. The problem of
        defining your boundaries is relevant, too, to the extramarital
        relationships. Both of you have the same difficulty deciding
        "What's your problem and what's my problem?"

H: Yes! As long as we're not together, these relationships are his
        problem. As soon as we're together, I feel they're my problem,
        too.

A: It's always the same: as soon as I like someone else, she feels
        it's a personal insult.

H: When we're not together I think, Go on, do whatever you
        want! But when we're together it bothers me!

T: Sometimes I almost feel as if you need his girlfriends. If it
        weren't for them, you would both get too close.

H: Well that may be true. Clearly, it's easier for me to say "You
        don't need me" so that I can push him away. Probably the
        question is whether we ought to go on with therapy at all.

Heidi's attempts to apply pressure have affected me so that my
attempt to sustain the role of therapist unconsciously becomes an
abuse of this role. I feel aggrieved at her threat to divorce (thereby
ending therapy, too) and in turn hurt Heidi by making an "interpre-

tation." Heidi does not contradict me, but continues the collusion (with me) by questioning the value of therapy. Because of my own personal involvement at this point, I lose the chance to work therapeutically on the therapeutic collusion between myself and Heidi.

Over the next few months, the couple's relationship became more free. Inevitably, steps forward were followed by steps backward. Heidi remained inclined to believe the worst until Andy proved that the changes in his attitudes and behaviors were permanent. On his part, Andy's fears that these changes might make Heidi expect too much lead him to push her away. These reactions slow progress, but the narcissistic collusion becomes increasingly clearer. Again and again, Andy places Heidi in double-binds, evoking in her the need to fulfill contradictory expectations whose fulfillment, one way or another, will lead to her being punished. He wants absolute love without being under any obligation himself, an absolute love that no living woman, with her own dreams and expectations, can fulfill.

H: What he says, about my being too fat, hurts me very much. I get upset, thinking that nothing has changed in the least. How am I supposed to behave so that Andy won't have this fear of me, and would I lose myself, cease being myself?

T: (To A) How did you feel then?

A: I saw that I had hurt her, but I hadn't expected that afterwards she'd react so violently. What especially hurt me were the conclusions she drew, the way she said, "All right, now I'll get a divorce. I don't want anything more from you." It's the way she jumps to conclusions and demands that I take a stand.

T: How would you have reacted if she had said that to you?

H: Not so violently. I'd wonder instead what to do to make myself attractive again.

T: Then you'd like to be what the other person expects?

A: Yes, if the other person's opinion matters to me.

H: That's something I simply won't do. Besides, you said you didn't know if you could love me even if I lost the weight.

A: Outward things don't really matter if people get along well in other ways. Look, when all I say is that I find it hard to get close to you, you think I don't like you. Then you say, "Now I want a divorce."

H: I really don't do so many things depending upon Andy.

T: (To A) How do you feel about that? If Heidi knew more clearly
          what she wants, would it be easier for you to get over your
          ambivalence?

A: Maybe so.

T: I can understand how Heidi feels. She's repeatedly said that
          your ideal woman is completely devoted to you and very close;
          and yet you push her away the moment she tries to behave
          the way you want. That really confuses her.

The tragedy of every collusion is that each partner exhibits those
very behavior patterns that make it most difficult for the other partner to make any progress toward improving the situation. In fact,
each is compelled by his own problem to prevent the other from developing in a direction for which the latter may have a desperate need,
for to allow this would put himself at risk. Andy's secret expectation
that Heidi will unite with him and his pain at her attempts to assert
her independence make it doubly difficult for her to overcome her
personal limitations because these attempts threaten the continuation of the relationship. Therefore I try to show Andy that he would be
less afraid of intimacy with Heidi if he could accept her as independent of himself.

     The couple are now aware of the collusion and also see how each of
them has to change. But both find it hard to give up inappropriate
behavior because each fears that any tangible change might lead the
partner to develop exaggerated expectations. Therefore each acts in
accord with the idea: Because I cannot live up to my partner's image
of me, I must nip my partner's hopes in the bud to forestall disappointment. This reaction is typical of this stage of therapy. When someone
gives up a symptom, others raise their expectations. It takes courage
to get well because each secretly fears being cheated in the end.

A: Heidi has always said she wants to live with me. So I really
          believed it was just a question of my making a decision. And
          now finally I say I'm ready to come back to her and she says
          she hasn't made up her mind yet!

T: I can imagine that you, Heidi, are very much afraid of being
          hurt and that you, Andy, are afraid of being pressured. Now
          you face the hard question: when you're living together
          again, how will you manage to keep yourselves sufficiently

separate and not too close? I imagine that scares you both quite a bit.

A: (To T) She gave me a final date and I've tried for a whole month to get close to her. (To H) That's why I want to talk about what we're feeling now. I can't understand why you don't see that. And if we can't get closer, then we'd better call it quits.

H: I haven't noticed you trying to get closer.

A: Then why are we talking? Why am I trying to get back together with you?

H: Yes, Andy, you wanted to get closer to me. I am trying to keep you at a distance because I'm afraid of your being close. I'm afraid that I won't be accepted.

T: Is this an all-or-nothing situation for you?

H: If he'd accept me three-quarters, all right.

T: How about one-tenth?

H: That's not enough for me.

T: He's talking in terms of small steps. I have the impression if you make it "either-or," he'll make it "neither-nor."

H: I find this extreme way of dealing with things very hard to put up with.

H: But if I have no hope of living on at least five-tenths, I say no. One-tenth isn't enough for a relationship. I'm afraid that he has only two-tenths to give. Even Social Security gives you enough to live on.

T: How do you know this?

H: Because he says, "There's not enough there. There might be something more later on, but I don't feel anything for you as a woman. And so then I say to myself, "I have Peter!" Then I use Peter and say, "You can go to the devil!"

As the collusion is unravelled, both partners are less reactive and more free with each other. Increasingly they see the disorders in their relationship as stemming from their own personal problems. Andy now realizes that the demand that he fully account to Heidi stems not only from her but from himself. His pain at being unable to live up to this ideal makes him react with guilt and hurtful behavior toward Heidi.

T: You're both hypersensitive, and troubled by whether you're really accepted or not. There's a fear when one becomes involved that one can feel betrayed because the other person doesn't feel what one expected her to, not loved the way she expected to be loved.

H: I think we've made considerable progress just to see that we share the same problem. I think: "Oh God, Andy has had just as rough time over that as I have!"

A: Basically, we've realized that we're alike in our fear of being disappointed.

H: My trouble is even if you told me ten times over that you think I'm pretty and you like me, I still wouldn't believe it.

A: Everything you've said about yourself, I think the same thing applies to me.

Now that both partners see their common ground, they hope to help each other overcome their problem. But Heidi's hope of obtaining validation from Andy still causes him to back away from her.

A: I've always had the feeling that you like me more than I like you, at least recently.

H: (Hangs head in frustration)

T: We've often talked about the fact that you share the same problems. But perhaps it would be good to ask now, "What's the best way for us to work together to solve these problems?"

A: We should draw up an inventory.

H: We should tell each other where we stand only when we know it and then say it.

A: But often one can't tell where one stands until somebody demands that he take a position. The more one is required to take a stand, the more clearly one can unravel what one feels.

H: But naturally, there's the problem that he may—to avoid a certain situation—decide not to be completely honest.

Andy's remarks are an unexpected and startling reversal of the position he took at the beginning of therapy, and they stimulate Heidi's questioning whether this requirement is realistic.

T: My impression is that Andy senses your demand that he affirm you 100 percent and so he believes: "I can never fulfill her expectations, and so it won't work anyway."

H: Yes, I should lower my expectations. But it still hurts.

T: It's already accomplishing a lot to be able to perceive the hurt so clearly and also to be able to express it.

H: I just don't feel at all free in your presence, Andy.

A: No doubt that's why you try to hurt me. But often it's just too much for me. Sometimes I think I might be jealous that she's capable of so much feeling.

H: That's funny! The other day, I thought, "Maybe Andy's jealous because he can't feel strongly the way I do.

A: Yes, I like and admire your spontaneity and I don't simply resent it. The rejection I do feel may stem from the fact that I'm not as good at that as she is.

As therapy continued, Heidi became increasingly desperate and depressed. She finds it difficult to give up her absolute demands on a love relationship and feels she cannot live up to the ideal of being more herself and not allowing Andy to rule her feelings. Andy feels responsible for her survival, which causes him guilt and fear.

A: At the beginning, I was looking for a mother substitute, and you accepted this role. I severed the mother-son relationship, and you're having trouble finding another role for yourself. You think there's no other kind of relationship.

H: That's not so. You look for a mother in every woman.

A: You treated me like a child, you determined my life. Now I've separated from you exactly like a son separates from a mother, and then the mother has lost the relationship and has problems.

T: (To H) A year ago you talked about how Andy grew up and back then I felt there was a mother-son relationship on both sides. That is why you took Andy's part like a good mother.

H: That's been over for two years. It stopped when I had my own children.

T: (To A) Were you afraid of losing your mother, that she might die? (Andy had lost his mother at age 10.)

A: Not die, but be lost. I imagine it's a fear of getting too used to something.

H: You're not afraid of losing me, but of something ending!

T: I'm struck by the fact that when Heidi says she wants a divorce, you are much more affectionate with her.

A: When it gets final, I'm afraid. Otherwise I don't have such a need to be with her.

T: So she gets the most affection when she doesn't want it anymore.

H: We've played that game for years.

A: But now we're playing it without getting hurt.

H: It bores me now.

T: Probably it would be better if each of you could behave more as you really feel, and not simply react to each other's behavior.

A: If you let me be annoyed without always immediately reacting to me, it would be better.

H: All right. Then I'll be "me" without regard for the consequences.

Andy demands that Heidi define herself and accept his doing so, also, and live with the friction of being separate but close individuals. But he also admits that it would be hard on him if Heidi did not keep the relationship suspenseful, for he finds this stimulating and would not like it to become boring and pedestrian. Thus when Heidi behaves aggressively toward Andy, she is fulfilling his deeper expectations, even though consciously he is annoyed by her behavior.

There was a long holiday break at this point, after which Heidi returned with the announcement that she had finally decided once and for all to divorce.

H: I no longer have any expectations. I'm not motivated for therapy. Now I've decided I'd like a divorce.

T: (To A) And you?

A: I still feel hopeful we could have a better relationship and get closer to each other. And things could develop that one day I'd want to live with her.

H: Things went well on the holiday because I made no demands. I didn't ask him to say I was pretty or that he accepted me. But all in all, I don't want a relationship in which I have to do without those things.

T: (Sharply, to A) Can you understand that?

A: Yes, she's broken free but it seems forced to me. She wants to destroy what we've built up and that's why she doesn't want to stay on friendly terms afterwards. It's forced because she really doesn't want it at all.

H: (Fighting back tears) You always gloat that I want a divorce and yet I'm always at your beck and call. This isn't an attempt to pressure you.

T: It's more of a slow, painful decision.

H: I expected something different when we entered therapy. I thought we'd come out a happy couple. I kept hoping. But I'm not sorry it didn't; it would have turned out that way anyway, and I'd have been a lot more disappointed even though it hurt a lot.

At the moment, Heidi doesn't feel motivated to undertake further therapy, and given the circumstances, neither does Andy. In a follow-up two months later, Heidi had taken no steps to obtain the divorce. The two have established a subtle balance by which, while preserving their outer and inner separation, they are able to display and to accept delicate signs of love without immediately trying to pressure each other or become defensive. Heidi's wounds that therapy did not validate her ideal of marriage seem to be healing. Her withdrawal is permitting Andy to show Heidi affection for the first time.

H: Physical separation is really important to me because unless we're a long distance apart, we still see each other very often and that always hurts, which wouldn't happen any more if there's lots of space between us.

T: (To A) And how do you feel about that?

A: (Sighs) When she says something like that, I think she's already decided in Peter's favor.

H: No, I just don't have any wish to commit myself or try anything new with you anymore. At least now I no longer react so strongly in my relationship with you. There's something between us, but I don't know what it is.

T: The new thing for me is that both of you are able to hint and to accept without resistance that you are very fond of each other and really don't want to go your separate ways, but that you can't get too close either. You're accepting that without bitterness.

A: I'm not so tense anymore; that makes it easier for me to get close to her. (To H) But I still feel you're suppressing something, getting this divorce.

H: What if that's true? What use is it to me if I love you? The way you are and the way I am, there would be tension every time we got close. So it's better for us to get a divorce.

T: I wonder whether you can get closer if the external separation between you is clearer and by having a less intense relationship?

Both partners increasingly see that divorce would not end their relationship, for they could continue to see each other. Too many people, therapists included, regard divorce as something final. In reality, the years a couple have spent together can never be erased; they are an indelible part of their lives. While people can try to forget an earlier relationship in a second or third marriage, it always lives on, in one form or another, in the later relationship.

Heidi feels highly ambivalent about the change therapy has produced in her. She believed that relinquishing her absolute demands would decrease her ability to feel. Instead, such clinging prevents intimacy by alienating the partner. In this sense, more "realistic" attitudes make it possible for people to get close. This truth may deprive love of some of its magical and mystical qualities, a loss which can be experienced as painful and hard to accept.

T: (To H) What's new is that you no longer feel that this situation is intolerable. In the past you said, "I can't stand it anymore; it's better to end it than to go on in this suspense."

H: Yes, but then I was really still hoping that we'd get back together completely. Maybe I needed to realize that it was over for good, a thing of the past in order to behave this way.

T: I think we have to wait and see how things develop.

A: In any case I won't get a divorce until after our tenth anniversary, because I'll be entitled to a pension, and of course, I'm not going to give that up!

Heidi needs the idea of divorce in order to feel and accept the internal separation from Andy, to accept the frustration of remaining separate in the experience of love and to take into account her partner's limited abilities to relate to her.

I saw the couple at three-month intervals after this last meeting. They continued living apart, but Andy had grown away from his girlfriend, and was determined to get back together with his family as soon as circumstances permitted. While they have not achieved a marriage that corresponds to the conventional model, I believe they have found a form that is possible for them, given their present stage of personal development.

Many people are offended by the suggestion that a close marital relationship may not be conducive to their health. They feel that they are not fully worthwhile if they cannot adhere to traditional norms. But the facts show that an intimate form of marriage is unsuitable for many people who are otherwise capable of meaningful and fulfilling relationships of other kinds.

The acceptance of one's own limitations and the desire to find a form of relationship that suits each person are not symptoms of a limited personality, but rather a sign of maturity. In this sense, Andy and Heidi made progress in therapy. They no longer use affairs to regulate intimacy, nor to hurt each other and find compensation. They are no longer so polarized, nor do they need each other as before to make up for their own deficiencies.

And so in examining collusion between couples and its resolution, we come full circle: the vicissitudes of daily living entail many losses that must be accepted so that we can move on. As the Japanese proverb puts it: Meeting is the beginning of parting. In this way, we never lose what we have relinquished.

NOTES

1. This term was coined by Christopher Lasch in his book, *Culture of Narcissism* (W.W. Norton, 1979).
2. As each member of the family is added, both the needs and possible avenues of fulfilment correspondingly increase until the lines of obligation become an intricately interwoven pattern.
3. See Sheldon Cashdan, *Object Relations Therapy* (W.W. Norton, 1988) for a set of four projective identification themes labeled dependency, power, sex and ingratiation.
4. In projection the unconscious fantasies of person A are projected onto person B, who may be entirely unaware of them unless person A now "responds" to the perceived projection. In projection identification, on the other hand, person A induces person B to *behave* in a way that A personally disowns in him- or herself.
5. Willi's concept of collusion is similar to that of *projective identification* in which B manipulates A to feel and enact, say, the dependency that B disavows so that B can be "active" and strong. In this exchange, B hopes that A will go along with the "setup," and that A's dependency will enhance her weak self. Unknown to B (because it is unconscious) is the downside risk of this transaction: that A will reject the projected identity and B will end up feeling the badness associated with dependency that she sought to discharge onto A for reworking. The collusion concept has the advantage of highlighting the latently encouraging role of A in the interactive process.